library of

the SIMSERS

Deco H.

THE MOUNTAIN IS MOVING

PATRICIA MORLEY

THE MOUNTAIN IS MOVING

JAPANESE WOMEN'S LIVES

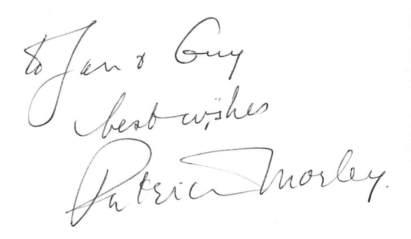

UBCPress / Vancouver

Printed in Canada on acid-free paper

ISBN 0-7748-0675-3

Canadian Cataloguing in Publication Data

Morley, Patricia, 1929-
　　The mountain is moving

　　Includes bibliographical references and index.
　　ISBN 0 7748 0675-3

　　1. Women – Japan. 2. Japan – Social conditions –
1945- I. Title.
HQ1762.M67 1999　　　305.42'0952　　　C98-910608-X

UBC Press gratefully acknowledges the ongoing support to its publishing program from the Canada Council for the Arts, the British Columbia Arts Council, and the Department of Canadian Heritage of the Government of Canada.

Set in Electra and Felix
Printed and bound in Canada by Friesens
Copy editor: Camilla Jenkins
Designer: George Vaitkunas
Indexer: Robert Glen
Proofreader: Gail Copeland

UBC Press
University of British Columbia
6344 Memorial Road
Vancouver, BC V6T 1Z2
(604) 822-5959
Fax: 1-800-668-0821
E-mail: orders@ubcpress.ubc.ca
http://www.ubcpress.ubc.ca

To my mother,
Mabel Winsland Marlow,
a strong, quiet woman,
and my daughter,
Patricia Morley-Foster

CONTENTS

ILLUSTRATIONS

PREFACE

RESEARCH FOR THIS BOOK began in the early 1980s. I first went to Japan in 1961, by chance, as a tourist. I was instantly captivated, intrigued by a country with such a rich artistic heritage and a culture so different from my own. I have had Japanese friends and interests ever since, and have returned for nine long trips.

In the late 1970s, while serving as a professor in the Department of English at Concordia University, Montreal, I became a founding member of the Simone de Beauvoir Institute there and began to teach Women's Studies. By the 1980s I was ready to put together two long-standing interests, Japan and women's lives.

A Japan Foundation Fellowship (1991-2) greatly facilitated my research, which was carried out through four interrelated methodologies or sources of information, some relatively uncommon. The first was fieldwork, in the form of individual interviews with hundreds of Japanese women in Hokkaido, Honshū, and Shikoku over the last decade. The techniques of oral history can uncover data and reveal insights that have never been committed to paper. To my surprise, I found Japanese women ready, even eager, to tell a stranger about their lives. The diversity of the stories revealed both the patterns that concern sociologists and the exceptions that interest writers and philosophers. The women's voices became my eyes and ears, a lens through which much of the formal research was viewed. Issues raised in individual interviews became the target of further research in certain areas, and were sometimes one test of the credibility of written sources.

I have vivid memories of many of these women and of the astonishing range of their abilities and aspirations. Many interviews confirmed, however, that Japanese husbands could be very demanding, that their long work hours left little time for them to share in housework or childcare, and that the majority of women believed they had little choice but to conform to social norms and expectations. Rebels, unashamed nonconformists, are still uncommon in Japan but their numbers have been increasing in recent years.

The personal stories became a rich source of insights and a base for a deeper understanding of the more formal research materials in libraries, archives, books, magazines, journals, and government publications. This material constituted my second source.

For the third source, I combed Japanese English-language newspapers for articles on women, education, and the family, social topics that relate to women's lives. The Japanese media is still male dominated, but the old pattern of restricting 'women's' news to food and fashion slowly gave way in the 1980s to new practices of reporting on women's lives and on exceptional women. Nowadays articles in these newspapers, although scattered and incomplete, offer a valuable source of information that can be checked against other data. The two newspapers used most frequently were the *Japan Times* and the *Asahi Evening News*, both venerable and well-respected Japanese institutions with a reputation for accuracy and reliability. Many of the journalists from whose articles I quote are well-educated, bilingual Japanese women.

My fourth, and final, source of material was the work of contemporary Japanese women writers in translation, which I used as a means of understanding how women perceive their own lives. Fiction, poetry, and autobiography offer many insights, especially into the emotional reactions of the characters. This avenue would have been closed to me twenty-five years ago. In 1970, there were almost no English translations of contemporary Japanese women writers, but only of those in the classical period nearly 1,000 years earlier.

International Women's Year, 1975, and the international women's movement affected Japanese women in the 1970s, and by the end of the decade English translations of Japanese women writers were beginning to be published. The trickle soon became a steady stream. Geraldine Harcourt, winner of the Wheatland Prize for translation, observed in 1985 that a contemporary writer such as Yūko Tsushima was beginning to be termed simply *joryu sakka* (woman writer) instead of *joryu bungaku* (women's school writer), an earlier classification for all women's writing that set it apart from mainstream – read *male* – literature. By 1990, Harcourt noted that a representative selection of writing by contemporary Japanese women had been translated.

Women writers are voicing their feelings, their unease, their dissatisfaction, and their desire for change. I have been greatly assisted in understanding the lives of postwar Japanese women by the translated work of Fumiko Enchi, Minako Ōba, Sawako Ariyoshi, Yūko Tsushima, Harumi Setouchi, Shidzue Ishimoto Kato, Shizuko Gō, and many other Japanese women writers. Ariyoshi died in 1984, but I was fortunate to meet the rest of these writers, and other women writers, painters, and sculptors in Japan in 1986 and in the early 1990s. These creative women are commenting imaginatively and indirectly with irony and humour and anger on the changing realities of women's lives.

The longer my research continued, the more difficult my task became. I knew the exceptions that surrounded every generalization. The women I had met were as varied as people everywhere. And as women, they shared with the women of other cultures a vast commonality of experience and concerns. Nevertheless, the patterns, the ways of living and reacting and thinking unique to Japan, were inescapable. Sometimes they left me puzzled. Time and again I was forced to acknowledge that the underlying assumptions of the Japanese women to whom I was talking, often in English, were different from my own. Despite this, after the mid-1980s I increasingly encountered or read about Japanese women whose idea of 'fairness' and whose long-term goals and aspirations were similar to those of many Western women.

Could I do justice to the patterns, the puzzles, and the exceptions? And could I reflect the conservative bias of Japanese society, its resistance to change, along with the tumultuous shifts in recent years which some have termed a 'quiet revolution'? Like other writers, my seeing eye is strongly affected by the country where I was born and grew up – Canada – as well as by my gender. I speak very little Japanese. My acquaintance with Japanese culture and with the lives of Japanese women runs deep, however, as do my sympathies and interests. My perceptions have thus been extended and their limitations qualified by this exposure, and by the voices of the Japanese women and men that resound through this study. I respect and value individual cultures, but every culture has room for improvement, and each faces pressure to change amid changing conditions everywhere.

In closing, I note that names are given here in the Western order, with the family name last.

ACKNOWLEDGMENTS

I AM INDEBTED to many individuals and institutions for help with the writing of this book. In 1991, I received financial support and personal encouragement from the Japan Foundation (Toronto and Tokyo), the Canada Council (Ottawa), and the Ottawa-Carleton Arts Council. In 1993, I was assisted by the Canada-Japan Fund (Ottawa). Without their grants my research would of necessity have been briefer and much less thorough.

Personnel at the Embassy of Japan in Ottawa, always helpful, have provided data and research material such as the *Japan Times.*

For help translating interviews, both at home and in the field, and for kind hospitality, I am grateful to Mayumi Kurokawa and Shunko Sasaki. Hisashi Urashima, president of Joy International in Obihiro, Hokkaido, arranged interviews for me with former students. Professors Mary McCrimmon of Okayama and Miho Shimada of Kyoto lent their class time and students for some lively exchanges. Mary McCrimmon and Shunko Sasaki were also volunteer research assistants, who mailed fat packages of clippings from Japanese newspapers to Canada to help keep me up to date on news of women. Susan Caws helped to organize some of this material. Professor Kazuko Kikui answered many an urgent query by e-mail as editing proceeded.

To the hundreds of Japanese women who gave me their time and shared something of their lives with me in interviews I owe a special thanks. My understanding of more formal research material would have been different without this window into personal and individual experience.

I am also indebted to Kyōko Asakura, Mariko Bando, Mioko Fujieda, Hisako Fujiwara, Mariko Fukuroi, Yoshiko Furuki, Sumiko Gomi, Michiko Goto, Geraldine Harcourt, Nobuko Hashimoto, Junko Hayashi, Toshiko Matsui Hōga, Keiko Ichiba, Junko Ikegawa, Yasuko Ikeuchi, Mie Ishida, Suni Izumi, Willie Jones, Masako Kamiya, Y. Kaneda, Hisako Kanehira, Tamako Kataoka, Kazuko Kikui, Noriko Kimura, Mieko Kitajima, Fukuko Kobayashi, Setsuko Koyano, Takako Kuhara, Hisako Kunitomi, Noriko Mizuta Lippit, Sachie Mano, Keiko Matsuda, Yoshimi Matsuda, Tamiko Matsumura, Hideko Matsuo, Yoshinari and Tomiko Minami, Yuriko Mizuta, Kazuya Morita, Sumiko Morita, Yumiko Nagai, Yuri Nishibori,

Yuriko Oido, Teruko Ohno and the National Women's Education Centre, Atsuko Okada, Yoshio Okawa, Yasuko Ono, Donald Richie, Nobutaka and Miyoko Saiki, Noriko Saneyoshi, Mitsuyo Sawa, Reiko Sekiguchi, Eiko Shiraga, Yasuko Suginome, Tomoko Suzuki, Kioko Takagi, Kazuko Tanaka, Yukiko Tanaka, Takako Tani, Yayoi Taniguchi, Naoko Toita, Etsuko Tsutsui, Toshiko Tsutsumi, Tsuyako Wakimoto, Kazuko Watanabe, Noboru Watanabe, Mutsuko Yamamoto, and Masako Yoshida.

For help with many a computer tangle, I am greatly indebted to Gary McVeigh. Excellent editorial assistance has been provided by Laura Macleod and Camilla Jenkins of UBC Press.

For permission to reproduce small samples of their poetry, I thank Motoko Michiura, Ei Akitsu, and Kimiko Itami, each of whom is represented in *A Long Rainy Season: Haiku and Tanka*, ed. and trans. Leza Lowitz, Miyuki Aoyama, and Akemi Tomioka, illus. Robert Kushner, vol. 1 of *Contemporary Japanese Women's Poetry*, Rock Spring Collection of Japanese Literature (Berkeley, CA: Stone Bridge Press 1994). Stone Bridge Press also kindly gave permission to reproduce the work in English. For permission to use Janine Beichman's translation of a tanka by Akiko Yosano in 'Yosano Akiko: Return to the Female,' *Japan Quarterly* 37, 2 (1990): 244, I thank the journal.

Finally, I thank the Japanese writers who were kind enough to talk with me about a craft and a passion we share: writing. This sharing, and their work, has added greatly to my understanding of Japanese women's lives. The book would have been different, and poorer, without their input.

CHAPTER 1

IS THE MOUNTAIN MOVING?

The day when the mountains move is coming
I tell you, yet people refuse to believe it
The mountains have been sleeping for a long time
Long ago they moved passionately blazing with fire
You need not believe it
But ah! believe only this:
Women who have been sleeping
Begin to awake and move.

AKIKO YOSANO, 'The Day When the Mountains Move,' composite translation

In RECENT YEARS, the topic of Japanese women's lives has begun to intrigue the West. More than a few books and scores of articles have told us – what? That Japanese women are changing? Are not changing? Are happy with their roles as wives and mothers, content to leave the stress of fourteen-hour days in offices and commuter trains to men? Or frustrated by the limitations of this role?

In the last thirty years, women's lives in the West have changed enormously. Of course this change had been preceded by several centuries of struggle for women's emancipation. In the interim, modern medicine had altered the human lifespan, and family planning had slowly but inexorably diminished the size of families. Patterns that made sense when women had many children and lived some three-score years took on a totally different aspect when women lived for four-score years and had only one or two children. By the late 1990s, two generations of Western women have learned that it is possible, profitable, challenging, and, for many women, necessary to combine the bearing and raising of children with work outside the home.

The structure of Western society changed accordingly. It had to. Women do not live in isolation, and families everywhere, however defined, are at the core of societal patterns. Perhaps the fascination that Japanese women hold for the West lies in the different choices our societies have made, and the reasons for them.

As we will see in Chapter 3, Japanese society is group oriented and hierarchical. These comments are truisms, but there are different ways of understanding the obvious. The strength of the group, and the corresponding weakness of the value of the individual, are concepts that may require long periods of living exposure to Japanese culture to be truly understood. To a mind informed by Western concepts of individual liberty, freedom of conscience, and the equal value of all human beings, the power of the Japanese group to require and enforce compliance from all its members is learned slowly and reluctantly.

It may well be that the West, in its late-twentieth-century phase, has leaned too far in the direction of individual rights and will find itself in need of a corrective. Obviously any well-adjusted human society should be sensitive to both the individual and the group. The fact remains that Japan and the West are poles apart on this point. Japan remains an arch-conservative society where, as countless Japanese were eager to tell me, 'the nail that sticks up gets hammered down.' It also belongs to an Eastern tradition in which patriarchal structures have long dominated social and political thought.

Some critics believe that the last fifteen years in Japan have brought about profound changes in women's lives, making women the 'most dynamic sector' of the population.[1] It is true that many men are chained to the institutions they have established; that women benefit in their homes from new technologies and appliances; and that a few women are now working in areas that would have been closed to them a generation ago, such as construction, the police, and the self-defence forces. Women now hold responsible positions in government, law, and business, as well as in medicine and teaching, bastions stormed earlier. The same critics point to the current freedom of Japanese women to marry later, to choose their own husbands, and to dictate their own terms. Many women are quite openly in search of a tall, good-looking, highly educated man with a high salary. Arranged marriages are in the minority, and some men are experiencing difficulties in finding wives.

Men are expected to provide their families with financial support. They are 'salarymen' or 'money-carrying birds,' in a literal translation of one blackly comic Japanese idiom. Harsh working conditions for many men convince some that women have an easier lifestyle. Urban salarymen typically endure long journeys on crowded commuter trains. They are largely absentee husbands and fathers, since obligations to employers and co-workers absorb most of their time, strength, and even emotions. They take very few holidays in the year, and work extraordinarily long hours, so long that a phenomenon called *karōshi*, death from overwork, is now the subject of numerous articles, at least one book, and a number of legal suits.

Quite understandably, few women are in a hurry to compete with men under these conditions, but the price for women is dependence, exclusion from power, and ignorance of large areas of experience that many would consider necessary to full adult development. To call this 'freedom' is a half-truth at best. A web of entrenched values, attitudes, and customs have bound the majority of Japanese women to home, housework, and caring for the family. In Canada I was once asked if Japanese women still practise foot binding. After recovering from my astonishment at the confusion of feudal Chinese customs with those of modern Japan, I realized that the error had some validity as a metaphor. Later, a Japanese woman told me that in her view many customs regarding women amounted to cultural foot binding. The metaphor was a fact of life for her. Japanese women are bound to traditional roles by ties of silk and steel that go back hundreds of years.

As wives and mothers, women normally bear the sole responsibility for family life, and within that restricted sphere they do wield considerable power. They have been conditioned from childhood to expect to bring up their children by themselves. Help from a mother or mother-in-law is welcome, but babysitters are non-existent and daycare is in short supply. The number of daycares is increasing slowly, and in the early 1990s the Diet legislated longer maternity leave and parental leave for childcare.

Once their children are in school women have freedom for cultural and social activities that men do not. Many, however, are re-entering the work force in their thirties and forties, where they can count on being poorly paid and where the nature of the work usually bears no relation to their education or abilities. By 1990, 50 percent of Japan's labour force was female.[2] Yet the vast majority of women can find only jobs that are defined as part time, although they may involve forty hours or more per week. These jobs offer no benefits such as pensions, sick leave, or semi-annual bonuses. The hard fact is that Japanese women who return to work after years of childcare are not paid a living wage. Retraining is rare, and confidence may be low. Women accept what amounts to a supplemental family income which is often used for educational 'extras.' Observers of Japanese society point out, with good reason, that both sexes would stand to gain a great deal if the roles they are expected to play were made more flexible.

Many women have said to me, 'We are changing, but men are not changing.' The expectations of Japanese men have remained conservative and traditional, and entrenched customs make it very difficult for women to enter society's mainstream. Even an optimist such as social psychologist Sumiko Iwao of Keio University, who writes of women gaining a whole new range of freedoms in recent years, admits that the central organizations and groups in Japanese society are still almost exclusively staffed and controlled by men.

The current division of work according to sex may have suited pre-modern families with many children and shorter life expectancies. In a modern urban society such as Japan, where the birth rate was 1.46 children per couple in 1993 and a woman's life expectancy is eighty-two years, these roles make much less sense. Many Japanese women now have college or university education, and Japan was suffering a labour shortage until the early 1990s. In years to come, demographic changes will again bring labour shortages to an aging nation. The practice of restricting women to low-status jobs constitutes a tremendous waste of women's talents and potential.

Areas such as family life, care of the elderly, and women's work and activities outside the home can be understood only in the light of Japanese history, culture, and traditional resistance to change. Sociologist Chie Nakane wrote in 1970: 'While the outlook of Japanese society has suffered drastic changes over the past hundred years, the basic social grammar has hardly been affected. Here is an example of industrialization and the importation of western culture not affecting changes in the basic cultural structure.'[3] Kurt Singer, who varies the metaphor by speaking of the geometry of Japanese life, agrees that the culture follows its own organic logic, and that despite the legislative changes following the Pacific War, the fundamental, age-old pattern was not and 'will not be readily changed.'[4]

Women themselves are divided about the likelihood of change. When asked in the early 1990s if they expected significant societal changes to alter the patterns of their lives (a) soon, (b) within twenty-five years, or (c) never, roughly one-third responded in each category.

My interviews and other research left me equally uncertain. Many Japanese women appear happy with their lifestyles, and have managed, with ingenuity and creativity, to find or forge a space for their talents within the basic family role that their culture allots them. Others, radicalized by experience or more independent by nature, are frankly dissatisfied with current ways. Some are angry. They hope and work for change: for respect for women who choose to remain unmarried; for the right to continue working after marriage or after having children; for reasonable office hours so that working women are not forced into the harsh options of either marriage and children or a career; for a living wage for women who return to work in their thirties and forties; and for respect as full social, economic, and political partners at every level in the nation.

Certainly the last fifteen years have transformed some aspects of life for women in Japan, yet the basic 'social grammar' that Nakane saw as relatively static in 1970 appears to be much the same a generation later. Many promises remain unfulfilled and now appear as empty rhetoric. The prime example is the Equal Employment Opportunity Law, passed by the Diet in 1972 with the proviso that it should come into effect in 1986. Not only did the law come with a built-in delay of fourteen years but as is true of similar pieces of Japanese legislation, it has no teeth: no penalties for those who break it, no mechanisms for enforcement. Women who attempt the newly possible career-track positions are discouraged by the unusually long work hours expected and by male managers who have no idea how to treat them. Other office women, the secretaries and clerks who compose the army of so-called 'office ladies' in Japanese companies, often resent their privileged position.

Masks of illusion and reality shift deceptively in every culture, but nowhere are they more elusive than in Japan. The language itself, often deliberately ambiguous, bolsters the cultural preference for *tatemae*, or surface truth. *Honne*, deep truth, is harder to come by, and rarely simple. Japan's 'new' woman has far more in common with her prewar grandmother than media rhetoric would lead us to suspect. Japan may be unique among Asian countries in being modern and Westernized on the surface and very traditional beneath that veneer.

Norma Field, a bilingual and biracial Japanese American, describes Japan as 'the world's most orderly and prosperous society.' Obviously, there are benefits for both sexes in a stable and affluent society. Having spent her childhood in Japan and most of her adult years in America, however, Field finds the cost of belonging to Japanese society very high. For her, it would be intolerable. Despite an almost universal Japanese belief in the existence and importance of social harmony, she finds a repressive quality in everyday life. Field points to a 'coercive consensus' that prevents open discussion of any sensitive issue.[5] Japanese women who would like to diverge from the roles expected of them will understand Field's reaction. Japanese culture is based on social constraint and a deep-seated reluctance to contradict others.

There is a dark undercurrent in Japan's vaunted order, and as in any country women are sometimes the target of violence. Some of Field's views are shared by Japanese critics who point to a general increase in self-censorship following murders, bombings, and other forms of violence committed by political extremists of the far right. An American journalist notes that rising danger has caused 'a society of individuals already notoriously reluctant to express their views to become even less outspoken.'[6] Professor Yasuhiro Okudaira of International Christian University writes that journalists legitimately fear retaliation if they report critically on religious sects, gangs, and rightist organizations. Professor Keiichi Katsura of the University of Tokyo's Social Information Research Center observes that legally there is no suppression of freedom of speech, unlike prewar days, but that freedom of speech is gradually declining in social custom: 'A mood of self-restraint is becoming stronger.'

Such constraints affect both sexes but have a special relevance for women. Violent right wingers aim at restoring the emperor to his prewar status, tossing out the 1946 Constitution, outlawing racial mixing and re-establishing Japanese hegemony over Asia. These fanatics also favour the patriarchal traditions of prewar Japan. Women politicians and women who have spoken out strongly against sexual harassment have felt their wrath. In brief, right wingers oppose change, and women – many women – are working quietly and unobtrusively for change in Japanese society: 'We are changing, but men are not changing.' Not yet.

This study is primarily concerned with the lives of Japanese women since the Pacific War, but it is necessary to have some understanding of prewar conditions in order to appreciate the pull of tradition on the forces of modernization. Mavericks who work for social change and the betterment of women's lives are a minority in any culture. In Japan, such women stand on a brave tradition going back more than a century to the 1870s and before.

CHAPTER 2

BACK TO THE FUTURE:
THE WAITING YEARS

Tell him that when I die I want no funeral. Tell him that all he need do is to take my body out to sea at Shinagawa and dump it in the water.

FUMIKO ENCHI, *The Waiting Years*

Oh, women have the hardest part of life to bear ... Poor, poor women, how I long to do something to better your position.

UME TSUDA, letter, 7 December 1883

ROM SEPTEMBER 1945 until the end of 1947, Japan experienced a bloodless social and cultural revolution inspired by the occupation forces and welcomed by the vast majority of the population. Oxford historian Richard Storry writes: 'Once the war was over and the almost intolerable pressure of a police state was removed, all kinds of forces, dammed up for years, were suddenly released.'[1] The 1946 Constitution granted women the right to vote, to run for parliament, and to enter the national universities. It declared that men and women were equal and that marriage should be by mutual consent.

In the maelstrom of the early postwar years, many women must have felt exhilaration and hope. The new Constitution stressed the right to freedom of thought, equality of education, and the equal rights of husband and wife. Storry observes that *jinken*, or human rights, became a popular term of the day and captured the imagination of the Japanese people. The days when a woman would walk three steps behind her husband were over. Women had been fighting for many of these rights for nearly three-quarters of a century.

Over that period the Japanese state had curtailed freedoms for both men and women, but women had been handicapped far more severely.

The principle of *danson johi* (men respected, women scorned) was the prevailing norm. Even the rush to modernize the Japanese economy and society, begun in 1868, brought new difficulties for women. Ironically, restrictions that during the Edo period (1601-1868) had applied solely to the 10 percent of the population belonging to the elite samurai class were now extended to the other classes: farmers, merchants, and craftsmen.[2] The rigid separation of people into four classes was legally abolished, but in practice this meant that customs such as arranged marriage, which had governed only samurai wives since the fifteenth century, became widespread in the midst of modernization during the Meiji period (1868-1912).

Marriage was the sole destiny of any respectable woman. As a Buddhist proverb put it, 'Woman is without a house in all three worlds.' She was fated to leave her childhood home and her birth parents, to have her name struck from their register and added to that of her husband. She could return to her former home only rarely, on special holidays. When a girl married, her parents would break her rice bowl on their doorstep to signify that she was now dead to them. One strong woman saw it as banishment.[3] Despite the 1946 proclamation of equality, another half-century passed before the Japanese government would consider allowing women to retain their maiden name after marriage. Despite the initial sense of change in the postwar years, women would slowly come to realize just how little had changed with regard to the roles expected of them. Custom would prove far stronger than legislation, and far more difficult to alter.

Fumiko Enchi's novel *The Waiting Years*, published in Japanese in 1957 as *Onnazaka* but begun in the late 1940s, portrays the experience of women in Meiji and Taishō times, in the late nineteenth and early twentieth century.[4] The novel suggests that the anger and frustration experienced by the long-suffering heroine during some fifty years of loyal service to a self-indulgent husband was also felt by Enchi herself, born in 1905. With its searing attack on the institution of concubinage, the double sexual standard, and the absolute financial dependence of women on men, the novel dramatizes many of the issues that concerned early reformers from the 1870s to the Pacific War and beyond. This novel is a good place to start trying to understand the patriarchal and conservative ways of the society that rose out of wartime devastation to form the modern state of Japan.

Enchi's epic fiction follows three generations of the Shirakawa family through nearly half a century, from the late 1870s to the early 1920s. The ambitious Shirakawa, sprung from a low-ranking samurai family, has done well for himself in the political turmoil following the Meiji Restoration in 1868. As the story opens, he is chief secretary to a prefectural governor and sufficiently wealthy to send his wife to Tokyo to choose a concubine for him. Fifteen-year-old Suga is bought as a family 'maid,' and later registered as an adopted daughter.

The mixed emotions of pity, jealousy, hate, and guilt felt by Tomo, the wife, are powerfully portrayed. Married at fourteen, Tomo is barely thirty by the time she is charged with this onerous task. Moreover, she loves her husband. Why, she thinks, must she contribute to this cruelty that was 'little better than slave-trading'? She experiences two conflicting emotions: 'boundless pity as for a charming animal that was about to be led to the slaughter, and fixed hatred at the thought that eventually this innocent girl might turn into a devil that would devour her husband and sweep unchecked through the whole house.'[5]

Sacrificed for her family's fortunes, Suga is taken to bed by Shirakawa before she is sexually mature and becomes sterile as a result. Worse, life as a captive sexual toy cultivates a deep-seated, lifelong passivity in the girl and continuing guilt in Tomo for her part in it: 'For the change from the charming young victim to the apathetic Suga ..., dull as a silkworm's cocoon, there lay a responsibility that could not, Tomo felt, be attributed to her husband alone' (p. 112).

Tomo herself had been sexually initiated at an even younger age, and her first child is a maladjusted, boyish man who makes life miserable for those around him. Tomo believes that the blame for her son's 'eternal immaturity' can only be attributed to the immaturity of her own body at fifteen when she had given birth to him: 'Conceived in a womb imperfectly matured, he had been born with a mind incapable of growth' (p. 86).

After he becomes superintendent of the Tokyo police, Shirakawa receives part of his income from taxes on the Yoshiwara, a red-light district. In an incident that dramatizes the political struggles of the early 1880s, he is injured in a street fight with members of the Liberal Party. Tomo accepts unquestioningly what she is told by her husband and the governor's wife, namely, that those who defied officials governing in accordance with the emperor's command and who tried to stir up the people with talk of liberty and civil rights 'were rogues who deserved punishment in the same way as arsonists and robbers' (pp. 42-3).

The truly radical nature of the novel lies less in its historical accuracy, however, than in its portrayal of Tomo's inner self. This strong woman's bonds are largely internal, thanks to her social conditioning within a patriarchal society, which has taught her to accept the harsh treatment of reformers along with her own position within the family: 'Towards the Emperor and the authorities she showed the same vaguely submissive attitude as to the feminine ethic that had taught her to yield to her husband's wishes in every respect, however unreasonable they might seem. Born in a country district of Kyūshū near the end of the feudal period and barely able to read and write, she had no shield to defend herself other than the existing moral code' (p. 43).

As Tomo watches the innocent young Suga dance, she thinks her husband a monster of callousness, yet since serving him is the creed on which her life is centred, 'to rebel against his outrages *would have been to destroy herself as well*' (p. 28, emphasis added). Her tumultuous feelings are complicated by her one-sided love and her deep desire to have her husband understand her feelings.

Installing Suga in the Shirakawa household makes Tomo's own position very vulnerable. She has seen other powerful men discard their wives and replace them with concubines. She has been taught to be the chaste wife who lives only to serve husband and family, 'but now an unmistakable mistrust in the code that had been her unquestioned creed was making itself felt within' (p. 52).

The Waiting Years portrays a woman whose husband fears her strength. Secretly, he knows her to be an equal, a capable household and estate manager whose diligence earns no praise, 'an enemy entrenched in a fortress that no assault could reduce' (p. 75). As the years pass and political troubles multiply, he longs to be comforted by this strong wife, but he realizes that his behaviour has long since killed her love. Shirakawa's tragic loneliness matches Tomo's. This is one of the novel's central ironies, just as its title symbolizes Tomo's entire life. The metaphor is underlined by the sound made by her stiff silk sash as it unwinds, 'melancholy and monotonous, yet powerful as the waves on a wintry sea' (p. 75).

Tomo finds both release and revenge in her approaching death. She insists that her will be read by her husband before she dies. In old-fashioned women's language, Tomo has written of the money left from the sum entrusted to her thirty years earlier to buy a concubine in Tokyo. Fearful for her future, she had saved and invested it: 'Again and again, as he read, [Shirakawa] felt himself reeling before a force more powerful than himself. There was not a word of complaint from Tomo against the outrageous way he had oppressed her: nothing but apology for not having trusted him fully and for always having kept a painful secret from him. Yet the words of apology bore down on his heart more heavily than the strongest protest' (p. 200). By adhering to the moral code, Tomo forces her husband to see that he himself has betrayed its spirit.

Next, Tomo insists that Shirakawa be told she wants *no funeral*, but that her body should be dumped at sea. Implicit is the suggestion that this is the value he has put on her life. The women forced to convey the message understand perfectly; they had been married and had suffered themselves. The bizarre message, taut with a lifetime of pent-up emotion, strikes the husband like a body-blow: 'The shock was enough to split his arrogant ego in two' (p. 203). Enchi's fiction reveals the individual suffering behind historical facts.

Concubinage in the Japanese family system has been documented by many historians, but few can match the power of Enchi's fiction to reveal its emotional effect upon women. Male reformers such as Arinori Mori and Yukichi Fukuzawa, writing in the early 1870s, claimed that the treatment of women in Japanese society was barbaric and inhumane; that reform must begin with the family; and that the concubine system, symbol of male power and privilege, could only be supported 'by men whose self-interest and self-indulgence made them less than human.'[6] Attitudes towards women bred through centuries of concubinage in Japan have continued to manifest themselves throughout the twentieth century.

Ume Tsuda (1865-1929), a pioneer educator of women in Japan, was equally critical of the Japanese patriarchy. The youngest of five girls sent by her government in 1872 to be educated in America, Ume turned seven on the voyage out. This curious experiment of sending girls abroad for education appeared to be sparked by the realization that higher institutions for learning for young women were utterly lacking in Japan, and that education was essential to modernization.[7]

Ume's ten years in the United States were happy ones, spent with foster parents Adeline and Charles Lanman, well-to-do and cultured people. Her separation from the other girls, however, meant that Ume completely lost her Japanese language ability and took years to regain it once back in Japan. When she returned in 1882, full of hopes and plans for the education of Japanese women, she saw with the eyes of a foreigner and was shocked at the condition of women.

A second shock came with the gradual discovery that the government that had paid for her education, perhaps on a whim, had no plans to make use of an educated women such as herself save as the wife of an important man. Faced with the hard choice of marriage or a career as an educator, Tsuda chose the latter. Eventually, with financial help from Americans, she founded a college for girls that survives today as Tsuda College, a prestigious women's university.

The recurring topic in letters to her American foster mother was the low status of Japanese women: 'God knows, life is hard enough anyway, but a Japanese woman's, oh, how sad! In blinding ignorance, she does everything – a most respectful, obedient and dutiful way must be hers to her husband. Her children are more his than hers ... She is not often loved, often a plaything, oftener like a servant – ... the very magnitude of the work overwhelms me.'[8] Tsuda realized that virtue and discipline were valued far above individual character and intellectual vitality and that in trying to instill the latter in her students she was working against the policies of Japanese schools.

It is not surprising that Tsuda found little or no support for her ideas. There was a popular rights movement in Meiji Japan and a Liberal Party, but the latter was dissolved in 1884 as civil unrest intensified. As well, the majority of male reformers were uninterested in women's concerns. A few bold women mounted public platforms despite the increasing violence of political meetings.

Toshiko Kishida (1863-1901), Japan's first woman journalist, undertook a two-month speaking tour at the age of twenty and drew crowds with standing room only. Earlier, she had served the empress at court but had found the atmosphere stifling. She believed that excluding women from the nation's work was irrational, that the principle of *danson johi* was unethical, and that equality between the sexes was the mark of a civilized state. Daughters, she told her listeners in 1883, were like flowers. They needed a nourishing environment in order to develop their full potential and should not be confined to the home, a play on *hako-iri musume* (daughter in a box), a Japanese idiom for a sheltered maiden who had been carefully reared. This speech earned Kishida eight days in jail.[9]

Hideko Fukuda (1867-1927) heard Kishida speak on women's rights in 1883 and was deeply affected, as she later wrote in her autobiography, *Half of My Lifetime*.[10] She remained a strong advocate for freedom and justice for both sexes. Fukuda was also inspired by a biography of Joan of Arc, translated by her father. Involvement with a circle of radical liberal activists led to several years in prison, but in 1889 a general amnesty in honour of the new constitution released Fukuda and her friends. She founded one journal, *Women of the World*, and contributed to many others. An article on socialism that she contributed many years later to the feminist journal *Seito* led the government to ban and seize the issue.

Meanwhile the ruling elite, far from considering the possibility of suffrage for women in the late nineteenth century, set out to ban them from taking any part in political activity. In 1882, women were forbidden to make political speeches. The constitution of 1889 formally excluded women, for the first time in the nation's history, from accession to the Japanese throne. In 1890, under Article 5 of the Police Security Regulations, women were denied the right to participate in politics *at any level*. They were banned from joining a political group and even from attending a political meeting, subject to fine or imprisonment.

Ironically, the actions of reformers such as Kishida and Fukuda, along with Japan's first strike in 1886, had resulted in further repression. As Sharon Sievers observes, 'Japanese women, after a decade of valuable political experience, were now unable to mount a campaign against the regulations without violating them.'[11] In short, for over sixty years prior to the Pacific War, the state attempted to bar women from having or expressing political opinions.

Shidzue Ishimoto's observations in the 1920s and '30s echo those of Ume Tsuda and Fumiko Enchi and are relevant to both the nineteenth and the twentieth century. Ishimoto (b. 1897) was just eight years younger than the novelist. Born into a rich and noble family, reared delicately and married at sixteen to Baron Keikichi Ishimoto, Shidzue's real education, like that of Ume Tsuda after she returned to Japan, might well be called shock treatment. It was begun in the rural mining communities of Kyūshū, where her husband served as a mining engineer with Miike Coal Mines. Women miners, Ishimoto writes, went down the mines half clothed to labour alongside naked men in the humid heat: 'Often pregnant women, working until the last moment, gave birth to children in the dark pit.'[12]

Shidzue's traumatic education continued in the slums of New York, where her husband left her alone for six months to learn English and typing while he toured Europe. She was determined to become wife, mother, and partner by taking 'an energetic part in public work' (p. 243). When the Baron switched his political allegiance

Writer Shidzue Ishimoto Katō in her home in Tokyo, 1991.

from liberal humanism to conservative nationalism and became a supporter of Japanese expansion in mainland China, Shidzue declined to follow. After years of hardship she obtained a divorce in the 1940s and married a socialist reformer, Kanju Katō. In the late 1980s, Shidzue Ishimoto Katō was honoured by the United Nations for some seventy years of work in family planning.

By her thirties, Shidzue had fiercely repudiated the attitudes to women that had dominated her early life. For centuries, a neo-Confucian tract by Kaibara Ekken (1631-1714) had served as a guide for female education in Japan and a shaper of male views of women. Katō calls the discipline of the *Onna daigaku* (Great learning for women) fantastically rigid. Rules for a man to divorce his wife included jealousy, talkativeness, and failure to bear an heir.[13] Talking is described as breaking the harmony of the family. The 'way' of women is summed up as obedience. Women's 'sins' or failings include disobedience, anger, envy, and stupidity. Katō quotes from Kaibara Ekken, who concludes that these failings make women inferior to men: 'Above all, shallowness of mind is her worst fault ... In bringing up her children, she merely follows instinct and not reason; so she cannot educate them properly. Utterly devoid of wisdom, she should humbly follow her husband in everything' (p. 280). Shidzue, who found these ideas common in the 1920s and '30s, calls *Onna daigaku* 'the moral code which has chained Japanese women to the past' (p. 38).

The influence of this neo-Confucian moral code could be seen as Japan struggled to modernize its infrastructure in the late nineteenth century. Labour-intensive light industry such as textile manufacture earned the foreign exchange needed to import material and equipment for capital-intensive industries such as steel. Silk and cotton mills required relatively little capital and a large labour force. In Japan as in the West, there was no shortage of daughters accustomed to hard labour. Indeed Meiji leaders considered these young women one of the country's major resources. By 1914, female mill hands had made Japan the world's leading exporter of silk and the world leader in cotton manufacturing: 'Without the work of Japan's women, the apparent miracle of Japan's economic growth [pre-1940] might not have been possible.'[14]

The social costs of ill health and death paid by the female workers were enormous yet, paradoxically, their work did nothing to change the country's view that women belonged in the home. Patricia Tsurumi writes that Japan's industrialization preserved rather than dissolved the traditional order: 'By helping the landlords, girls and women in the textile plants helped perpetuate the hierarchical and exploitative relationships of the pre-Meiji countryside.'[15] Because of women's work and endurance, the state could continue to ignore widespread poverty. As women marched to work through the mountain passes, they sang to lift their spirits and recall their goals: 'For ourselves, for our parents. / For men, the army, For women, the mills. / Spinning thread is for the country too.'

It is surprising to realize that women dominated the Meiji work force, constituting an average of 60 percent of Japan's industrial labour from 1894 to 1912. Well-documented sources show that economic historians have ignored or downplayed the important part played by these women, and their hardships: 'Women bore the brunt of Japan's industrial revolution in its early stages.'[16] Their work brought them neither upward social mobility nor economic independence. The latter was considered unimportant, an attitude that has continued into the 1990s, thanks to what Sievers calls 'the comforting myth' that women would be protected for life by a benevolent family structure. Then as now this myth conveniently ignores the realities of divorce, death, and various common economic hardships, while exploitation continues to mask itself as paternalism.

The mill owner's contract was made not with the worker but with her family, usually farmers in desperate conditions. A cash advance to the father established the traditional relationship of obligation. In the 1870s, a few model mills fostered the illusion that conditions were safe for the workers. By the 1880s, conditions had become intolerable yet Japanese recruiters were still able to secure the daughters of impoverished families, just as immigrants continued to supply labour to mills in New England.

Workers lived in prison-like dormitories, where locks, barbed wire, and guards discouraged escape. Few workers lasted more than a year. The annual turnover rate in Meiji times was 50 percent. Food was poor and unvaried. The average workday in the 1880-1900 period was twelve to thirteen hours, with two fifteen-minute breaks. Lung disease was endemic, with high humidity added to poor nutrition, long hours, and wretched sleeping conditions. Many workers left the mills only to die of tuberculosis and other diseases.[17] Women suffered more than any other group in the Japanese work force, both during and after their period of employment in the mills.

Women workers courageously organized boycotts, walkouts, and strikes from the 1880s on. These elicited little sympathy with farmers, who associated the strikes with lower prices paid for cocoons. One young farm woman who knew nothing of the harsh conditions in the factories considered it 'shocking and indecent to force someone's hand by refusing to work,' while her older brother warned her not to become 'a shameless girl, always demanding more than her due.'[18]

Twentieth-century Japanese historians continued to characterize the mill workers as 'ignorant farm girls,' incapable of protest, unorganizable, impermanent workers. (The idea that women are content to be temporary workers is still in force today.) Sievers calls the broken promises of turn-of-the-century owners and recruiters a parody of traditional worker-employer relationships. Women were considered commodities to be bought and sold.

Despite the growing importance of women in the work force, the ideal woman continued to be seen in terms of *ryosai kenbo*, 'good wife, wise mother,' a phrase coined by Meiji reformer Masanao Nakamura that remains current in the twentieth century. The theoretical elevation of motherhood was a prominent icon in Victorian England. In Japan, it co-existed with the principle of *danson johi*.

Social divisions unfortunately prevented women in the popular rights movement of the late nineteenth century from identifying with young factory women. After the 1880s, as we have seen, women could no longer make political speeches. Published articles had far less impact and failed to reach women with little formal schooling. Moreover, the long-suffering mill workers, often sexually exploited by male managers, were looked down on: 'In the popular mind, being "sold" to a textile mill was akin to being "sold" to a brothel.'[19] As for brothels, they were sanctioned by the government, and many impoverished families sold their daughters to geisha houses or brothels in urban centres.

The elaborate hair styles required for geisha, and indeed for nearly all prewar Japanese women, meant that hairdressing provided steady work for women. There were over 100 traditional hairstyles, many of them involving painful and unhealthy tugging and binding of the hair.[20] Scrupulously neat hair was part of female virtue. Small wonder that Meiji rebel Akiko Yosano chose *Tangled Hair* as the title for a book of love poems. Her image connected tangled hair with women's emancipation and sexual freedom.[21] Earlier reformers active in the struggle for women's rights had cut their hair at home. The Meiji government reacted by banning short hair for women, a quite extraordinary act seen by Sievers as a message to Japanese women that they should symbolize their country's past rather than make any attempt to participate in its future.[22]

By the late nineteenth and early twentieth centuries, new areas of employment were opening to women in hospitals, schools, and telephone and telegraph stations. The first Japanese women doctors were licensed in the late 1880s, the same decade when Canadian women doctors began to practise. Insufficient education barred rural women from many of these jobs. Office work remained relatively closed to women until after 1945. It was largely men, not women, who carried the endless cups of tea to their superiors in prewar Japanese offices.[23]

In the Taishō era (1912-26), women were allowed to teach in the early grades of elementary school. The first appointment of a woman principal of an elementary school came in 1931.[24] Because of the high esteem traditionally accorded to teachers, this field would gradually become an excellent one for women, one of the few in which they were not automatically dismissed when they married, a practice that continues in Japanese banks and major companies today.

The patriarchy continued to pretend that women were cared for within the family system, but this was simply not so. Many fell outside the net. Impoverished women could be street vendors, newsgirls, or domestic servants. Servants were often cheated of a fair wage by means of the prevailing etiquette that any initial discussion of wages was 'not nice,' and that upper-class employers could be trusted to act fairly.[25] Girls were often put into domestic service as young as eight or nine. One survivor, born in 1909, concluded philosophically in 1987, 'I don't think you can really blame anybody in particular for this; it's just that everyone like us was poor, and the world as a whole was much less advanced then.'[26]

Mikiso Hane writes that poor women suffered not simply the economic hardship and injustices that members of the underclass have always endured 'but also the restrictions and discrimination that all Japanese women had to put up with.'[27] A double bind. Fumiko Kaneko, who was executed for an alleged plot against the state in the 1920s, was the child of unmarried parents who had neglected to enter her name in either family register. This meant that she had no legal standing whatsoever and could attend school only as an auditor. The endless injustices encountered by Kaneko developed her keen sense of natural justice. Poverty fed the leftist political movements that the government so fiercely suppressed.

After the suppression of efforts in the 1880s, a second wave of reformist energy began to gather force in the early years of this century. In September 1911, the first issue of *Seitō* (Bluestocking) was published by a group of single, upper-class women who sought a vehicle for their writings and a place to air feminist grievances. The first article in the by-laws of Seitōsha, the Bluestocking Society, which published the journal, stated, 'We will strive for the development of female writers.'[28] The founding editor was Haruko Hiratsuka (1886-1971), better known as Raichō.

Seitō's first issue featured Raichō's now-famous manifesto: 'In the Beginning Woman was the Sun ... / Now Woman is the Moon. She lives through others ... / Now we must restore our hidden Sun.' It also contained Akiko Yosano's forceful verse, comparing women to a long-dormant volcano now ready to erupt. There were articles by other influential women, such as Toshiko Tamura. The journal that described itself as the only female literary magazine in Japan was off to a strong start.

Members of Seitōsha proudly identified themselves as 'new women.' Within a year, any newspaper reader knew the tag, but its negative aspect predominated. Several foolish escapades by Society members had contributed to the view that a new woman was inconstant, lustful, and lacking in maternal love: in short, fine fodder for the gossip columns but not to be taken seriously. Often the attack was led by members of the Real New Women's Association, a conservative group in favour of traditional norms.[29]

September 1911 was also marked by the first performance in Japanese of Ibsen's landmark feminist drama, A Doll's House. Tokyo audiences were stunned, by the play itself and by the performance of Sumako Matsui as Nora. Even male critics succumbed to the power of Nora's great speech as she prepares to leave home. Seitō devoted an entire issue to commentary on the play and on the issues it raised. In an open letter to Nora, Raichō expressed concern for her future, since her levels of social awareness and self-knowledge were still relatively low.[30]

Meanwhile, the self-awareness level of Seitōsha members was being steadily raised through generally harsh media reaction to their articles and public behaviour. As they were forced to realize that art is not easily separated from politics, they were moving slowly to the left, to an analysis of the difficulties women encountered in social life. Few, however, were prepared for Hideko Fukuda's article on women and socialism in the February 1913 issue. It upset both members and police, since Fukuda insisted that all women should be liberated, not simply an elite, and that a 'communist' system was the way to accomplish this.[31] The government banned the issue, with a warning that the journal was disturbing the traditional virtues of Japanese women. The Seitōsha found itself unable to hire a hall in which to continue its lecture series.

By late 1914, Raichō was preoccupied with a love affair and was finding the journal a burden. Colleagues had been gradually withdrawing as opposition mounted from both the public and police. The Society's youngest member, Noe Itō (1895-1923), had edited the October and November issues by herself, and her confidence was growing. In November, Itō asked that the position of editor-in-chief be transferred to herself, although the founder would remain the senior representative of the group. Raichō agreed. Twin editorials marked the January issue. Noe, barely twenty, wrote that she intended to provide 'a magazine without isms, without policies, without regulations.'

Seitō survived under Itō for just over one year, until February 1916. The new editor had to cope with increasing pressure from family responsibilities, a complex love triangle, and mounting government opposition. In 1913, the Seitōsha had pruned from its founding statements anything that limited the journal to literature alone, and its later issues concentrated on social and political issues as they affected women. There was, however, little consensus among the members, and defections continued.

Itō opened the pages to discussions on abortion, prostitution, and motherhood, debates that would continue long after the journal had ended. As Sievers writes, these issues challenged society's power over women's bodies, as well as the double sexual standard; in *Seitō*, sexuality was discussed openly and in relation to the politics of women's condition.[32]

Itō and her common-law husband Sakae Ōsugi were picked up by police during the confusion that followed the Great Earthquake in Tokyo on 1 September 1923. Soon after, they were strangled in their cells by a police officer. The women's movement to which Itō had contributed so much was not stilled. New journals, new movements were increasingly drawing together the Meiji struggle for women's political rights and the Taishō emphasis on women's creativity. Fusae Ichikawa would later summarize the goals of the suffrage movement in the 1920s as the desire to reform the legal system, increase welfare, clean up politics, and pursue peace.

Peace would be a long time coming. Life during the late 1920s and '30s was increasingly dominated by the military, and the only women's organizations to be tolerated became those that carried out government policies. Individual women and the voluntary groups that had been active during the first sixty years of Japan's modernization were co-opted in the 1930s into a new pattern of organization, one that was neither a political party nor an interest group. These mass organizations were controlled by government ministries that defined their agenda and the interests they served.[33]

The three chief organizations of this type were the Great Japan Federated Women's Association, the Great Japan National Defense Women's Association, and the Patriotic Women's Association. The first was founded in 1931 to promote household economy, public health, and moral education. The Defense Women's Association, founded in 1932 and directed by the army, was instructed to exorcise the materialism of Western thought and to encourage women's traditional morality. After the invasion of China in 1937, their membership grew rapidly to 7.5 million members. The Patriotic Women's Association, founded in 1901, had always enjoyed government support but was overhauled by the Home Ministry in 1933.

Early in 1942, these three bodies were amalgamated into one, the Great Japan Women's Association. Then, as earlier, activities included assisting soldiers and their families, raising money for the war effort, imposing frugality within the house, and increasing personal savings. Women were expected to bear more children, help with civil defence, and work, as assigned, in war-related industries and neighbourhood associations.

Gregory Kasza draws a comparison between the tightly controlled women's organizations and the mass conscript army. Both targeted an entire category of people for membership – all women except unmarrieds under twenty in the case of the Great Japan Women's Association. Both prohibited alternative organizations. And in each, key administrators, along with goals and activities, were chosen by the state rather than by the membership. In short, the Great Japan Women's Association was a women's army, the female half of a 'conscription state.'[34]

Most Japanese women were patriotic, but many also believed that these state-controlled women's organizations were achieving certain aims of the independent women's movement. Some women activists, such as suffragist Fusae Ichikawa, were offered official posts in state agencies.[35] This unprecedented access to government appeared to many as a step forward, despite the minimal influence women could bring to bear on policy making.

Shizuko Gō's beautiful novella, *Requiem*, captures the experience of girls and women during the Pacific War and stands as a strong indictment of all wars. This fiction is autobiographical, as Gō, like her young protagonist Setsuko Ōizumi, was born in 1929 and was sixteen in August 1945, as the fighting drew to its inevitable close. *Requiem*, a lament for a nation gone astray and for all the dead of those terrible times, is cast as the fevered flashbacks of Setsuko as she lies dying from malnutrition, tuberculosis, and exhaustion in a hand-dug bomb shelter.

Until her last weeks and months, Setsuko is a fervent believer in the military propaganda that controls her life. As a young girl, she had written to unknown Japanese soldiers at the front to encourage them. Each defeat was a Glorious Sacrifice in the sacred war for the Japanese goal of a Greater East Asia Co-Prosperity Sphere: 'So Setsuko had been taught, had believed, had lived.'[36] Japanese would never surrender. The 'Invincible Army of the Rising Sun' would fight to the last man (p. 49).

Setsuko has two friends who think differently. Naomi is the daughter of a professor who had opposed the war and who is imprisoned for ideological crimes. Shōichi Wakui is the older brother of her brother's friend. He too is imprisoned for being a pacifist and a communist. Through letters and occasional encounters between the young people their opposing views are discussed in an atmosphere of tolerance and love. Increasingly, Setsuko's patriotic views must confront the realities of war on the home front.

Soon high school girls are enlisted to work in munitions factories. Setsuko's job is making vacuum tubes. Every day she must make the long, arduous walk from Yokohama to the factory. Her health is so poor that she has been advised to leave the factory and return to school, as pupils in ill health were allowed to do. But Setsuko, a 'true Japanese' and a model student, is ready to sacrifice herself and longs to make some small contribution to the war effort. Her idealism has even prevented her from accepting black market food sent by a friend: 'When I think of the soldiers at the front, I just can't' (pp. 42-3).

Slowly, slowly, Setsuko begins to see that war is neither sacred nor glorious but meaningless and horrible. Her mother has searched for her father's body amid charred heaps of corpses until she felt herself becoming one of them. Later, her mother is machine-gunned from a low-flying American plane as she stood on a bomb site with other survivors waiting for rations. 'Why do we make war,' Setsuko wonders, 'when we're all the same human beings?' (p. 72).

Writer Shizuko Gō in her home in Yokohama, 1990.

In the final scene, as the Occupation forces are arriving on 16 August 1945, neighbours recall the rape of Nanking and advise Setsuko to hide in the mountains, 'or else.' Men are all the same at a time like this, the neighbour adds, whether they are Japanese or Americans. As a male figure approaches Setsuko in her last moment of consciousness, the girl confuses the American soldier with her dead brother, Hajime.

This closing image brings the warring sides together into one man, thus reinforcing the credo that Gō's heroine has gradually forged for herself, one of love, hope, tolerance, and individual questioning. Pacifism would continue to be a goal pursued by women's groups and women writers in the half-century to come. The author's own health was badly damaged during the war. Her moving requiem for 'the military nation girls' was not written until 1972, when Gō had sons of her own and the Cold War was causing concern to mothers everywhere.[37]

This brief survey of women's lives during the three-quarters of a century before the modern period makes the latter more comprehensible, since the weight of tradition continues to bear heavily upon Japanese society. Sharon Sievers emphasizes that policies affecting Meiji women 'were not the product of some vague accumulated social inertia' but were a calculated response by the authorities towards women 'who attempted to define their own roles in a rapidly changing society that seemed to invite such redefinition.'[38] The heavy hand of government planning is self-evident, but we should not discount the strong influence that centuries of devaluing women – *danson johi* – must inevitably have had on the male autocrats who controlled Japanese society. Social inertia, alias cultural conditioning, is not so easily dismissed.

Historically, Japanese women have shared with women everywhere the devaluation of their work, a lack of legal rights, the double sexual standard, and the determination of many males to control women's lives, minds, and bodies. These hardships differ in degree from culture to culture and from age to age. Nevertheless, the experience of Japanese women before the Pacific War was exceptionally harsh. 'We received democracy [after the war], and it was delicious,' I was told by one woman. Since 1945, however, cultural change has been remarkably slow. The next chapter examines aspects of Japanese culture that have influenced the daily lives of women in the last half-century and are only recently beginning to change.

CHAPTER 3

CULTURE:
THE MASTER KEY

What angered her even more was the unladylike way in which Keiko sat with one thigh crossed over the other, as if to show off her legs and stockings – such conduct in a young girl had been unthinkable before the coming of the Occupation Forces ... Here was a threat, it seemed to her, to the whole structure of Japanese womanliness and morality.

MASAKO TOGAWA, *The Master Key*

I could not hope for sympathy from friends whose eternal moral code was feminine sacrifice.

SHIDZUE ISHIMOTO, *Facing Two Ways: The Story of My Life*

Aт FIRST SIGHT, women's lives in contemporary Japan appear to resemble those of North American women in the 1950s and early '60s. The similarities are often illusory and can be misleading. Japanese history and culture underlie current differences, social patterns, and rates of change. The threat to 'the whole structure of Japanese womanliness and morality' expressed in Masako Togawa's mystery novel, *The Master Key*, is perceived in a high school student by an older woman teacher in the early postwar years. Togawa's thrillers have been compared with the fiction of P.D. James. In *The Master Key*, the subtle subtext and the key to the mystery is the importance of the individual.[1]

The perceived threat is really the confident assertion of individuality in the face of entrenched patterns of obligation, hierarchy, and group consensus. These social norms encourage and enforce the acceptance of practices that Shidzue Ishimoto Katō sees as an unreasonable submission on the part of women, one that benefits neither sex.

By the average Japanese, individualism is understood as selfishness. It represents antisocial behaviour.[2] 'Human rights' and 'women's rights' may be common phrases in the West but are understood differently in Japan. The 1946 Constitution cast a thin veneer of democracy over a feudal society. That veneer would prove far weaker than traditional ways.

In any nation, a process of lifelong conditioning begins early and is reinforced daily. In Japan, however, the priority given to group harmony (*wa*) reinforces other customs and traditions. Many commentators insist that the conservative character of Japan makes for 'a deeply ingrained reluctance to ignore or change the established order,' and it has naturally affected the experience of women in postwar Japan.[3]

Chie Nakane's analysis of Japanese society as one based on hierarchical principles and reciprocal obligations is a good place to begin. Without it, the average Westerner may be puzzled by behaviour and situations that seem obvious to the Japanese. Nakane's *Japanese Society* is a work of social anthropology that concentrates on individual behaviour and interpersonal relations. She explores her country's structural core and the reasons behind the sturdy persistence of prewar values and norms. Her theme is the working of the vertical principle, the bond that links individuals and groups to one another. This relationship between two human units of *unequal* status forms Japan's basic structural principle.

Nakane's social analysis depends on two criteria, one based on individual attributes, the other on a situational position within a given frame, or field. A frame may be a place, an institution, or a relationship, and depends on circumstances or situation. It establishes a boundary and provides a common basis for a set of individuals located or involved in it. The Japanese tendency to stress this framework is seen when workers typically introduce themselves as belonging to a certain company. It is the company or institution that bestows identity, not the worker's role as secretary, lawyer, or engineer.

Nakane describes the company as providing employees with their entire social existence and as having authority over all aspects of their lives. She compares this deeply emotional bond with the extended family or *ie*, the fundamental social unit in prewar Japan. The *ie* was framed by kinship and local residence. Moreover, it was often a management organization. Human relationships within the *ie* took precedence over all others.[4]

Nakane argues, convincingly, that the old role of the *ie* has been played in postwar Japan by modern companies: 'A company is conceived as an *ie*, all its employees qualifying as members of the household, with the employer at the head ... The employer readily takes responsibility for his employee's family, for which, in turn, the primary concern is the company.'[5] The social consciousness that made this possible has been justified by traditional morality and promoted by slogans.

Nakane takes this startling analogy further by showing that the new employee is received by the company 'in much the same spirit as if he were a newly born family member, a newly adopted son-in-law or a bride come into the husband's household' (p. 14). The relationship is closer than that between husband and wife. This metaphor for engrained social patterns helps non-Japanese to understand why the typical salaryman will work longer hours than those accepted in other developed nations, will work to the point of endangering his health, and will endure job transfers that remove him from his family for years on end.

The salaryman's loyalty to company and co-workers within a structure of group consciousness and hierarchical relationships provides him with a social life and with security for himself and his family. Nakane notes that loyalty to an employer is a lifelong commitment and embodies an ideology far removed from any sense of contract. For many Japanese, emotional security is a primary requirement.[6] The enormous strength of the husband's bond with his company is a basic given laid upon the lives of Japanese housewives. In return, they share in the security that many salarymen enjoy. At least, this was so until the early 1990s.

Over the last decade the bond has been loosening. Some husbands and wives are finding such security not worth the high price it exacts. One irate woman told me that for as long as her husband had worked for a large, international company she had had to meet him at the train station every evening near midnight. The parking lot was filled with other waiting wives. The woman considered that her husband had been 'a slave' to the company, whose prison-like premises – her image – were locked and guarded each day beginning soon after 8:00 AM: 'Once I start telling the complaints I can't stop!' Few, if any, would dare to publish such views in the media. The couple had decided that it would be better for the husband to take a less prestigious job with lower pay, shorter hours, and less commitment to the employer.

Talking with a group of nine women cafeteria workers in 1991, I encountered more conservative attitudes. In hopes of making my queries and attitudes more understandable, I explained that although I enjoyed close relationships with family and friends, in the last analysis I relied on myself. The women looked puzzled and sympathetic as to one in an unenviable situation. One after another they reiterated their own position, saying, 'I feel secure.' Some said it twice. These women were all graduates of universities or two-year colleges. They worked thirty-five hours a week, were paid one-quarter or one-third of a minimum living wage (without benefits) and therefore depended on their husbands for present and future support.

I wondered how many Western women in the last two decades of this century, married or unmarried, would make such a confident assertion.

Sumiko Iwao argues that the hierarchical structure of relationships and institutions affects only men and that women's groups tend to be horizontal, with structures based on qualification or task.[7] This ignores the fact that a housewife depends on her husband and he, in turn, on his company. Moreover, hierarchical structures strongly affect women as workers, barring them until recently from management-stream jobs and affecting their pay scales.

Hierarchy affects every relationship. Within it, age and sex are superseded by status. Japanese women are nearly always ranked as inferior because they are almost automatically assigned lower social status. Even at the supper table of an ordinary family, members are seated and served by rank: 'Last of all come the mistress of the household and the wife of the successor. The sequence of serving thus clearly reflects the structure of the group.'[8]

Chance encounters on the street are equally regulated. Wives behave towards each other in accordance with the ranks of their spouses. The depth of the bow, and the honorific language used would be appropriate to the relationship between the women's husbands. Nakane notes that a relationship among equals is rare in Japan but is most closely approached by two individuals of the same sex and school year. In any gathering, the frequency with which someone offers an opinion, and the initial order in which those present speak are also indications of rank: 'To this extent, ranking order not only regulates social behaviour but also curbs the open expression of thought' (p. 35).

The importance of harmony and the acceptance of the authority of the group is inculcated in early childhood. Vertical structures are rooted in childhood training and the indulgence commonly accorded to Japanese children. Takeo Doi argues that *amae* (dependence or passive love, the confident expectation that self-indulgence will be permitted) is a key to the Japanese mentality and the chief characteristic of the parent-child relationship.[9] Ruth Benedict discusses child training at greater length, and demonstrates that home is a haven of safety and indulgence, with the mother as the source of constant and extreme gratifications. A boy, in particular, can gratify or indulge even his aggressions.[10] Many of the prewar child-rearing practices described by Benedict remained in place in the postwar period and continue to affect the behaviour and attitudes of both sexes.

A recent study takes issue with the common view of young Japanese children as overindulged and shows how preschools work to provide sheltered children with a chance to learn how to function as members of a group."[11] Starting from Takeo Doi's later model, *The Anatomy of Self* (1986) and its concept of the two-tiered Japanese self with *omote* and *ura* (outer and inner) dimensions, Joseph Tobin argues that Japanese preschools teach children aged three to six not merely to distinguish between public and private behaviour but – more important – the art of *kejime*, the ability to move easily from one to the other. Japanese put a high value on formality, or the behaviour proper to public spheres of life. Western societies used to value formal behaviour, as we are reminded by a recent televised production of Jane Austen's 1813 novel, *Pride and Prejudice*. Currently the West values *omote* less and *ura* (spontaneity) more, a change that has tended to complicate mutual understanding between North America and Japan.

Children have always been very important to Japanese women, not only for emotional satisfaction but also because it is largely as a mother that a wife gains status. Before 1945, a wife could be returned to her parents if she failed to bear a child. Japan has been called a children's paradise, where small children may do as they please and are rarely scolded. A baby sleeps beside the mother's futon until the age of one and thereafter, for some years, under her covers. The child is commonly nursed, and for a substantially longer period than in the West. Before the war, and for the first postwar generation, the infant or small child was carried in a double sash on the back of mothers and siblings. She or he is still taught respect-language very young, and when the mother bows, she inclines the child's head with her hand.

Benedict, in a prewar study that has relevance today, notes that teasing is a common disciplinary measure for preschool children. Mock threats, quickly rescinded when the child's behaviour improves, become 'rich soil for the fear of ridicule and ostracism which is so marked in the Japanese grown-up ... The sense of being laughed at fuses with the panic of the child threatened with loss of all that is safe and familiar.'[12] This practice, along with group solidarity, is the basis of what has been called Japan's shame culture, in contrast to the part played by guilt in the Western psyche.

Small children are generally free of the sense of shame (*haji*) that governs the behaviour of adults. Japanese, however, are especially critical of difference. Children tend to ridicule other children whose clothes, shoes, or school supplies differ from the perceived norm or who make mistakes. To avoid being laughed at by the world at large, the Japanese child must learn a whole series of restraints and must learn to recognize his or her indebtedness to neighbours, family, and country. Failure to live up to moral obligations and reciprocal duties will result in ridicule. Such lessons become, in Benedict's words, 'a new and serious extension of the pattern of babyhood teasing' (p. 273). A Japanese child must learn restraint, self-discipline, and complex patterns of indebtedness. If a child is criticized for local mischief, family members become 'a solid phalanx of accusation' (p. 273). The family name is at stake. Schoolmates, too, will use ostracism as a disciplinary measure. Benedict calls this failure of family and other groups to protect their own members a very uncommon sociological phenomenon, quoting Geoffrey Gorer to reinforce her point: 'By this mechanism the approval of the "outside world" takes on an importance probably unparalleled in any other society.'[3]

The child thus learns the importance of being *accepted*, rather than any absolute standard of virtue. Fear of rejection by family, neighbours, or co-workers is one of the strongest motivating factors in Japan. The need for acceptance makes the average salaryman work late on a regular basis, refuse to take holidays owing, and become, in effect, an absentee father. For a woman, the shame factor might make her stay in an intolerable marriage, fail to take action against sexual harassment, or silently suffer an infringement of her rights in the workplace.

A 1991 interview I had with a forty-year-old businesswoman comes to mind. The woman, a graduate in economics from the University of Tokyo, had no children and had worked in business all her adult life, first with her father and then with her husband. She regularly put in long days at the office along with cooking for her mother-in-law, her husband, and herself. Twice yearly she was responsible for ordering and sending gifts to some 500 clients of the family business. To represent her husband she regularly attended weddings, funerals, and other ceremonies involving clients. The woman was overtired, frustrated, and deeply angry. Habit, anger, and the formal ties of marriage seemed to be all that bound her to her husband. Since the couple was wealthy, I suggested hiring help in the house. She said that her husband said his mother had never needed help and therefore neither did she. I suggested making use of some ready-to-serve convenience foods, which are readily available in Japanese supermarkets. Her husband had anticipated this measure. His mother had never used such food and he refused to have it at his table.

This experienced businesswoman had considered and rejected divorce many times. Why? Not because she found her situation tolerable but because divorce meant that *people would talk*, a phrase repeated three times in our half-hour discussion. Obviously the woman considered the prospect of gossip, and perhaps ostracism, to be a fate worse than her currently unhappy situation. A thirty-year-old Japanese woman who had spent some years in Canada responded to this story by commenting, with an ironic laugh, 'To bring shame or embarrassment to your family is the first sin!' Compare the verdict of Norma Field, a bilingual Japanese American: 'To create an awkward moment is a sin in Japan; to cause disruption puts one beyond the pale.'[14]

An analysis of *amae* (dependency and indulgence) in Japanese society and in the parent-child relationship clarifies the dependency bred in childhood and the fondness for security. As Chie Nakane demonstrates, large companies typically treat their employees as family members. Companies provide housing, hospital benefits, recreational facilities for the entire family, monetary gifts for special occasions such as marriage, even counselling on family planning. Employers really employ the total man, as shown in the expression *marugakae* (completely enveloped).[15] This reflects the *amae* that Japanese children grow to expect.

Psychiatrist Takeo Doi considers *amae*, which is found in every culture, to be particularly strong in Japan. He relates this very Japanese emotion to the hierarchical social structure, going so far as to reason that it is the *cause* of the emphasis on vertical relationships. In short, Doi argues, *amae* forms the basis of both the social system and the national character.[16] His analysis grows from the premise that a national language reflects the national character. He quotes American linguist Benjamin Whorf, who describes language as a vast pattern system built on culturally ordained forms. Language builds the house of consciousness. Since there is no word corresponding to *amae* in Western languages despite the universality of the desire – 'Even a puppy does it,' as Doi notes – this word and its rich linguistic associations must bear a special relevance to Japanese relationships and social patterns.

A woman's life is bound by a web of *amae* in the form of expectations and needs of husband, children, employers, parents, and even ancestors. It is usually the woman who cares for the family shrine in the house. On the one hand, this web restrains the freedom and initiative of the individual. Through honorific or respect-language, for example, a bond is created, one of expectation and obligation.[17] On the other, Doi suggests, by becoming one with the group Japanese may find a strength beyond their own.[18] Constraints upon children are imposed largely by members of the same age group, for the group is conceived of as the individual's better self.[19]

The idea of protective constraints, actual or symbolic, is certainly more attractive to Japanese than to Westerners. I was surprised to learn from a Japanese woman that the doors used by employees to enter the bank where she worked in the 1980s were locked in the morning after the start of the workday and not unlocked again until quitting time. My mind presented the image of workers locked in, while she saw that non-employees were locked out from the benefits offered by the employer. These included rooms in which to rest or exercise and a cafeteria in which food and drink were free.

A prominent politician recently described the Japanese as a people who take government protection and guidance for granted: 'Japanese prefer to have regulations not only to prevent accidents but to govern all societal needs.'[20] Companies as well as individuals welcome regulations as protective shields. In a society that respects not majority rule but unanimous consensus, there is little room for the concept of individual responsibility to develop.

Japanese ideas of law and public debate are also tied to the central principle of harmony within the group. Avoiding friction is more important than eradicating injustice. Kurt Singer points to the very different traditions of East and West in this respect:

> The concept of public affairs being discussed among equals ..., everyone assuming responsibility for his own words; the value of the spoken word arising from such debates; the habit of competing for power by peaceful means, by persuasion; the joy of attacking, and of defending oneself, ably and brilliantly; ... finally and supremely, the emergence of a new form of life centred in the creative and critical powers of mind, continually shaping and reshaping the legacy of the past ... all this, with few exceptions, was absent from old Japan.[21]

The Confucian respect for silence rather than argument and the demand for unanimity make Western law and public debate, with their roots in ancient Greece and Rome, appear as strange guests of uncertain authority in modern Japan (p. 71).

Psychiatrist Masao Miyamoto believes that the desire to avoid friction at almost any cost is what lies behind the tendency of many teachers to ignore the bullying common in Japanese schools. Victims of this cruel practice have been driven to suicide. Miyamoto describes suicide as anger turned inwards and bullying (*ijime*) as anger and frustration projected onto the weakest member of the group. He calls the syndrome 'part of the psychopathology of Japanese society.'[22] Teachers who ignore bullying do not want to see that group harmony and consensus have been disturbed. To acknowledge the existence of *ijime* might be an admission of failure on their part. It might jeopardize their careers in a bureaucracy that punishes failure rather than rewards success. Miyamoto suspects that many teachers share the bureaucratic mentality of the education ministry.

Most Japanese, he argues, view bullying as a part of life for adults as well as children. They justify it by saying that the struggle to overcome it 'will enable the victim to develop a capacity for strength and harmony.' In short, *bullying is a tool to ensure conformity.* Miyamoto has little patience with a cultural goal that interprets sameness as harmony. He calls this principle 'the constitution of Japan.' The resulting suppression of feelings only breeds anger and frustration, while the goal of levelling down to a common denominator acts to eliminate exceptional talent and creativity.

To illustrate, Miyamoto points to the way in which English is taught in Japan. Students study the language for six years yet are unable to speak it, since the system focuses on the examination of fine points of grammar and not on communication. He believes that foreignness is perceived as a threat by the bureaucrats in charge of education, who wish to maintain a psychological barrier between Japanese students and foreign culture. (I am reminded of a Japanese woman who told me that she felt herself to be a different person while speaking English. 'In what way?' I naturally enquired. 'Bolder,' she replied, 'and more aware of myself as an individual.')

In the second article of his two-part analysis, Miyamoto describes bullying and envy as related mechanisms 'used to maintain the structure of Japan, Inc.' He himself was bullied when he took up a position in the Ministry of Health and Welfare after ten years of studying and teaching in the United States. His director told him that this unpleasant pressure was actually a form of love, calculated to train Miyamoto to become part of the work group: uniformity was essential, difference posed a threat, and criticism of prevailing practices disturbed the harmony of the workplace.

Miyamoto compares the Japanese view of envy as a useful social tool with the Western condemnation of it. Japan views envy as 'a form of social righteousness' used to condemn difference, including talent and creativity. Again, the process involves levelling down: 'It is only in Japan that a talented person becomes a victim.' Protecting oneself against envy consumes the energy that might have been used creatively. In his view, envy and bullying work together to maintain group harmony, or rather the superficial appearance of it that is accepted in Japan.

This Socratic gadfly or social critic was accused by a ministry investigator of having fundamentally different values from those held by most Japanese.[23] Perhaps he is merely more outspoken than most. His hard-hitting diagnosis of bullying in Japanese society makes more sense than anything else I have read on the matter.

An attempt to avoid confrontation is also evident in Japanese divorce procedures. Prewar conventions considered it offensive to go to court. In modern Japan, divorce law avoids the confrontational patterns of the West and employs counsellors to work with the contending parties towards a mutually acceptable settlement. Law is deemed inseparable from the stream of common life, hence community demands for consensus and harmony take precedence. For single mothers, however, this often means pressure to accept a less than equitable support payment.

Similarly, the widespread noncompliance of Japanese companies with a 1986 law concerning equal employment opportunities for women can be better understood in the light of the general concept of law in Japan as a cultural guide, a desirable direction for society to take rather than a matter to be enforced by fines and courts.

The idea of individual human rights is as foreign to traditional Japan as is the Western concept of law. In the West, the value of the individual was nurtured by the Reformation and the Renaissance, while the concept of rights emerged from the great eighteenth-century revolutions, American and French. Individual Japanese writers have taken up these ideas from Meiji times on, but they have never become rooted in the popular mind and remain unfamiliar today. Thus tradition, combined with an intolerance of difference, can lead to treatment of individuals that Westerners find repressive.

Norma Field blames the Japanese government for practising 'a sort of psychic quality control.' She sees its roots not merely in tradition but in commodity gratification amidst relative economic affluence: the age-old distractions of bread and circuses. Field writes: 'In a society such as present-day Japan's, where the overwhelming majority of citizens believe they belong to the majority, and where that belief is daily reinforced as the core of national identity, the burden of the minority struggle for the rights of all is all but unbearably onerous.'[24]

That struggle is dramatically illustrated in her study of three disturbing individual case histories, in which she targets the national context and official attitudes that make dissent a dangerous activity in Japan. *In the Realm of a Dying Emperor* examines these cases in detail as a microcosm of Japanese intolerance of dissent and of freedom of speech. The study describes the circumstances of an Okinawan supermarket owner who burned the Rising Sun flag at a national sports meet held in his town; a middle-aged Christian housewife who fought in the courts for fifteen years to try to prevent the Self-Defense Forces (SDF) from 'deifying' her deceased husband; and the mayor of Nagasaki, who became a target of rightist assassins after publicly expressing the opinion that Emperor Hirohito bore some responsibility for the war.

Yasuko Nakaya, the second of Field's 'extraordinary resisters,' was unsuccessful in her legal battle to prevent the state from turning her husband, who had died in a traffic accident, into an object of veneration. She endured public vilification and a quantity of hate mail, which Field found unnerving to examine: 'The malice burned my finger tips' (p. 134). Nakaya also received many letters of encouragement. Field notes that even in a society accustomed to court decisions consonant with government wishes, the Nakaya verdict – a fourteen to one decision by the Supreme Court – met with considerable scepticism.

Some letter writers thanked the housewife for giving them fresh courage in daily life. A man of seventy-seven wrote that the verdict 'corroborates the fact that the tendency to elevate men and to denigrate women remains an ineradicably powerful force in Japanese society today.' A female law student saw the Nakaya trial as an example of a basic contradiction in the country, namely, the postwar attempt to establish a liberal democratic state while retaining the emperor cult (pp. 153-4).

Reviewing Field's book, Donald Richie writes that it is impossible to subscribe to ideas of a willing national accord after having read *In the Realm of a Dying Emperor.*[25] The continuance in the 1990s of attitudes that favour the superficial appearance of social harmony and the suppression of dissent affect women in every area of their lives.

The concept of human rights is linked to the idea of equality, which is in turn closely related to culture. Since hierarchy, consensus, and gender roles have been accepted by the majority of women in Japan until relatively recently as normal, ideas of equality and fairness are understood within this normative framework. The result is that Western and Japanese women may differ in their views of what constitutes equality. Some Japanese women see nothing unfair in practices they have been conditioned to accept. Anthropologist Takie Sugiyama Lebra noted in the mid-1970s that in Japan there was neither consensus over what equality meant nor unanimity over whether it was possible or even desirable from the standpoint of women's welfare: 'In the meantime, male dominance in most institutions remains unchallenged.'[26]

Wives consider themselves equal to their husbands *within the household.* And dependency cuts two ways. Japanese husbands are physically and emotionally dependent on the wives who remain financially dependent on them. Lebra suggests that such interdependence requires trust and entails both mutual appreciation and guilt (p. 285).

Writing in the early postwar period, Hiroshi Minami points to traditional habits of submission, acceptance, and endurance and credits them to a kind of fatalism encouraged by Buddhist belief in karmic suffering. Duty, he writes, is not seen in opposition to rights but is part of the suffering of life. This belief provides some immunity to unhappiness. Fatalism affects both sexes, but Minami finds that habits of resignation and endurance are particularly strong in women.[27] Women are more likely than men to resort to the proverbial *shikata ga nai* (It can't be helped. There's nothing I can do).

Social psychologist Sumiko Iwao sees the average Japanese view of equality in the 1990s as consisting of 'a balance of advantage, opportunity and responsibility achieved *over time*.'[28] She believes that a long-term perspective, based on perseverance and endurance, preserves stable relationships. Since Iwao admits that Japanese women have been left out of the mainstream for the last century, it would seem that patience is a key requirement. Here again, behaviour can only be understood in the light of the cultural patterns that have shaped personality, habit, and expectation for generations.

Iwao notes that Japanese women are basically reactive. They are more likely to respond to conditions around them than to initiate action. Above all, they are pragmatic and nonconfrontational. Neither family life nor educational methods aim at encouraging independence: 'In place of independence, they develop and maintain a high degree of sensitivity to what their peers and other persons significant in their lives expect them to be and to do' (p. 9). Women are averse to absolutes, preferring to 'go with the flow,' as a Japanese idiom has it, and thus preserve harmony. In Japan, this deference is considered to be positive behaviour, especially for women. Both before and after the postwar Constitution, women were thoroughly familiar with a maxim that urged them not to be assertive but to act *oriai yoku* – namely, to compromise. Iwao sees the positive interpretation of deference as part of the reason why it is difficult to establish solidarity among Japanese women.

Deference and endurance, however, have been losing ground over the last decade to new values. Women's centres are being established in urban areas to offer assertiveness training, private counselling, and public meetings that feature the kind of personal sharing of lives that tends to embolden individuals. Judging from the women with whom I talked at two such centres, the temperament of Japanese women is becoming more martial.

The deference that was expected of women until recently was built into the tone of voice considered courteous for their sex. Japanese women have traditionally spoken in high voices, a phenomenon taken to postwar extremes by elevator attendants in department stores. An American journalist

Some of the founders and co-ordinators
of the Okayama Women's Centre, 1993.
Women's centres, many of them dating
from the 1970s, are relatively new to Japan
and have influenced and encouraged
many women.

likened the pitch to that of a dog whistle. Lower voices for women are becoming common, and are seen as a rejection of the submissive stance suggested by a high-pitched voice. Teenagers tend to find high voices comic. The voices of female Japanese announcers on television and radio have been dropping, as have female recordings played on subway platforms in Tokyo. The pitch of popular women singers is falling, as shown in a study of 200 songs from the 1950s to the 1990s examined by Tadahiro Murao. This professor of music found that the pitch of female singers has dropped dramatically since the 1980s.[29]

The 1946 Constitution states that all Japanese are 'equal under the law.' The problem for women remains one of equal opportunity and enforcement. Moreover, some women remain uncertain about what form they would like equality to take since men's work schedules appear unattractive. The United Nations-sponsored Decade for Women, launched in 1975, directed attention and respectability to the women's rights movement in Japan and slowly, very slowly, the government began in the 1970s to reconsider policies that discriminate against women in the workplace. Pragmatism and a culturally based view of equality leave many Japanese women convinced, however, that given conditions in the 1990s workplace and home they have no wish to hold permanent full-time jobs or to bear economic responsibility for the family equal to that of men. For the large numbers of women who must work of necessity, the discrimination is especially hard to bear.

Inequality for men and women is so entrenched in Japanese work practices that it is difficult to understand save in the context of history and culture. Writing of women office and factory workers in a large company in the late 1980s, Jeannie Lo stresses that contemporary attitudes to women workers are still rooted in upper-caste Tokugawa or feudal views of woman as homemaker and mother. Family survival depended on the eldest son. Daughters were *gokutsubushi*, grain wasters. *Mabiki*, literally thinning, or female infanticide, was a common practice justified by the economic survival of the family. Young girls were sometimes sold into the slavery of prostitution, and from the 1870s on factories and textile mills offered women harsh new opportunities, often at terrible cost to their health.[30] From prewar decades to the modern Japanese office may seem like a long jump, but Lo is not the only social critic to make the connection. Tomoko Bamba, writing of the affluence of young 'office ladies,' or 'OL's (o-eru's), in the 1970s, compares their situation with that of prewar textile workers: 'Behind their seemingly gay and envious life lies a modern version of the sad stories of female factory hands of half a century ago.'[31]

Bamba reviews the relentless social pressures that condition Japanese women to view marriage as their goal in life. Grandmothers of the young workers of the 1970s experienced an era when a childless wife was required to leave her husband's family and return to her parents in disgrace. Mothers of the 1970s generation were educated to be 'good wives and mothers.' Women of the first postwar generation were not only nurtured by these two generations but also experienced social pressures not so very different from those of prewar days: 'When these young women were kindergartners, they had to reply "I want to be a bride" to the question "What do you want to be in the future?" No bitter lessons of their mothers or grandmothers have been transferred to them. The feudalistic way of thinking is still with today's third generation' (pp. 244-5).

Other social commentators believe that such attitudes have become unpopular and dated, save with older men. Until the last decade, the term 'career woman' suggested a tough and unattractive woman, an object of curiosity because of her scarcity. Proper women stayed home, kept house, and cared for their families. Etsuko Yamashita, in a forceful analysis of Saiichi Maruya's novel *Onnazakari* and of the film made from it, argues that the box-office failure of the film followed from the nature of this male writer's heroine. She is a career woman, a journalist in her forties, who nevertheless behaves like a geisha, demurely and deferentially, towards her married lover. Such a woman, Yamashita claims, would appeal only to men over fifty. Women in their twenties and thirties are rejecting the image, the attitudes, and the behaviour.[32]

Young women have been indoctrinated by the notion of the 'right' marriageable age. This was twenty-three to twenty-five for most of the postwar period and is currently twenty-six. *Tekireiki*, literally 'the suitable age,' was reinforced by the taunt of *kurisumasu keeki* (Christmas cake, presumably stale and unwanted after the 25th), applied to unmarried women over the desirable age. Kittredge Cherry notes that the concept of a 'right' age to marry is emphasized by health textbooks in Japanese schools. It is also exploited by advertisers. Cosmetic firms, for example, used for decades the catch phrase 'Your skin is at a turning point when you are 25.'[33] A mature unmarried woman may still be called *hannin mae*, or half-person, a phrase never applied to men despite the fact that Japanese society expects men to marry too.

While an increasing number of women pursue career goals and independent lifestyles, young women remain subject to strong parental pressure to marry. In 1993 a woman wrote a letter to the editor of a large daily newspaper to wonder aloud if she should feel guilty for not having married by the age of twenty-seven. This elicited a flood of responses. Clearly, women in their late twenties face considerable social and parental pressures to marry. One woman, about to marry at twenty-eight, confessed to having felt 'gloomy' for four years prior to making this commitment. Another was experiencing at her workplace daily enquiries about marriage plans. Some testified that their parents were ashamed of their unmarried state or were too anxious to sleep at night. One mother wrote that she could not feel she had fulfilled her responsibility until her daughter married. There were also letters urging the unmarried woman of twenty-seven to seek out her own interests. And letters from parents whose most urgent worry was their sons' inability to find a wife.[34]

The compulsion to marry, and to marry before a certain age, remains an important factor in Japan's social and economic structures. Analyses by Tomoko Bamba, Jeannie Lo, and others show that most Japanese women still view marriage as the route to 'happiness,' that division of work according to sex was strongly supported by society from 1945 to 1990 and beyond, and that large numbers of women can still find no alternative save marriage to working for low salaries with little prospect of long-range employment or promotion. Since women's office work is often boring, strong incentives to resist the social pressure to marry and quit the workplace are lacking.

In *Blueprint for a New Japan*, a visionary plan for social and political change in the 1990s, Ichiro Ozawa argues that many of the methods that worked for Japan in postwar decades will not help the nation to flourish in the future. A senior Diet member and co-founder in 1993 of the Japan Renewal Party, Ozawa contends that increasing internationalization requires decentralization, deregulation, and stronger political leadership. The goal of all these reforms, Ozawa stresses, is the autonomy of the individual.[35] The Japanese must be re-educated to take responsibility for themselves. These are brave new words from a Japanese leader, and do indeed constitute 'the rethinking of a nation,' his book's subtitle. Like Ozawa, former prime minister Morihiro Hosokawa is beginning to emphasize that Japan needs 'a creative society, rich in individuality.'[36]

Ozawa's *Blueprint* calls for increasing choices for women and the support systems necessary to make them meaningful, such as substantially more participation in household work by men, children, and seniors. Women should no longer bear the sole responsibility for child rearing and for all the work done in the home. Men should also have new support structures that would enable them to participate in domestic work. Presumably this means substantially shorter working hours at their companies. Ozawa believes that Japanese society is currently suffering from the loss of responsible career women who are forced to leave their jobs just at the height of their experience and capabilities. What chance for success have such ideas, this blueprint for change, in Japan today? Traditionally, change has been very slow except in times of crisis.

In 1994, Harvard scholar Michael Blaker took a conservative view of the prospects for radical or rapid change in Japanese society: 'Despite the fervent wish for national purpose, identity, leadership and vision, these remain desirable, not feasible or realistic, goals in today's Japan. No crystal ball is needed to predict that what changes do occur will unfold through the gradualist, reactive, risk-minimizing processes of the past.'[37] This prediction, safe enough in earlier decades, may be overly cautious. Social change is in the air, and women are its leading catalyst.

Studies on Japanese cultural identity, called *nihonjinron* or *nihon-bunkaron*, have long been a staple of Japanese scholarship. The genre has been popular commercially, as well as among largely male researchers. With the notable exception of American anthropologist Ruth Benedict, it is only since the early 1970s that women scholars have entered the field, focusing on gender studies and the status of women in Japanese society. Numerous monographs on women by women have been published from the early 1980s on, and many female researchers of Japanese social studies have become well known. Their tone, understandably, has been critical. Prior to 1980, the stance favoured in *nihonjinron* studies by both Japanese and Western scholars was generally positive. Concepts such as harmony, homogeneity, and the 'ninety percent middle-class society' were seen as admirable. Writing in the late 1980s, Patricia Tsurumi attacks this stream of seemingly endless books as biased: 'Such attractive portrayals of how Japan supposedly functions as a polity, economy and society ... are amazingly one-sided.'[38]

In the last fifteen years, then, the focus of *nihonjinron* has been on diversity, individuality, gender, and issues of conflict. The serene cultural relativism achieved by Ruth Benedict is now harder to come by, and the pressures for change exerted by those who feel themselves disadvantaged are stronger than ever before.

CHAPTER 4

HOUSEWIVES: THE SMILE OF A MOUNTAIN WITCH

Strangely enough, when she died she had a mysteriously naïve face with the innocent smile of a newborn baby. Sobbing and clinging to this woman who had died in
peace, the daughter, with swollen eyes which told of her indescribable relief, said,
'Such a beautiful death mask – Mother, you really must have been a happy woman.'
Her husband cried silently with wide open eyes full of tears like a fish.

MINAKO ŌBA, 'The Smile of a Mountain Witch,' *Stories by Contemporary
Japanese Women Writers*

THE VAST MAJORITY of Japanese women are married, by choice and,
in a very real sense, of necessity. Marriage has always been the cultural
norm expected of women in Japan. Other norms, including workplace
practices, continue to make it difficult to buck the expectation despite
recent changes. Family life, where the housewife controls most of the family budget, forms the exception to the general rule of male dominance in
Japan. The average woman considers marriage and motherhood to constitute her real career.

Traditional norms and expectations are reflected in language. To the
bride's family, marriage means 'to dispose of' (*katazu keru*) a daughter, a
term never used for sons. Marriage meant an alliance of two families until
legal reforms in 1947 ruled that a new couple must start a new family register. Recognizing the economic basis of marriage, brides called it 'eternal
employment' (*eikyu shushoku*). In a shrewd and comic assessment of what
Japanese words say about women, Kittredge Cherry notes that a Japanese
wife, unlike her husband, can never retire from her work of caring for home
and family and that men are the usual subject of a different wedding verb,
'to stabilize oneself' (*mi o katameru*).[1]

For prewar women, marriage was usually arranged by relatives and trusted go-betweens. The custom of meeting the prospective spouse by formal arrangement, or *o miai*, held true for the first postwar generation and gradually lost popularity. By the 1990s, perhaps one marriage in three is arranged, through a much looser process than prewar *o miai*, while the idea of freely choosing one's own spouse has become common.

Despite the attractiveness of love marriage as an idea, the boom in what is now a matchmaking industry indicates that many men and women have difficulty in meeting people. In Tokyo alone, there are some 2,000 matchmaking companies, which arrange parties and occasions for singles to meet. The Japanese rarely entertain in their homes. Combined with the long hours worked by most men, this makes it very difficult for young adults to meet and talk.

The high fees that working women are willing to pay to dating clubs indicate the importance they attach to finding a man with 'the three highs,' namely one who is tall, highly educated, and highly paid. One Tokyo dating club limits membership to medical doctors and dentists. There are no educational prerequisites for women, but they pay ¥3,000,000, roughly $3,000, to join, ten times the annual membership fee charged to men.[2] A company spokesman at one dating service believes that many women are persuaded to join by their parents. Comments by members suggest that the women are self-driven. One young woman disparaged the practice of finding a mate at the office. At club parties, prospective partners were sure to have the right social status: 'Sure, love is the most important thing in marriage, but I guess solid economic foundations are just as important,' she told an *Asahi* reporter.

Not even a doctor's income will secure a small house in the Tokyo area. Land is very expensive, especially for the 75 percent of Japan's population living in urban areas. The 'bubble' economy of the 1980s pushed land prices to record highs. Surveys show that a detached house with a garden is the dream of 70 percent of Japanese but most have little hope of achieving it. More than a million families in the Tokyo area live in apartments that do not meet the minimum living standard of fifty square metres for a family of four.

Since 1945, Japan has given priority to developing its economy. Unlike the former West Germany, which made housing one of the main pillars of its reconstruction process, the Japanese bureaucracy left the building of homes up to individual effort. Minimal government schemes for low- and middle-income housing could be entered only through a lottery procedure in which the odds of obtaining a home were astronomical. Without strict land-use regulations or an appropriate property tax system and with construction entirely in the private sector, it is not surprising that land prices rose out of all proportion to the increase in wages and gross national product. Assuming constant and rapid inflation in the value of land, companies used it as collateral to obtain financing to modernize plants and equipment. In this sense, writes the editor of the *Asahi Evening News*, 'rising land prices were a necessary ingredient in Japan's high rate of economic growth.'[3] Construction costs for Japanese homes are twice those of American houses. The result of all this is that most Japanese live in cramped apartments and spend at least two hours a day on commuter trains. A distinguished economist writes, 'Many Japanese believe that they live in the smallest houses of any advanced nation – and they are probably right.'[4]

Japanese families, and particularly housewives, have paid the price for governmental neglect of housing problems. Crowded living space affects a housewife's life in many negative ways. Kitchens are small, with limited cupboard and refrigerator space. Many women shop daily on foot, preferring to patronize local shops and to use fresh food. Traditional Japanese bedding is spread out at night, aired over railings in the morning and then put away. Japanese-style cuisine is beautiful to the eye and very time-consuming to prepare. A schoolchild's packed lunch (*o bentō*) is a work of art. The husband's habitually late return from work often entails serving up two dinners, since children and elderly parents may be unwilling to wait. With or without modern appliances, it requires time, much time, to run a Japanese household. Even the large, deep baths of which Japanese are so fond are prepared by women.

Kittredge Cherry calls *Meshi! Furo! Neru!* (Food! Bath! Bed!) a cliché for the lifestyle of a salaried man and his wife. The husband's conversation, as he arrives home late and perhaps slightly tipsy, may be limited to these three commands. Since Japanese rarely express feelings of love or other emotions in words, women joked in the 1960s and '70s that their husbands were so busy contributing to the economic miracle that these were the only words they uttered.[5] The stereotype was still valid in 1993, when a nationwide survey revealed that household 'conversations' were distinctly one-sided: 'Many wives complained that their conversations were one-way, with husbands often grunting or nodding agreement to what they said.'[6] Since most Japanese women are well educated, their dissatisfaction is perfectly understandable. They are left alone to manage households and care for children and often parents, and must also supervise their children's education. This includes the extra study on which success in this highly competitive society often depends.

All societies expect certain duties of their members, and roles determined by gender and other factors are common. In Japan, however, the roles expected of men and women are more rigid than those found in most developed countries in the late twentieth century, and seem to be changing more slowly.

Postwar constitutional reforms stripped the old family system of its legal backing, but cultural norms and economic pressures prove stronger than legal niceties. It was economic necessity that drove many women to work outside the home in the late 1940s and '50s. And it was the economic 'miracle' of the 1960s and '70s that revived and reshaped the prewar role of women as 'Mrs Interior,' the literal meaning of *okusan*, wife.[7]

Again, the past illuminates the present. From the 1880s, the emperor was cast as the nation's father, and ideology advocated merging the patriarchal family, the *ie*, with state power. Family structure and nation state should reflect one another, a concept enshrined in the Meiji Constitution (1889), the Imperial Rescript on Education (1890), and the Meiji Civil Code (1898).

Military expansion on the mainland in the 1930s meant that many fathers were absent from their families, and the state began to shift its emphasis to the mother. The Ministry of Education saw women's role as crucial to preserving the family system, a role analogous to that of soldiers fighting the 'sacred' war for the Japanese family-state. Women were urged to have large families, and until 1944 their procreative role took precedence over their mobilization for work in munitions factories.[8]

The biggest shift in postwar family structure was from country to city, from those engaged in family enterprises such as farming to those headed by salaried workers. This shift, as Keiko Higuchi observes, also resulted in a substantial increase in the number of full-time housewives.[9] During the rapid economic growth of the 1960s, policy concerning the family (termed 'human resources development') was one of the government's primary concerns. The echo of Meiji, Taishō, and early Shōwa ideas concerning women could be heard in postwar reports that stressed the reproductive and care-giving roles of women.

Higuchi notes that a 1966 government report termed the household the site for the 'human reproduction' that was needed for economic development. In 1968 the Ministry of Education stressed girls' special abilities as homemakers and laid plans to make home economics mandatory for female high school students: 'During the period of rapid economic growth, even as more and more women joined the work force on a part-time basis, the principle of a sexual division of labour – men at work, women at home

– was becoming entrenched in government policy' (p. 52). Role differentiation progressed alongside urbanization and the growth of nuclear families.

The UN Decade for Women drew attention to women throughout the world. A six-nation survey of women's attitudes in the 1970s showed Japanese women to be 'exceptionally traditional, conservative, and amenable to the conventional division of labour' (p. 53). Just at this time, however, some Japanese women were beginning to study these trends with a critical eye and to call for change.

In her role as full-time homemaker, the Japanese wife frees her husband to work the long hours demanded by employers. In exchange, she has in recent decades gained increasing control of the family budget. Some women consider this a dubious privilege, since the more expensive or important the item the more likely that the husband will share in or control the financial decision.

Others consider the housewife's control of family finances to be a major gain. Yōko Abe, in a lyrical piece in praise of the happy housewife, calls Japan's 'affluent' housewives the chief beneficiaries of the nation's growth. This view conveniently ignores an opposing claim, that Japan's economic success has been accomplished by exploiting women in poorly paid jobs. Each is a partial truth. Abe describes the Japanese housewife as inundated with countless electrical appliances made possible by a husband's salary that ranks among the world's highest. Her analysis, in a slightly abridged translation unsupported by any documentation, emphasizes that women usually control the family purse strings.[10] A survey made in the early 1970s suggested that 97 percent of wives in urban housing developments controlled the family budget, compared with only 66 percent of rural housewives.

Writing in the early 1990s in a prestigious newsletter aimed at foreign scholars, Sumiko Iwao also emphasizes women's control of the family budget and the average salaryman's acceptance of this. Her recent book, written in English, develops the optimistic theory of an earlier article, namely that contemporary Japanese women wield considerable control even beyond their own households and that most, given their practical and non-confrontational bias, are happy with the long-range security of the status quo. Iwao concentrates on urban, college-educated women who were born between 1946 and 1955 and came of age in the 1970s.[11]

Iwao (b. 1935) is a director of the Japanese Institute of Women's Employment and an adviser on women's issues to both the Japanese government and many international companies. Her knowledge of the field is clearly extensive. Her point of view, like that of any writer, is subjective.

Many other Japanese women – social critics, creative writers, and hundreds of my interview subjects – are less satisfied with current conditions for women. Even Iwao modifies her rosy view of the 'quiet revolution' as her argument proceeds. This clash of opinions over what constitutes a satisfying life adds spice to debates that have no easy answers.

As we have seen, Japanese women take their status primarily from their husband's position. A large company or powerful ministry bestows high status on both employees and their families. Iwao claims that women's self-esteem remains high because family management has always been considered central to stability and prosperity in Japan. This is unconvincing, given that in recent decades it is extremely common for a Japanese husband to describe his wife as 'just a housewife.' Wives, speaking fluent English, will commonly use the same demeaning modifier to describe themselves. Perhaps knowledge of the multiple roles being played by women in other countries casts doubt on the exclusive nature of the housewife's role.

In a curious reversal of freedoms, Japanese men remain trapped by peer pressure and social norms within the companies and institutions they have created. Their work hours would be considered unacceptable by most developed countries. They remain utterly dependent on women for physical and psychological support. Is this privilege, or misfortune? Or both, as a creative writer like Minako Ōba reveals? Some see men as exploited even while they cling to the illusion of superiority and control, since women's lives in the second postwar generation have been eased by fewer children and more household appliances. Such an argument ignores the social life that men enjoy in sharp contrast to the relative isolation of a housewife with preschool children. It also overlooks women's responsibility for the elderly; their lack of political, legal, and financial empowerment; and the major difficulties they experience in the workplace. The pleasures of meeting and mastering responsibilities and challenges in areas outside the household are denied to many Japanese women.

One peculiarly Japanese phenomenon that places a severe strain on family life is the company transfer. A male employee required by his employer to work in another city at a branch office too far for a daily commute is known as *tanshin funin*. The transfer may last a few years or for a much longer period, and the situation is common. The custom is for the transferred husband to move alone. Education is given priority, and it is widely believed that children would be handicapped if they were transferred to a school in another prefecture. The husband may return home once or twice a month, or the wife may leave her mother in charge of the children and travel periodically to her husband's second residence. The latter system has the added advantage, for the husband, of allowing his wife to clean the apartment, do the laundry, and perhaps bring a week's supply of home-cooked frozen dinners. Cleaning, cooking, and operating laundry machines seem to be quite beyond the ability of the average Japanese man. An alternative solution for some husbands, according to a Japanese informant, is to find a local mistress who will double as a cook and cleaning lady.

Obviously children may suffer from the lack of a father. Behavioural problems are traditionally blamed on mothers, but some teenage problems are now being linked to absentee fathers. Women feel the loneliness acutely but have been taught from childhood to *endure,* to suffer silently. 'It's a huge issue,' in the words of one Japanese woman, a problem that leads to many personal tragedies. Young men are beginning to resent being transferred away from their families. A company's right to do so, however, was vindicated in a recent court case, and the practice is increasing.

Government reports released in 1992 and 1994 indicate that job transfers are forcing nearly half a million men each year into living apart from their families. Such enforced separations have soared by 15 percent over the figures for 1987, although employment for the seven-year period rose by less than 10 percent.[12] Further increases in the practice are anticipated. The larger the company, the more likely that some of its employees will be posted to other cities without their families. Most transfers affect men in their forties and fifties in middle management. The men, typically workaholics, seem surprisingly tolerant of the situation. Wives have little choice. Stress takes its toll on family members in many ways.

How do Japan's contemporary women writers view family patterns and married life? Ironically. And quite critically. Novelist and social commentator Ayako Sono (b. 1931) was one of the first women writers to emerge after the war. In 'Fuji,' she depicts the life of a young married woman during the first two years of a four-year separation caused by company transfer. The ambitious husband is pleased to be sent on a special training program that includes a college-level curriculum. He comes home once a month. His small son finds him a stranger, and the fictional wife suspects that he is turning into a different person. Childcare confines her to their apartment and neighbourhood, and her talk of local trivia bores and irritates the husband. The two share nothing but sex, and the wife finds his monthly visits an 'agony.' Sono's story shows that this wife pays a high price emotionally for her financial security. She is, however, resigned to the suffering and her fate.[13]

Minako Ōba (b. 1930), one of Japan's foremost contemporary writers, spent nearly twelve years with her husband in Sitka, Alaska, from 1959 to

1970. Her fiction is concerned primarily with women's lives and often expresses psychological truths through mythic images and situations. The fog and mist of the Alaskan coast become a metaphor for loneliness and the need for freedom. In her 1973 story 'The Pale Fox,' a woman's former lover suddenly reappears after an absence of seven years. His appearance reminds her of a fox in the moonlight. It may be his melancholy look, the sharpness of his chin, or the cock of his head. Her father's sharp eyes and jaw also resemble those of a fox, so that the image expands to suggests Japanese men in general.

The Pale Fox tells the woman of his marriage and divorce during the interval since they were lovers. He is scornful of his former wife, calling her a crying doll and a dried-up moth: 'Finally, that's all she was, just a spot on the wall. She was the sort of woman who dreams of finding happiness in ordinary family life.'[14] Is Ōba satirizing a typical Japanese woman? The Pale Fox found that his wife's inability to talk with him left him exhausted: 'I always do what I want, and yet while my own life-style was selfish, I feel some responsibility toward my thoroughly unselfish partner. At the bottom of my heart I suppose what I really want is a woman who'll be a slave to me' (p. 342).

The woman warns the Pale Fox that a tyrant is always bound by 'a tyrant's debt.' The Fox believes that women renounce their freedom as a means of binding men to them. The narrator reflects, 'If a woman chooses to be a slave, presumably the man's guilt is resolved and this allows him to behave as he pleases. The woman understood this man's fantasy very well' (p. 343). She tells her former lover that his kind of marriage depends on someone who has 'lost her identity as a woman.'

They make love, they talk, they eat dinner. The images portray a symbiotic relationship of shared entrapment, where each preys on the other. In the morning, the woman leaves the hotel, remembers that she has left a hair ornament and goes back, only to find that the man has returned before her with another woman. The black humour of this symbolic tale of mutual bondage heightens the message that men can free themselves only by freeing the women to whom they are connected and that a master-servant relationship has an unpleasant way of reversing itself.

The psychic cost to both parties of a 'thoroughly unselfish partner,' as the Pale Fox calls his wife, is depicted even more forcefully in Ōba's symbolic tale, 'The Smile of a Mountain Witch' (1976). Ōba is not the only Japanese woman writer to use the well-known folk tale of a *yamamba* as an image of a Japanese everywoman.[15] This legendary, witch-like woman runs through the mountains devouring any man she meets. Ōba's tale traces the life of a woman from early childhood to death at sixty-two from cerebral thrombosis. The little girl learns early that adults like flattery and that keeping her real opinions to herself smooths relationships. She senses peoples' minds, and assumes whatever behaviour is expected of her towards those whose affection she wants.[16]

As the bride of an 'ordinary' Japanese man, 'typical for one who had been doted on by his mother,' the woman realizes that her husband wants her to be a mother substitute, magnanimous and dignified. He also expects her to act in a helpless and dependent manner. Playing the part actually fosters these feelings. He likes her to be jealous, yet is ready to pontificate: 'Women are utterly unmanageable creatures, so full of jealousy, capable only of shallow ideas and small lies. They are really just timid and stupid. In English, the word man refers to human beings, but I guess women are only capable of being human by adhering to men.'[17] Ōba turns the husband's thoughts into an amusing parody of Kaibara Ekken's neo-Confucian tract, the *Onna daigaku*. 'Unmanageable, jealous, shallow, stupid' echo Ekken's very words.

The patriarchal attitudes that shape the husband's thoughts and language leave the woman overwhelmed by loneliness. As the two age, the husband becomes a hypochondriac and the wife his nurse. She hates nursing, but the husband is convinced that 'as far as nursing was concerned, women were blessed with God-given talents against which no man could compete' (p. 189). Her own ailments have been ignored for some twenty years or diagnosed as 'menopausal' until she collapses one morning and is taken to hospital.[18]

Called to the bedside, the adult children soon become concerned not that their mother may die but that she may live on as an invalid requiring costly care. They have other responsibilities. She has ceased to be useful, and her death brings tremendous relief to her family.[19] The woman wills her own death and her *yamamba* spirit returns to the mountains. The narrator describes the husband as 'a deranged old man' with tears like a fish, an image that casts doubt on the genuineness of his grief.

Ōba's biting portrait of a Japanese wife as *yamamba* is very revealing. The fictional wife both hates and loves her husband. She is trapped by a culture that has conditioned her behaviour from childhood and that offers no socially acceptable alternative. As for the accuracy of Ōba's portrait of the husband, the tendency of Japanese men to seek a mother substitute in a wife is a cultural cliché, the subject of numerous articles. By the 1980s, the physical and emotional pampering required by many husbands was beginning to be resented. As Aki Gotō observes, 'more and more women want to escape from taking care of immature, spoiled husbands with mother complexes.'[20]

Ōba's fable shows that a mother's excessive self-sacrifice breeds selfishness in husband and children, along with a damaging dependency that runs counter to their best interests. The failure to achieve self-reliance is seen by Michiko Nakajima and others as a cause of the increase in divorce in the 1980s: 'Behind these dependent young people hovers the shadow of over-protective mothers who are not self-reliant either.'[21] Overprotecting children, adds her colleague, Itsuko Teruoka, prevents the free development of character.

The reaction of Japanese women to Ōba's fable is illuminating. Some forty middle-aged women in two study groups in the early 1990s saw absolutely no irony or satire in it. Instead – and despite abundant verbal clues within the story that highlight the satirical intent – they read it as *a model of admirable behaviour*, an example of *kikubari*, or giving one's heart for others. This, they told me, was the way they tried to behave.

Of course the Japanese translator, along with various colleagues and readers who knew something of Ōba's life and other writings, read the fable as satire. So did one young woman in Tokyo. Asked if Ōba expected the reader to admire the fictional woman who lived for her family, this recent university graduate said 'No. Because she had no choice.' By the younger generation, the traditional security of the Japanese housewife is seen as entrapment.

In a third story by Ōba, the narrator also dreams of being a *yamamba*. 'Candle Fish,' like 'The Smile of a Mountain Witch,' raises issues such as entrapment and the need for self-reliance. The translator writes that Ōba uses the *yamamba* figure to articulate repressed desires and to explore 'the dialectic between a woman's desire for independence and self-expression on the one hand, and the psychic pain resulting from her solitary existence on the other.'[22]

The narrator here is a middle-aged Japanese woman who lived abroad for many years beside an inlet 'at the northernmost point of the earth' (p. 20). Once she is back in Japan, the friend of her years abroad visits the narrator on sleepless nights as the spirit of the moon, travelling on the backs of candle fish. When dried, these small fish burn like candles. The narrator remembers the years spent in this northern land as a precious period, a time of searching for meaning beyond words. Olga's friendship was part of that search. The American woman had married a musician who became alcoholic, then verbally abusive, and finally violent. Olga had found the courage to divorce him while their two children were still small.

A book club discussion group meets
monthly in Chiba. This activity is common
and very popular.

The narrator comments that at that time divorce was quite rare in Japan, and no one would hire a single mother with small children.

During the questing period of this northern exile, the narrator knows that she is a writer even though she has not yet published any work. Olga is also in search of herself: 'I ran away from my husband naked, and took with me only one thing, the sense of myself, you see' (p. 35). The two women continue to commune with one another in spirit over the years. Both have seized and held what the narrator calls her 'precious self' (p. 38).

The need for self-fulfilment emphasized by Japanese women writers of fiction also sounds repeatedly throughout articles by and about Japanese women from the late 1970s on. In a sensitive analysis of middle-class housewives after the critical age of thirty-five, Aki Gotō writes in 1984 of the sense of emptiness she experienced after her own two children entered school: 'For the first ten years of my marriage, this powerful "self" had remained concealed while I led a comfortable life as wife and mother ... The question burdening women is not survival but how to make the best of their lives ... Women are emerging from their homes in droves in quest of self-fulfilment.'[23] In the '90s, this mood is even stronger.

Most Japanese writing on the family focuses on its traditional structure. In *Child of Fortune*, however, novelist and story writer Yūko Tsushima portrays a single mother with a part-time job and a teenaged daughter. The girl, Kayako, has come to prefer the comfortable home of her aunt Shōko, her mother's sister. Shōko's traditional lifestyle contrasts strongly with the insecurity and relative disorder of the divorced Kōko's life. Just before taking the entrance examinations for junior high school, Kayako has chosen to move in with her conventional aunt. She returns to stay with her mother on weekends.

The rebellious Kōko is surrounded by women like her sister who accept Japanese gender roles. Their mother asked only that her granddaughter turn out to be 'the kind of girl who could put her heart into the cooking and the washing.'[24] Kayako herself, at a moment of crisis, declares that she hates people like her mother: read *unconventional*.

Kōko's stubborn individuality has come, in part, from her love for her mentally retarded brother, who died in childhood. His world was peaceful and loving, free of hypocrisy. From him she had learned 'the meaning of life and death' (p. 88), of life lived outside the sphere of social expectations and social pressures. Kōko's own life, as a woman and a mother, is continually subject to these pressures, with Kayako forming the intimate link between rebellion and conformity: 'Kayako, who rejected her mother and was fascinated by her aunt's world' (p. 43). Kayako finds her mother's failure to conform 'weird,' and urges her to 'look nice' for the school interview.

A more dramatic challenge to social convention presents itself as Kōko becomes convinced that she is pregnant by a lover. She grows fat and awkward. Feeling a lack in her life, she both wants and fears the illegitimate child: 'There was no point in worrying about what people thought' (p. 42). Her dead brother becomes a symbol of the independence she craves for herself and the unborn child: 'No one is going to force him to live in servile deference to other people's wishes' (p. 116).

Shrines for dead children and aborted babies have many *o-jizō-sama* figures decorated with baby clothes, toys, food, and other offerings. These touching shrines show the high emotional price paid by women who undergo abortions, the commonest method of birth control in Japan.

Eventually, a medical examination convinces Kōko that she is not pregnant but in a physical condition similar to pregnancy. Imaginary pregnancy is not abnormal but, like many ailments, is deeply associated with the mind. It was, she finally admits, a case of self-delusion pure and simple, save that it is not simple. Kōko struggles to come to terms with this self-knowledge and with her loneliness.

The novel depicts the multiple layers of a woman's consciousness, her fears and longings, her willingness to endure suffering yet resistance to pressures to conform: 'We're stubborn, we solo mothers' (p. 103). Like Ōba, Tsushima dramatizes the forces of conformity and the strength of the human spirit to resist.

Nonconformity has been taking subversive new forms in recent years as the birth rate continues to fall. Many Japanese social critics of both sexes view the record lows as a form of silent protest by women against the many irritants and impediments that make their lives difficult. Crowded living conditions, lack of privacy, an expensive and high-pressure system of education in which mothers play a key role, and a largely absentee husband add up to high levels of stress for any housewife, even in a nuclear family without the mother-in-law whose word was law for earlier generations.

The birth rate has been falling since the 1970s. On average, the first postwar generation had four children, and the second, two. The trend worries government planners, who foresee labour shortages, fewer taxpayers to support an aging society, and fewer care givers for the elderly. In 1993 the birth rate dropped to a record 1.46, down from 1.5 per child-bearing woman in 1992 and 1.53 in 1991. If the 1.5 rate had continued, the population would have decreased by 25 percent in one generation. The decline has been especially notable among women aged twenty-five to twenty-nine. The Population Policy Studies Institute of the Ministry of Health finds growing divorce rates and later marriages to be major factors.[25]

Statistics suggest that women's views on marriage are changing and that these trends will continue through 2010. Childless couples in their early thirties are expected to double to 29 percent of marriages from 14 percent in 1990. Nearly 40 percent of couples in their late twenties will be childless in the year 2000. The number of unmarried people of both sexes will increase sharply.[26] Men in their early thirties were finding it increasingly difficult to find brides in the early 1990s.

It seems unlikely that the Japanese wife and mother is threatened with extinction, but social patterns and working conditions, as they affect both sexes, are in flux. The new emphasis on the importance of the individual, being made in 1994 by leading politicians such as Ichiro Ozawa and Morihiro Hosokawa, indicate that the ship of state is beginning to steer a new course. It will affect women and the family with measures to promote better housing and shorter working hours.

On the plus side, Japanese society does not have the phenomenon termed by sociologists 'the feminization of poverty.' In the West, the majority of those living below the poverty line are women. Single women. Japanese women often choose not to leave an unsatisfactory marriage because the financial prospects are forbidding.

On the minus side, many Japanese housewives are de facto single mothers not only because of the common practice of job transfers but also because fathers typically spend very little time at home. A 1994 government report, quoted above in connection with company transfers, reveals that more than 50 percent of teenagers aged thirteen and fourteen and 40 percent of all fifth-graders say that they never talk with their fathers.

The report stresses that the role of the father is important in the family 'in order to teach just enough of the contradictory elements of care and discipline, protection and independence to the child.'[27] The emphasis on independence, even within a context that recommends balance, suggests that Japanese ideas of the value of indulging and protecting children may be changing. A substantial percent of adults surveyed said that families are losing the ability to educate children and that parents have become too indulgent. The report, which ends by urging society as a whole to recognize once again the importance of socializing children, is surprising in a nation that has traditionally emphasized the centrality of the family and the division of work roles by gender.

One encouraging recent sign is the presence of Japanese fathers with their children in parks and other recreational areas on Sundays. And a paternity book published in 1994 has been selling well. *Fushi techo* (Father and child pocket book) is co-authored by two assistant professors of the University of Tokyo and a public health nurse. The book describes pregnancy and ways in which new fathers can take over physically demanding chores such as laying out and folding away futons. It emphasizes good communication and spending time with babies and children to nurture good relationships. The book sold 20,000 copies in its first few weeks. Perhaps wives were presenting it to their husbands?[28]

CHAPTER 5

EDUCATION IN A
ONE-CHANCE SOCIETY

Let us search and test more educational methods which will be conducive to gen-
uinely free development of the individual ... Recognizing that social transformation
is imminent, we must rejuvenate the fundamental life force within each of us that
lies dormant under the suffocating weight of the old system.

MOTOKO HANI, 'Stories of My Life,' *Heroic with Grace: Legendary Women of Japan*

FOR MODERN JAPANESE WOMEN, education wears two faces. They
must pass through the system themselves, engaging in the types of postsecondary education now common for women and making use of their education in the ways that they are encouraged or permitted to do. This
experience prepares them for the key role they are then expected to play in
their children's education. Mothers are central to their children's struggle
to place highly within the fiercely competitive educational system, on
which a child's future largely depends.

As a group, Japanese women are among the most highly educated in
the world. The old idea that they should use their education primarily to
encourage and assist their children has continued well into the late twentieth century, however, and is still reflected in social patterns and hiring
practices. The blunt truth is that expectations surrounding marriage
prospects and limited employment opportunities affect young women and
their parents very strongly. Many Japanese men shy away from women with
impressive academic credentials. This has led to a system of two-year junior
colleges with curricula calculated to appeal to women who will become
housewives and mothers. Moreover ageism, the notion that certain activities are suitable only to certain periods of life, has restricted the personal
growth that should accompany longevity. Over the last decade, as Japan
begins to plan for its aging population, this concept is loosening its grip.

Appeals for an education system that would encourage a freer development of the individual are now being made by influential Japanese writers,
bureaucrats, and politicians. The words with which this chapter begins, curiously, were written in 1928, in the military atmosphere and instability of East
Asia before the Pacific War. Prophetically, they link the public education of
Japanese girls in the early years of this century to the ideas of modern reformers some three-quarters of a century later, as a system based on rote learning, strict discipline, and intense competition begins to come under attack.

Japan's elementary school system, established by the Education Act of
1872, was open to both boys and girls, but girls remained a small minority
in elementary schools until the twentieth century, and their elementary
curriculum stressed cooking, sewing, and flower arranging. Secondary
school for women grew very slowly from the 1880s; it was not until 1932 that
female secondary school enrolment reached 50 percent of male enrolment.
For a select few, secondary school could be followed by a women's college
or teacher training school. Women were not eligible for most four-year
universities and were barred until 1946 from the prestigious government-
sponsored imperial universities.

Japanese women's postelementary education in the late nineteenth
century was pioneered by British and American Christian missionaries.
Between 1877 and 1889, secondary and higher education for women was
carried on almost exclusively by eleven Christian schools founded by foreigners, schools that aspired to mould individual character and to advance
women's social status. Protestant values such as self-reliance, a responsible
work ethic, and a sense of mission were readily accepted by Japanese students, perhaps because of their similarity to samurai ethics.[1] The Christian
schools taught monogamy (in opposition to the socially sanctioned custom
of keeping concubines) and encouraged women's identity as individuals.

Motoko Hani, who became Japan's first female reporter and a pioneer
educator, was exposed to these ideals in 1891 at Meiji Women's School, a
postsecondary residential institution founded by foreign-educated Japanese
Christians. She and her husband would later incorporate similar goals and
values in their own Jiyu Gakuen (literally, Freedom School). The couple's
school synthesized Protestant and Confucian ideals of self-sufficiency, hard
work, and independence. Chieko Mulhern explains that the school managed to retain the almost taboo word *jiyu* throughout the repressive military
era thanks to Hani's insistence that her concept was both Christian and
Confucian and did not imply a wilful libertinism.

Hani's success, and the school's survival within a social climate that
defined female virtue as unquestioning obedience, was truly remarkable.

Her concept of education, as outlined in her autobiography and in articles written for various publications, aimed at the integration of personal and professional life and the harmonizing of female self-awareness with traditional roles: again, surprisingly modern goals.

The features of Japanese education that have supported postwar economic success stem from the late-nineteenth-century reforms of the Meiji Restoration. From the start, these included an emphasis on competition and central government control, both of which have turned modern Japanese women into *kyōiku mama*, or 'education mothers.'[2] The issue of 'examination hell' – the intensely stressful period during which students sit the entrance exams for the universities they hope to enter – was first raised in the legislature as far back as 1905. The Japanese people have supported their strict education system for a century because it provides the illusion of a meritocracy along with the promise of good employment and higher social status.[3]

Postwar reforms under the American Occupation (1945-52) were intended to remove ethnocentrism and militarism and to institute an American system of education. When the Occupation ended, these reforms encountered stiff resistance from the government, which promptly set about counter-reform. Its changes were strongly resisted in turn by the leftwing teachers' union, which supported more liberal theories of education. The struggle ended in modified counter-reforms that moulded an education system designed to serve a rapidly growing economy, a system that left the bureaucrats of the Ministry of Education firmly in charge.[4]

The 1946 Constitution guaranteed education as a fundamental right for every Japanese. The educational level of women improved rapidly, as did the ratio of female students going on to upper secondary school (grades 10 to 12). Since 1969, the percentage of girls entering upper secondary school has exceeded that of male students. By 1990, 95.6 percent of girls and 93.2 percent of boys were entering this level. This impressive record sets Japan apart from a great many nations where the education of girls lags far behind that of boys.[5] As Amano Ikuo observes, the fact that 95 percent of Japanese children go to high school leaves no doubt about the basic efficiency of the education system.

Ikuo also points out that a system of education with nationally standardized textbooks, a system that is homogeneous, compulsory, and free up to grade nine, has conveyed a common culture and played a major part in creating a strong sense of equality among the people. The corollary is a system of education that has ignored individuality and freedom of choice for children and teachers alike.

In a society of more than a hundred million people, Japan's education system has almost eliminated illiteracy and innumeracy and produced a well-trained work force that has served the needs of industrialization very effectively. And it has done this with the lowest rate of government expenditure and taxation among industrialized countries in the postwar period. The gender bias of women's education at the upper end of the educational scale, however, where women are encouraged to attend two-year colleges rather than universities, is much less publicized than the high rates of literacy, numeracy, and school attendance.

Until the late 1980s, the system supported the Japanese economy by turning out highly skilled, compliant workers.[6] Over the last decade, criticism of Japan's education system has been mounting, generated by students in revolt against harsh discipline and over-regulation; by mothers irritated at the financial and emotional costs of secondary and postsecondary education; by physicians who are seeing a generation of children with stress-related illnesses and weaker physiques; and by education reformers in search of a more flexible system designed to foster individuality and creativity.

Bureaucrats, writes journalist Clayton Naff, invented the *kyōiku mama*, despite the concept's roots in Confucian tradition. And they boasted of their success. As I, too, learned in interviews, any deviation from the normal lock-step progression through the education system was likely to result in rejection by the large companies that paid high wages and offered generous benefits. An extra postsecondary degree, initiated by a change of interest or vocation? A year abroad, travelling or working? I met university students who were fearful that such peccadillos would be unacceptable to large companies that train their own workers and value not maturity or initiative but a disciplined intelligence and a willingness to comply with expectations. Employers consider that malleability and complaisance have been proven by a successful passage through 'examination hell.'

Mariko Sugahara charges that Japan is weak in basic research, thanks to a 'clubby, exclusive, controlled atmosphere that dominates almost every field of endeavour, combined with a lack of transparency in regard to procedures and regulations.'[7] Sugahara blames the education system for making many Japanese excessively dependent, both economically and emotionally. Companies, she argues, have built on the educational system of rote learning and competitive exams to mass produce '"salaryman" clones,' workers whose imaginations never extend outside the framework of the corporation.

In a study dealing with the lack of freedom of expression in Japan, Norma Field describes the country as 'a society where proper execution of Chinese characters has been equated with not only intellectual but moral worth, an ideology mobilized to produce a statistically stunning literacy in the postwar decades, thus contributing to the sense that traditional virtues underpin economic might.[8] Along with many other observers, Field believes that the lack of free time engendered by this system is robbing Japanese children of their childhood.[9]

Field's criticism is illustrated by school practices such as secret reports and recommendations. The information, called cumulative guidance records, includes teacher evaluations of students' daily academic lives. It is used as the basis for comments on report cards and for recommendations sent to junior high schools of the students' choice. The records are retained by schools for twenty years and are not disclosed. My interviews reveal that mothers involved in PTA activities are afraid to voice any criticisms for fear of adversely affecting their child's secret record. Public opposition to the system is mounting.[10]

Parents must also cope with the high financial cost of senior high school and university. Women's work outside the home typically goes towards education costs. Japan's traditional view, that raising children is a private affair, has meant that a relatively low level of public spending has imposed a heavy burden on families. This is only just beginning to change in the public school system, in response to the sharply falling birth rate.[11] Recently, however, the costs for *juku*, or 'cram schools,' have soared, and these have come to be seen as part of the normal process of schooling. In 1990, extra schooling cost parents more than US$2,000 annually for primary children, over US$3,000 for public high schoolers and roughly double that for private senior high school students. More surprisingly, expenses for private lessons for kindergarten children were averaging $1,000. The cost of the extra tutoring that most Japanese parents consider essential has risen steadily through the 1990s with jumps of 20 percent annually.[12]

Despite the cost, attendance at *juku* is up sharply. Some five million elementary and junior high students were studying at *juku* in 1993, and percentages had increased for every age bracket. Even a ministry official found the figures 'abnormal.'[13] Smaller *juku* are being driven out by large, nationwide ones with computer systems capable of analyzing huge amounts of entrance examination data. The giant *juku* promise students a high probability of passing their exams.[14]

What drives this fierce competition and the dependence on extra schooling, uncommon in most other countries? In Japan, a good job depends on the status of one's university, the final link in the education chain. Large companies offer high status to their employees and the kind of social benefits or safety net that is provided by governments to the citizens of many

Western nations. School background is particularly important for appointment to the key government bureaux, which carry the highest social prestige.[15] Every university in the country is ranked. A prestigious preschool will prepare a child to win entrance to a prestigious elementary school, which in turn should lead to prestigious high schools and thence to success in the entrance examination to a prestigious university. Some private universities maintain their own system of elementary and secondary schools, where attendance guarantees entrance to the parent university. One observer describes a 'reasonably ambitious' mother as placing her children in cram school by fourth grade, whereas a mother who is 'only mildly driven' may wait until junior high. Mothers have little choice but to play their expected roles as coach and cheerleader:

> Excluded from jobs and abandoned by their spouses, Japanese mothers concentrate on education for their offspring. Classes have sprung up for pregnant women to teach their unborn children English: mum intones vocabulary into a tube, which is attached to a funnel strapped to her belly. Fully 42% of preschool children are shepherded off to special lessons (mainly sports or music); by the early teens the ratio hits 69% (mainly because of cram school lessons). A 1992 survey in Tokyo found that more than one in five children in their early teens had no time on weekdays to talk to mother. Small wonder that women think twice before devoting their lives to them.[16]

To call the process arduous for both mother and child is an understatement. The older the child gets, and the closer to the dreaded university-entrance exams, the higher the tension in the home. Norma Field writes: 'Men described as suffering from "home refusal syndrome" have had their places usurped by their children, especially those preparing for entrance examinations, who therefore command the unremitting devotion of their mothers.'[17] Mothers dance attendance on children, providing snacks and other comforts. Some mothers go to the length of attending *juku* themselves and taking notes in order to provide superior help at home.

Girls and boys favour different types of *juku*. These are divided into academic coaching in the English and mathematics required on entrance examinations and instruction in special fields such as music, calligraphy, and martial arts. National surveys have paid little attention to gender preferences in *juku*, but they do show that as students progress to high grades many fewer boys are involved in cultural, artistic, or athletic lessons. And after failing entrance exams far greater numbers of men spend one or more years of full-time extra study in an attempt to win admittance to a university.

The role division that has shaped the lives of postwar men and women extends to children and teens, whose sole responsibility is to study and do well in the examinations on which their future depends. Sons, in particular, are regarded as having *no time* to help with household chores, a practice that perpetuates the failure of adult males to help in the house. The division of labour by roles based on gender is learned in the home.

Clayton Naff is one among many who criticize the unhealthy preoccupation with study that the *kyōiku mama* encourages, especially in sons: 'She cooks his meals, washes his clothes, cleans his room, helps him with his home-work, drills him on material for his exams. As he reaches puberty, she struggles to discourage him from all outside interests, including dating, until he has won acceptance to college. Of course, not all mothers or children adhere to this pattern, but it is common enough to stand as representative.'[18] Cultural ideology makes the mother solely responsible for her children's success in the education system, although her control over the outcome is minuscule and the social measurement of success narrow. Not even a full-time job excuses her, but the father's job legitimizes his withdrawal from family life.

Amano Ikuo sees the problems created by the cramming of facts, excessive standardization, and the poor quality of university education as inextricably joined to the good features of the system: 'These problems are the price Japanese education has paid for its successes.'[19] Both virtues and defects can be traced to the strong control of education exercised by the ministry, control that it remains unwilling to relinquish.

Social problems connected with the system have been increasing since the early 1980s. These include violence against teachers and other students, truancy, absenteeism, and other antisocial behaviour that suggests children are resisting the strict discipline and lack of choice found in schools. Stress-related illnesses such as premature balding, ulcers, high blood pressure, and chronic fatigue are now found in Japanese children along with declining physical strength and flexibility. Social skills are also diminishing. Alarmed, the ministry cancelled one Saturday per month in 1992 from the normal six-day school week, but many parents said that *juku* would consume the freed hours.[20]

Bullying is a phenomenon found in every culture, but Japan's education system has fostered new and extreme forms. Groups of bullies have murdered fellow students or driven them to suicide.[21] Ryuzo Sato blames not only a society intolerant of difference but an education system that creates 'a pressure-cooker atmosphere.' Norma Field connects bullying with insensitive or weary teachers who tacitly condone it, or with overindulged children whose sole responsibility is study.[22]

The editor of a leading newspaper notes that the Ministry of Health and Welfare hired 14,000 welfare workers nationwide in 1993 to monitor the occurrence of bullying, truancy, and child abuse and that a total of 22,100 incidents of bullying involving varying degrees of violence were reported in the 1991-2 school year.[23] Is there some possible connection, the editor asks rhetorically, between such deviant behaviour and the constant demand for rigid adherence to the many rules and regulations imposed by schools? The same newspaper, shortly after, suggested that bullying in schools was 'a dark face of Japan's need for hierarchy, pride in its strongest, and disdain, rather than compassion, for its weakest.'[24] Pressure, and a system that forces students to repress their feelings, is the commonest explanation for a phenomenon that holds a morbid fascination for the Japanese and affects both parents and children deeply.[25]

Another set of forces strongly affects parents and children, especially daughters, but has drawn little attention from the Japanese media, perhaps because cultural bias can be invisible to those who live with it. Mary Brinton's excellent study of gender and work in postwar Japan reveals a sharp gender bias in the education system. Parents and students alike consider success in the education race to be more important for boys than for girls: 'Women are more active as *investors* in their sons' education than as students in whom investments for labour market success are made. They play an important indirect role in the economy through their own investments of hope and time in their sons' future success.'[26]

For both sexes, education is a crucial factor for success, but girls are encouraged to strike a delicate balance between too little and too much. The costs of higher education are borne by parents to a greater extent in Japan than in most other industrialized countries, since most Japanese youth have no time for part-time work during their high school years, and scholarships are uncommon. Male graduates of prestigious universities are hired immediately into permanent positions with top employers and ministries, while women, even graduates of the same universities, have been automatically relegated to non-promotional tracks until relatively recently. Education aimed at preparing students for the labour market is hardly unique to Japan, but the consequences for women, as Brinton points out, *are* distinctive. Why should Japanese parents invest as much in a daughter's education as in a son's? Public demand for education and the government's practice of restricting the total number of four-year universities have led to a 'peculiarly Japanese outcome' (p. 198), the junior college system for women.

Education is not meant to set a woman on a lifetime employment track but to co-ordinate her track with that of a successful male. The two-year junior college system, used almost exclusively by women, evolved after the war to meet this need. The first such colleges were established in 1950. By the early 1980s, there were over 500, almost all of them private. Four-year universities are concentrated in urban areas, whereas junior colleges are dispersed across the country. Many young women can attend one while continuing to live at home, a situation that employers have long considered 'chaste' and hence desirable.

Statistics tell a tale. Rates of high school graduation are virtually identical for the sexes, but rates of attendance at colleges and universities diverge sharply by sex. In 1980, women made up 91 percent of the students at two-year colleges. In the same year, 39.3 percent of male high school students were advancing to universities, and only 12.3 percent of female students. By 1988, women's rate of attendance at both university and junior college had increased, but the rate of increase at colleges had been much more rapid and colleges had become almost exclusively a female track.[27] These figures contrast sharply with those of American universities, where men and women are fairly evenly represented at both junior colleges and universities. By the late 1980s, the proportion of women at four-year universities in Japan was lower than that of any Western industrialized nation.

College curricula focus on home economics, education, and the humanities, although social science, social welfare, art, music, and industrial arts are also offered. Universities offer a wider range of humanities and a 'law' major, which is taken by many men.

The statistics reflect the educational aspirations and social attitudes of Japanese families. As Brinton points out, it is inside the family that gender roles crystallize and expectations form about the obligations of the sexes and the generations towards each other. Most Japanese parents believe that boys should be raised as boys and girls as girls. Nearly three-quarters of Japanese mothers hope for a university education for their sons, but many consider college or high school sufficient for a daughter: 'Japan is the only industrial country where a yawning gap exists between educational aspirations for sons and daughters.' These attitudes differ markedly from those of parents in the United States and especially in Sweden, countries that show more gender-equal attitudes towards the education of girls.[28]

I talked with a Japanese professor in 1992 who told me that graduates of a prestigious women's university in Tokyo were not desirable marriage prospects: 'Too smart,' he said with a sneer. Such attitudes are changing slowly, but they continue to influence many Japanese. The continuing perception of sex discrimination in the labour market actively discourages some parents from making the financial sacrifices necessary for a daughter's university education. By the time men and women begin to work, they have been strongly socialized for gender-segregated roles, and this socialization continues in the workplace.

Calls for a freer, more flexible, and more liberal education system have a new sense of urgency, driven by changes in the economy and a growing need for more independent workers. Since high schools and universities operate under strict ministry control, they are unable to change and adapt to new demands by employers or social planners. Bureaucrats and reformers alike fear that relaxing controls might cost Japan its high levels of literacy and discipline and that antisocial behaviour might increase even further, but urban, affluent Japanese are demanding a system that allows self-realization. The question now is not whether changes can be implemented but how quickly.

Two small but indicative changes affect women because they affect men. Textbooks are becoming a little less sexist, and home economics became a required subject for all senior secondary students in April 1994: small steps, perhaps, but revolutionary in Japan, where the vast majority of textbook writers are male, as are most ministry planners. Senior high school texts introduced in 1994 have modified the stereotypes of men earning money and women keeping house. Prior to this date, societal changes over the last twenty years were not reflected in most civics courses. Curriculum guidelines for 1993 did not point out to students the changing roles of women. Civics texts still make only passing references to working women, and only two mention the Equal Employment Opportunity Act of 1986. Only one mentions the Child Care Leave Law and problems with sexual harassment.[29] A few small changes to elementary texts in home economics date from 1992. One illustration portrays a woman jogging while father, complete with apron, vacuums the home. Another shows a woman reading a newspaper and a man washing dishes. The texts, approved by the government for use nationwide, were welcomed by women and termed 'unnatural' by some men.

A shortage of trained home economics teachers as of 1992 was expected to be met by providing volunteer teacher applicants with one year's training in subjects relating to food, clothing, and homemaking and allowing educators to acquire a licence to teach home economics while continuing to do their regular work. One enthusiastic male teacher was quoted as saying that home economics had the power to change students' outlook on life.[30]

Judging by my own questionnaire put to some 100 male students at a provincial university in 1992, many did not know how to prepare food and considered cooking to be a woman's job. Housework was also considered the wife's responsibility, whether or not she worked outside the home. Ministry research, however, found that many male students had some interest in home economics, believing it to be 'knowledge useful for living.'[31] Regional differences between Tokyo and more conservative parts of Japan might account for the discrepancies.

New senior high school courses include three subjects: general home economics, living techniques, and living in general. Lessons will no longer focus solely on cooking and sewing but will cover a broad range of topics such as the aging of the population, consumer education, and the environment.[32] Some instructors plan to include topics such as real estate in order to teach the importance of contracts and responsibility. Students, many of whom have no siblings, will study childcare. Teachers welcome the new home economics course as a less structured option functioning outside the area of competitive examinations.

A change in the way school rosters are used is another small indication of a new attention to gender issues in education. Schools have many rosters, lists for attendance, guidance, graduation, and so on. It has long been customary to divide students by sex in composing rosters and to read the boys' names first. A trend to use mixed rosters began in the mid-1980s and is slowly spreading throughout the country. One editor sees the change as significant: 'If people are made to think from their childhood that "men first and women second" is the natural order, they will naturally develop fixed ideas concerning the relationship between men and women. It is desirable for children to grow up daily and personally experiencing in practice as well as in school rosters that the two equal sexes are creating society together.'[33]

Less encouraging is the type of activity undertaken by some high school girls in aid of male sports teams. The girls, usually students from the same school as the players, call themselves team managers but their work consists of preparing food and drinks for players, cleaning the dressing room, and even washing players' socks and uniforms at home. The 'manager' girls, known as *joshi-mane*, are widely accepted in Japan, but the objections of some women teachers brought the situation to the attention of the media recently. One woman insisted that the girls' duties are exactly the same as the work of housewives at home: '*Joshi-mane* is nothing more than sexual division of labour.'[34] Some girls become managers because there are no sports teams for girls; others seem devoted to the players. Teachers opposed to the system have been unable to get it banned. Obviously the manager girls face attitudes concerning suitable activities for women that are entrenched in the wider society.

Ageism is another entrenched view that is gradually losing its power. Since the 1960s in North America mature students of all ages have been starting or returning to universities to upgrade their skills, find fulfilment, or prepare to enter the work force. Japan has yet to discover this cure for universities facing a steadily decreasing number of young students. The hierarchical patterns that govern Japanese relationships include the conviction that age takes precedence and that people of differing ages cannot mix easily.[35]

The North American phenomenon of university graduates in their thirties or forties returning to take a second degree was very rare in Japan until the 1980s. Such opportunities are of special interest to women with children. Japanese universities have strict entrance examinations for graduate school as well as for undergraduate programs. These include exams in two foreign languages. I was told by many Japanese women that it was 'impossible' to re-enter university after an absence of more than one or two years. It is still uncommon to find mature Japanese women who have taken a university degree after spending some years outside the educational system, but it is no longer unheard of. Women who found the traditional role unfulfilling have taken a first or second university degree and begun teaching in schools, colleges, or universities. These pioneers may be the wave of the future, as Japan will be facing a severe labour shortage within a few years.

Far-sighted politicians like Ichiro Ozawa agree. He notes that the permanent employment system in workplaces such as teacher organizations, hospitals, and insurance companies makes it impossible in principle to become an elementary school teacher in mid-career. He believes that the practice must be changed: 'It is obviously important that teachers have experience, but there is no reason that every teacher must have acquired that experience in his or her twenties. There is no reason why well-educated women cannot begin teaching in schools in their forties, after they have raised their own families. Fresh blood of this kind could improve the level of education, not undermine it.'[36]

Japan has been called a one-chance society because of its examination system and lifetime employment practices. The recession of the early 1990s upset the latter pattern, and the current mood of the country has led people to question the former.[37] Women's talents, in particular, have been underused for decades. Human resources are also wasted when students fail to win acceptance at any university at the time of high school graduation. Students usually hedge their bets by taking the entrance exams for several institutions. Failure on all fronts turns the student into a *ronin* (literally, a masterless samurai, an outcast) for one or more years of continuing struggle. This results in appalling stress and expense to the individual and wasted work years for the nation. It costs hundreds of dollars to take the examinations for any one university. Such fees provide a substantial percentage of the operating budgets of many institutions.[38]

Wasted time and talent often continue once students are enrolled. After frantic competition to enter the university of choice, formal learning may play a relatively small part in the years that follow. Many Japanese believe that after the extended trauma of examination hell, students deserve a four-year rest. University years, often called 'leisure land,' are a time for students to socialize with peers and to have part-time jobs – called *arbeit* from the German for *work* – before entering the companies that will teach and train them. Much of the senior year may be spent job hunting, to the detriment, one professor complains, of their studies.[39]

Keen students may be discouraged by fellow students' aimlessness and lack of purpose.[40] In universities, as in schools, Japanese students are not expected to ask questions and there is little interaction between students and teachers. I was once asked by a professor at a respected national university if it was true that Canadian and American students asked questions during class. I assured him that this was so, whereupon his brow furrowed and he said, in a sympathetic tone, 'That must be very difficult for you.' I found it almost impossible to make him understand that what I found difficult was the reluctance of most Japanese students to engage in dialogue.

One reformer recently founded an open university with classes only on Saturdays. Tokyo's Jiyu Daigaku (Free University) was established in 1992 by a renowned economic anthropologist to protest corruption and staleness at his university. In principle, the university is open to anyone regardless of race, sex, age, or nationality. The entrance examination consists of an essay, an interview, and questions in English. Courses focus on comparative culture, economics, and modern politics. Some students are attending the open university while enrolled in a formal institution. Others, like vast numbers of North American students, combine studying with paid work. Educational experiments along the lines of Jiyu Daigaku are still rare in Japan.

The education system and the kind of worker it produces enabled Japan to catch up with and overtake the economy of the West in the 1960s, '70s, and early '80s. The same system, however, is ill equipped to nurture original technology in the 1990s. Japanese companies are risk averse, and *kaizen*, the relentless improvement of existing products, will not enable Japan to take a technological lead.[41] In recent years it has been losing market share even in once dominant areas such as consumer electronics.

Ozawa takes aim at the education system which has failed to foster creativity. He quotes, approvingly, the criticism of Japanese high school students made by an American cultural anthropologist who compared the examination system to foot binding. The anthropologist observed that students are encouraged not to attempt new things but to adapt to their surroundings and to favour external appearances. 'They do not learn to express their thoughts,' Ozawa writes: 'They are not encouraged to talk or to write. They are not trained to think or debate. They do not even learn that there is more than one way to interpret a single issue. Memorization takes priority over analysis, and the official curriculum places little or no emphasis on the students' artistic natures, their personalities, or their humanity.'[42]

Ozawa goes on to compare Japanese teachers with computers, which always have the right answers. The system that has allowed students to achieve the highest marks on international tests for evaluating educational achievement cannot be all wrong, he argues, but it is deeply flawed. Independent thinking should be encouraged, and local governments should control part of the curriculum in order to enable each area to root its education in local culture and to develop a diverse population (pp. 205-6).

The diversity that Ozawa sees as desirable has long been sponsored in Japan by local governments: prefectures, cities, towns, and villages. In recent decades, women's centres have begun organizing large numbers of workshops, courses, and lectures. Subjects range from practical and technical matters to academic courses of university standard given by university teachers. Typical themes or course names include 'Creating New Roles for Women,' 'Women Looking to the Year 2001,' and 'Women's Economic Participation in Development.'[43]

These courses have little effect on women's position in the labour market but, like the women's studies courses offered in some universities over the last decade, they help to raise women's consciousness. Women's centres, co-operatives that have opened in large cities such as Kyoto and Okayama in recent years, are having the same effect.

Some of the widespread social attitudes that have driven women to choose junior colleges, to allow employers to discriminate against them, and to accept parental and societal pressure to marry and become full-time housewives are beginning – just beginning – to ease. Surveys conducted in the late 1980s and early 1990s, however, show the continuing power of traditional thinking and practices.

Japanese women are slowly becoming aware of their power as individuals and as a group. Meanwhile, the country experiences a sharply falling birth rate, a rising average age for marrying, and a looming labour shortage. Where will the raised consciousness of many women take them over the next decade?

CHAPTER 6

FACING TWO WAYS:
WOMEN IN THE WORKPLACE

> It is not a question of ability, but our fatal custom that holds women in subjection to man – a ridiculous tradition which does not remain so intact even in China, the birthplace of Confucius ... Our Japanese men have not yet realized that to encourage women to develop their personalities will bring more happiness even to men, for the sexes are deeply dependent upon each other in this as in all other respects.
>
> SHIDZUE ISHIMOTO, *Facing Two Ways: The Story of My Life*

STRONG SOCIAL EXPECTATIONS, many of them institutionalized through company practices, dictate the work experience and opportunities of most Japanese women. The basic expectation is that women will work until they marry and again, part time, when their children are in school or university.[1] As *sengyo shufu* (professional housewife), the woman bears sole responsibility for housework, cooking, and the care of family members, and thus is believed to have no time for permanent or serious employment.

The phrase *sengyo shufu* is a twentieth-century invention. Most Japanese women have always done work above and beyond household responsibilities, whether in farming, fishing, sewing, small business, or crafts. The relentless increase in urbanization in this century spawned both the salaryman and the full-time housewife.

It is a further irony, and a paradox, that despite gendered expectations and role division, Japan remains heavily dependent on women's labour outside the home. As factories and textile mills emerged in the early Meiji period, leaders recognized that Japan's greatest natural resource was the young women who were willing to work in wretched conditions for low wages in order to help their families and the nation.

The economic miracle of postwar Japan has been greatly assisted by the work of low-paid women in impermanent jobs. They have provided the perfect complement to the system of seniority and lifetime employment for men. In short, the flexibility and cheapness of the female work force has supported the stability and security of male workers. These complementary patterns help to explain what Western scholars consider 'a seeming contradiction,' namely high rates of participation by women in the Japanese economy combined with substantial gendered differences in wages, employment status, and occupational roles.[2]

Many women work full-time hours (forty hours per week and more, compared with a legal maximum of thirty-five hours for part timers) but are defined, paid, and treated as part timers. Women's wages are commonly considered to be roughly half those of men. When the semi-annual bonuses and other benefits given to most male workers are taken into account, the percentage becomes substantially lower.[3]

The Japanese tax system has contributed to keeping women's wages low. A women who earns less than ¥1,000,000 per year, which is well below a living wage in Japan, continues to be a full tax deduction of ¥350,000 for her husband. Both husbands and wives consider this an important factor in their financial planning. Feminist critics argue that the tax system plays a strong role in keeping women tied to the home. They suggest that such deductions should be eliminated in favour of increased personal exemptions.[4]

Female participation in the Japanese work force follows set patterns according to age. These show on a graph in the form of an M. Relatively few women work before the age of seventeen, reflecting the high level of secondary education. Labour participation peaks for the group aged twenty to twenty-four, standing at 73.7 percent in 1988 and 75.1 percent in 1990. It drops precipitously for the group aged twenty-five to twenty-nine and again for the thirty to thirty-four age group. After the age of thirty-five participation gradually increases again, then begins to fall slowly after the age of forty-five. The M-curve indicates that many women leave the labour force for full-time childcare and return to work afterwards.

Overall participation of women in the labour force grew steadily until the recessionary years of the early 1990s. Between 1975 and 1990, the number of working women over the age of thirty-five grew from 47.4 percent to 59.6 percent of the total female work force.[5] Women are working for longer periods, and the percentage of women working for the same company for ten years or more grew between 1980 and 1989 from 20 to 26 percent. The re-employment of housewives after child raising has enlarged the pool of female labour and greatly increased the average age of the working woman in recent years.

With 49 percent of adult females in the labour force in 1987, Japan stands midway between the higher rates of North America and Scandinavia and the slightly lower rates of Western Europe. Yet this figure masks three phenomena unique to Japan: first, Japanese women are much more likely to be piece workers or to be sharing in family-run enterprises; second, they are more likely to be in blue-collar jobs; and third, the male-female wage gap is greater in Japan.[6]

Marriage, the basic social expectation laid on both sexes, shapes the workplace for men and women. It also helps to explain the pay scales for both sexes, based partly on seniority, and the general constraints for women who would like to work outside the home. Marriage is viewed as part of a natural progression from adolescence to maturity and the acceptance of adult responsibilities. By marrying, a woman fulfils a basic commitment to her family and transfers her dependence to her husband's family. Marriage offers women not only security but escape from tedious and/or unchallenging work, and from the paternalism of home or company dormitories for single women. It is expensive, however, and savings made during the three to five years worked by women after leaving school or university are commonly used to provide the exorbitant sums needed for the wedding and honeymoon. During these years young women workers also enjoy travel, shopping, fashion, and entertainment. This period of employment may be the freest time of their lives.

The importance of young working women as consumers began to make news in the 1970s, when they were termed one of Japan's richest consumer markets. Women's clothing stores, travel agencies, and airlines began to rely on this lucrative market. As a group, these women are a curious anomaly in a country known since 1945 for much work and little play.

Most of the women live at home or in company dormitories. Indeed some companies, acting as chaperons, insist that they do so. Much of their income is therefore disposable, and many call them 'unmarried aristocrats.' Since they are not expected to work overtime, they are free to take lessons such as English conversation or flower arranging, to go dancing, or to play tennis. Such activities are expensive and provide a welcome change from office routine. The image of self-indulgent young women consumers is still strong, yet many do not fit the mould and some are ready to satirize the trend. In an iconoclastic exhibition of paintings in Tokyo in 1994, Miran Fukuda exhibited portraits of young women that parodied the big-consumer stereotype.[7]

Many women work either in factories or in stores and offices as sale clerks and secretaries. The choice depends on their educational level seems to reflect a class bias despite the insistence of the average Japanese that they are all 'middle class.' Clerks and 'office ladies' (a Japanese coinage) are usually graduates of colleges and universities. Factory women are high school graduates. Teaching has been a good field for women since 1945, and recently women have become principals, especially of elementary schools, and members of boards of education. Women have also found teaching positions in private *juku* or have established their own *juku* to provide the after-school coaching that many parents consider essential.

Despite the rapid growth of the economy since the mid-1950s, the feudal concept that women should perform domestic tasks and support the lifestyles of men remains alive and well in Japanese male culture. Women office workers still perform domestic functions as office housekeepers and hosts, along with their other work, and company policy still bars the vast majority from management positions. The number of women objecting to these patterns is increasing.

Equally damaging to women's career aspirations is the practice, common to banks and many institutions and companies, of 'encouraging' – forcing – women to retire when they marry. (No such pressure is laid on nurses, teachers, or government workers.) This is a tacit understanding, though prior to 1986 it might also have been written in a contract. I first learned of the practice in Hokkaido in the early 1990s. Henceforth I made it the subject of numerous enquiries in Honshū and found it to be widespread, although it violates the 1986 Equal Employment Opportunity Law. Some young women remain ignorant of the law, while knowledgeable ones know just how frequently and easily it is evaded by companies who consider it a mere guideline.

My Hokkaido informant was a twenty-six-year-old bank clerk at the time of the interview. She had been married for two years and had been forced to leave her first position in a bank at the time of her marriage. She had then obtained a job in a second bank at a lower salary. She knew friends who had suffered the same fate. I enquired if she knew anyone who had refused to leave. Yes, one friend had objected and had subsequently been given a transfer to another branch some distance away. Since this woman was about to marry a man who worked in the city where her original position was located, she had no choice but to resign. Hearing the story, a senior woman government worker commented dryly, 'If she objected she'd never get another job in the area.'

In a large provincial capital in central Honshū, a thirty-five-year-old ɔman found herself facing an unwelcome choice between marriage and job as a television producer. She worked for a private company in which female employees were forced to retire at the time of marriage. This interview also took place in the early 1990s. Evidently the practice extended even to relatively senior positions. Could the marriage be kept secret? No, Japan was a gossipy society and news was certain to reach her employer promptly. Could she live with the man she wished to marry without marrying? No, when news of this arrangement reached her employer it would also cost her the job she enjoyed and had taken a dozen years to master. The woman's frustration was keen, which is hardly surprising.

The practice of forcing women to retire when they marry was common in prewar years and continues to be so, although the media have chosen to acknowledge it only in the 1990s. Its unfairness was recognized long before it became illegal. Examining conditions for 'office ladies' in the late 1970s, Tomoko Bamba quotes the personnel department manager of a giant company as saying, 'We know we will lose if we are sued. But there will be few people who would resort to court. We will retain this system until we lose.'[8]

Dull work, no prospect of promotion, and heavy social pressure have combined to make many Japanese women take the marriage option. Bamba documents internal strife such as impatience, anxiety, restlessness, doubt, defiance, and resignation (p. 245). A male scholar, also writing in 1979, puts it more bluntly: 'Japanese companies do not promote women.'[9]

Suppressed frustration is now turning into militant and vocal resistance on the part of increasing numbers of women. The corporate bias against working couples, including those who are not working in the same company, remains strong in the male-dominated business world. Women who try to continue working after marriage are told, variously, that they are greedy to pursue a double income; that they would be incapable of taking proper care of a husband; that order in the company would be disrupted; and that the husband would not be given his normal promotions. A clerk at a major bank in Osaka was told, 'There are no women in our bank who stay with us after marriage.' A manager at a major securities firm, more honest than the average, explained that allowing women to remain in the labour force would increase costs, given the seniority-based system.[10]

The long-standing understanding that women will resign their jobs before marrying is increasingly being challenged. Companies are now afraid of lawsuits and prefer to force women to quit by indirect pressures such as reassigning them to unacceptable locations or restructuring their workloads to unreasonable levels. A woman head of a job counselling centre suggests that companies are irritated by the growing presence of married women and couples in the workplace and by the challenge to corporate assumptions of the past.

A sensitive and revealing portrait of what life is like for female office workers is found in Jeannie Lo's *Office Ladies/Factory Women* (1990). In the late 1980s, this young Asian-American researcher worked for Brother Industries in Nagoya as part of her Harvard project on the working lives of Japanese women. Lo worked at Brother for one year, first as an office worker, or 'OL,' and then on the factory line making typewriters. As an office lady, Lo worked in a typical Japanese office, a large undivided room with many desks arranged in clusters or work units. All workers are highly visible. One or two OLs came early each day to wipe desks, turn on lights and air-conditioning, and set the kettle to boil. Women served tea twice each morning and afternoon and did clerical jobs such as typing, using the facsimile machines, and answering the telephones. They were aware that one of their chief functions as 'office flowers' was to brighten the workplace.[11]

Lo found the office workers at Brother to be very concerned with fashion and their general appearance. Diets and men were frequent topics of conversation. The presence of men prompted the secretaries to act in a childish or *burikko* manner (from *furi*, pretence, and *ko*, child). Lo describes a typical OL at Brother Industries as follows: 'She may be sexually active, but she feigns innocence. The men enjoyed this pretence. One commented, "*Burikko* are cute. It's nice to have them around." Consistent with the *burikko* act, women cluttered their desks with toys and pins of Disney characters. By pretending to be children, OLs attempted to attract the attention of men who might take care of them' (pp. 42-3). Away from men, their manner was different, their voices louder.

Lo sought to understand why these women accepted the eternal tea service and the lack of challenge without complaint. She learned that they were sensitive to *shigarami*, the network of relationships that bound and held the workers as a functioning unit.[12] They might not enjoy serving tea but did so out of obligation to the work group in order to maintain the binding structure of existing relationships. Lo found Chie Nakane's analogy of company as extended family to be a living reality in the large office. It was clearly essential for an OL to be deferential and to observe the rules of the frame, or context, namely her work group. Those who disagreed had to adjust, or leave.[13]

A 1991 survey indicated that 80 percent of 1,700 companies still had their staff serve tea and that 90 percent of such service was performed only ⁓ women. By the 1990s, however, some managers and government bureau- ⁓s are beginning to recognize that women workers can be better ⁓yed. A municipal government in Tochigi Prefecture abolished the practice in 1994 and instructed women workers to concentrate on their jobs. Under the new policy, staff will pour their own tea, and visitors will not be served.[14] A small step. Letters to the editors of various publications indicate that the practice of tea service continues to be popular with men.

Lo found that company dormitories for men and women featured at least one marked difference that revealed the attitudes of male planners. The women's dormitory had small, primitive washing machines that required the user to participate manually at several points in the cycle – and one broken automatic. Doing laundry was an ordeal. Lo writes: 'Laundry is considered women's work. The men's dormitories, in contrast, are equipped with working automatic washing machines on every floor, saving time and effort.'[15] Consciously or subconsciously, the company was preparing women for their 'real' job as professional housewives.

Lo also served on the factory line at Brother Industries. These workers were almost exclusively women. The job was monotonous and fatiguing, mentally, spiritually, and physically: 'Frequently the workers actually run out of things to think about' (p. 32). The women factory workers were subjected to sexual harassment by male supervisors who would pat their bottoms while they were powerless to interrupt the flow of typewriters moving down the line. Men and marriage were the favourite topics of conversation among the factory women, who saw marriage and motherhood as an escape from the monotony of their work on the line and the best route to security.

In gender-conscious Japan, the concept of 'motherhood protection' has been hotly debated for most of this century. Prewar feminists argued primarily in economic terms: women were responsible for rearing children and should be enabled economically to do so. Male social reformers, on the other hand, sought to deny women access to certain jobs and to night work in order to protect the bodies of potential mothers. These varying concepts of protection, along with the basic view of women as mothers whose first duty to the state was to bear children, form a necessary background to understanding changes in work conditions for women in the second half of the twentieth century.

In the immediate postwar years, Japan was occupied by a foreign power that subscribed to the Potsdam Declaration, which called for male-female equality. The 1946 Constitution called for equal political rights for both sexes, and women hoped for legal changes concerning work. Jap was desperately poor, however, and millions of Japanese men were b repatriated from China and Southeast Asia. In this context, in Japa the West, women were encouraged to return home to open jobs fo ing men. This 'women at home' movement persisted for many

Male labour unions showed little interest in protecting women's interests. Barbara Molony writes: 'Government opinion generally applauded the removal of women from factory jobs as a means of controlling inflation and of bribing male workers into labour peace. Ironically, some women forced from railroad or factory work due to the enforcement of the prohibition of night work were pushed into prostitution ... The reinstatement of [prewar] protections reconcentrated women in female-dominated, poorly remunerated, dangerous jobs like those in textiles for which the protections of the Factory Law had been created in the first place.'[16]

Menstrual leave had been an issue since the late 1920s, when 500 women bus conductors staged a strike in Tokyo to demand it. Long hours on their feet and little or no opportunity to use a toilet made it a reasonable request. The issue resurfaced among women factory workers amid early postwar conditions. Molony explains: 'Women had no menstrual pads, there was no cotton available for that purpose. Rags were few. Factories had no heat or clean toilets, and many had broken windows. Menstruation leave was not inspired by women feeling weak or cramped or in need of protection for future maternity, but by women who had no easy way to deal with the physical aspects of their periods' (pp. 35-6). In the early postwar years, the majority of workers of both sexes approved of menstruation and maternity leave, but few believed that childcare leave or daycare facilities were needed. Mothers or other relatives of female workers were expected to provide care.

By the late 1940s the Occupation, fearing the growing radicalism of women's sections in the labour movement, froze any expansion of women workers' rights. Soon companies began pressing women to return to their homes. Menstrual leave was reduced from three days to two. Some companies tried to force women to leave by extending their hours and the time required to stand. As Molony notes, the real issue was not menstruation leave but the problem of institutionalized discrimination and sexism in Japanese employment practices (pp. 40-1).

From the mid-1950s to the early 1970s, the postwar 'women at home' movement provided even working women with their primary self-image. The number of working mothers with small children dropped, then climbed steadily from the mid-1970s. Menstrual leave was abandoned as the focus shifted gradually to maternity provisions.

As the postwar position of working women in industrialized countries anced, Japan came under increasing pressure from the international com-'y to amend conditions for women. In 1972 the Diet passed the Equal ment Opportunity (EEO) Law with the proviso that it should come t in 1986. Such laws are drafted by bureaucrats in consultation with special interest groups. Despite extensive consultation and further revisions passed by the Diet in 1985, the EEO Law clearly conflicts with established work norms and company practices in Japan. The law was opposed by many feminists as well, not merely because it contains no penalties for offenders but also because 'equal' treatment meant that by the yardstick of male norms women's work as mothers would be devalued. In other words, identical treatment would produce discriminatory results (p. 144).

The Japanese tendency to interpret law as a cultural guideline encouraged many employers to continue their time-honoured practices. Low-cost female labour had helped to keep down prices for international markets, while lifetime employment for workers at the largest companies, one-third of the national total, had earned the devoted loyalty and unstinting overtime of male employees.

By the 1970s, relatively small numbers of talented and well-educated women began to find permanent employment in government and high-technology industries. Faced with a growing shortage of skilled labour, major electronics firms were training women software engineers in the early 1980s. The growing importance of women in the consumer market led to job opportunities for women in product development and marketing. Meanwhile, the educational level of women was rapidly rising.[17] Companies such as department stores and supermarkets began to use women's creativity in project teams, the better to penetrate the market. There was, however, no formal link between such teams and career advancement. Female group leaders were also outside established career paths. Such positions were informal and ambiguous. The basic situation, that women entered the clerical stream and men the managerial, remained unchanged.

In the years leading up to the putative implementation of the EEO Law in 1986, employers had strongly resisted any new legal obligations in the areas of recruiting, job assignment, and promotion. Accordingly, the law merely *exhorted* employers 'to endeavour' to treat women equally with men in these areas. As Alice Lam writes, company managers argued that such changes would cause chaos in personnel management systems and would eventually destroy the vitality of the Japanese economy (p. 207). The hortatory provisions were purposely ambiguous and the definition of 'equal opportunity' narrow and limited. Companies were urged to 'make efforts' to offer women *some* opportunity. The Ministry of Labour had aimed no higher than removing the most blatant forms of direct discrimination against women and had left systemic or institutionalized discrimination firmly in place. Bureaucrats merely intended the law to serve as a moral mark future employment practices and an educational tool for employers.[18]

The immediate effects in 1986 were to change job advertisements and to move towards equalization of starting wages for new recruits. Women complained that the changes in advertising only created false expectations and confusion in dealing with companies that had no intention of offering them equal career opportunities. Companies moved towards indirect yet still institutionalized ways of segregating the vast majority of female employees into positions that offered no chance for promotion.[19]

Some major firms, however, began offering women a choice of positions: career-track or managerial (*sōgō shoku*), or clerical (*ippan shoku*). These broad specifications were often no more than a set of behavioural expectations, including the commitment to relocation. Men continued to be assigned automatically to the management track, while only exceptional women were selected for it.

Alice Lam's study shows that women's career aspirations did not rise in the first few years after the introduction of the EEO Law. Women displayed instead a greater degree of uncertainty about their career futures. Government surveys revealed a decline in the proportion of young women intending to pursue a continuous career, from 20 percent in 1979 to 14.4 percent in 1989. Lam notes that the intensive demands on employees in career tracks to work excessively long hours and to commit themselves to relocation appear to have driven more women into the common two-phase pattern of working before marriage and after children have grown. Lam calls this a pragmatic choice 'in a system which does not allow career jobs to be compatible with family life, and in a society which expects women to take up sole responsibility for raising children' (pp. 216-7).

Japanese companies fear the cost of expanding the number of permanent employees. They may also fear that resentment on the part of male employees accustomed to traditional privileges will lead to a drop in the high levels of commitment that have brought remarkable successes over the last forty years. The work norms that men have accepted are unrealistic for most married women. The current struggle is to create a workplace where women *and* men in career-track positions can be home in time to see and care for their children in the evening. Many employers have no sympathy with this goal. Molony writes that evidence since 1986 suggests companies are making particularly stringent demands on women for out-of-town travel and overtime. These employers hope to dissuade women from sticking to career-track jobs: 'In affluent, contemporary Japan, "motherhood protec-" has come to mean protecting the right to a full life, including work he enjoyment of one's family.'[20]

Amid current conditions, this is far from easy. The Japanese social support system for working mothers of small children is inadequate, as it is in so many other countries.[21] In Japan, however, long hours of work and the social expectation that mothers bear sole responsibility for childcare make extra problems for working mothers. The co-ordinator of an international preschool in Tokyo found Japanese society 'cold' towards working women. In her initial efforts to register her school, she encountered numerous road-blocks from officials who asked why she did not simply quit her job and 'be a housewife.'[22]

Under the Labour Standards Law in the 1980s, working women were given six weeks leave before childbirth, and eight weeks (six of them compulsory) after childbirth. The employer could not dismiss a worker during this period of leave or for thirty days following it.[23] With the falling birth rate pointing to worsening labour shortages and many other social problems to come, the government has a stake in women's attitudes to work and motherhood. In April 1992, the Diet passed the Child Care Leave Law, granting either parent the option of one year's leave without pay and the guarantee of returning to the same job at the same level. Benefits such as pension and medical insurance continue throughout the period of leave. Later that year, surveys conducted by the Economic Planning Agency showed that many large companies were totally unwilling to make changes to help working mothers. A thousand childless working women were asked what kind of changes would enable them to continue working while bringing up children: 30 percent said fewer working hours; 28 percent said the ability to work at home; and 22 percent called for daycare centres within the company. Responding to a matching survey, most large companies said they did not have such practices *nor any plans to introduce them.* Shorter hours were the only option that a few companies were even willing to consider.[24]

The law concerning childcare leave, like the EEO Law of 1986, carries no penalties for violators. A union survey in 1993 showed that only 22 percent of companies surveyed granted such leave. Other surveys showed that very few women and almost no men had taken such leave in the first year of its availability. Women cited a lack of understanding from their bosses and a lack of co-operation among co-workers that created 'a kind of psychological restraint on such leave.'[25] The lack of pay is also a crucial factor.

Problems surrounding daycare are legion. Transportation is time-consuming, and a general shortage of places can mean that parents with tv small children must deal with two different facilities. The vast majorit daycares close at five or six in the afternoon. Only about 5 percent stav later, and only 0.1 percent provide nightcare. Few accept babies ur age of one. A child's illness, however minor, creates major problems for the working mother and often guilt feelings.[26] Even the extra paperwork that mothers, but not fathers, must fill out when they apply for space in a day-care reflects the double standard for men and women workers.[27]

The EEO Law is now being taken more seriously by both women and the Ministry of Labour. Gradually, the ministry began telling companies to abandon discriminatory practices against women. The report of a ministry official in 1994 noted that 655 companies had been investigated, including financial institutions, construction firms, and broadcasting stations.[28] The ministry, with characteristic ambiguity and understatement, had found 'much room for improvement' in all areas of employment.

Also in 1994, the ministry prepared to mediate the first suit against discriminatory employment practices brought against Sumitomo Metal. Seven women workers, all regular office staffers with between nineteen and thirty-five years of service, claimed that the company had barred them from promotions and transfers on the grounds that they were married. Male colleagues had been promoted faster and as a result earned almost twice as much as the women bringing suit. Since applications for mediation by the ministry had been rejected in previous years, there is progress.[29]

Are Japanese women prepared to accept the current pace of change? Some are not. Some ambitious women, frustrated by discrimination, are seeking work abroad. A spokesman for a large recruiting firm with branches in Japan and Hong Kong noted the steep rise in the number of Japanese women registering with his firm between 1991 and 1994 and finding career-track jobs in Hong Kong.[30] Hong Kong has a tradition of providing equal job opportunities for men and women and employers treat women in their late twenties and early thirties the same as younger women. Best of all, women find themselves allowed to do challenging work in a comfortable atmosphere.[31] One woman working as a manager in Hong Kong noted that in Japan women are subordinated to men, 'and there's a subtle feeling that women shouldn't be too capable. Here in Hong Kong you don't have to worry about that.' Another testified, 'In Japan, men and women work, but only men have hopes of advancement'; and a third, 'In Hong Kong, things are different, capabilities are rewarded, regardless of gender.'[32]

The United States is also a popular destination for job seekers of both sexes. Since 1991, when America introduced a lottery system to determine who would be granted permission to immigrate, more than 130,000 Japanese have applied for the necessary 'green card.' Many said that their was to escape Japan's work-oriented lifestyle and stifling social mores, develop their own abilities.[33]

Ambitious women are further motivated to work abroad because of the special pressures associated with career-track work for them in Japan. Many experience stress-related illnesses such as insomnia, sore shoulders, irregular menstruation, and stomach pains. Problems include isolation, a lack of role models, and dirty jokes.[34]

In the recessionary years of the early 1990s Japanese women experienced severe difficulties finding jobs after graduation. Working during the crucial premarital years has been part of the rhythm of urban women's lives for two generations. Surveys show that the majority believed their gender was a disadvantage at every stage of the job hunt, from getting initial information to getting an interview, and many complaints noted sexual harassment at interviews. Women university graduates, in particular, were finding themselves frozen out of the job market. Men were even being preferred for positions in areas traditionally filled by women. Employers cited the tendency of women to stay in their jobs for many more years than previously as part of the problem. A senior Cabinet official acknowledged in 1994 that companies had *systematically* discriminated against women during the four-year economic downturn and that the EEO Law was being widely disregarded.[35]

These difficulties have fed a growing mood of militancy among young women. Working abroad is one way they are expressing their dissatisfaction. Another is fighting for married women to be allowed to retain their own surnames. Professor Reiko Sekiguchi of the University of Library and Information Science in Tsukuba has been a leader in this effort. Under current civil law (Article 750) married couples must choose *one* surname to register. In 98 percent of cases this has been the man's. Professional women are hampered by the restriction, and even women who identify themselves as 'ordinary housewives' consider the practice a symbol of subordination. By 1994 the education minister was assuring women that the convention would be changed 'eventually.'[36]

None of the options under review in the early 1990s regarding family names could solve the two main problems, the perceived weakening of the marital tie and children's names. The matter is an emotional one. Shuhei Ninomiya, Professor of Family Law at Ritsumeikan University in Kyoto, calls it a question of dignity and a symbol of individuality: 'There's a sense of paternalism that aims to keep family united under the authority of husband or father – the traditional thinking that men are superior to women.' Akira Ishihara, a member of the Japan Federation of Bar Associatior believes that a shared name provides a family with 'spiritual' stability togetherness and that the current regulation should not be changed some 80 percent of the people call for it.[37] Opinions on married surnames changed considerably between 1990 and 1994, but Ishihara's conservative preference is widespread and will not be altered overnight.[38]

Another example of discrimination against professional women is the practice in many private companies and government offices of requiring female salesclerks, office clerks, and even store managers to wear uniforms. In some, they are optional, but peer pressure and individual managers enforce compliance. Some employers believe that company uniforms for female staff increase sales. Uniforms are not worn by male employees.

Surveys show that both men and women believe uniforms place women in 'auxiliary positions.' A few company presidents are actually calling for more individuality and creativity and are abolishing uniforms for female employees as a step in this direction. A policy counsellor to a prefectural governor is convinced that uniforms deprive women of a sense of responsibility.[39] The EEO Law helped to discourage the use of uniforms. Curiously, the same currents of social change that are discouraging the general use of uniforms are helping pregnant women to retain their jobs, and the maternity uniforms introduced by several large department stores are reputedly popular with workers.[40]

Colourful uniforms are also proving popular with young college graduates determined to find jobs. Part-time women cleaners aged twenty-five and under are working in teams to tidy and vacuum high-speed passenger trains between trips. The uniform features short culottes and a jaunty hat. College graduates are also willing, indeed eager, to clean toilets at Disneyland. Admirable spirit and appalling waste? Or good discipline? This is the job market for young women in the early 1990s. One cleaner remarked: 'I know now that I can do things if I try and I won't be beaten by men.'[41]

Despite all the pressures to conform that Japanese women have experienced from childhood on, the will to explore, to find and face personal challenge, is strong in many. Women have long been physicians, and indeed some pioneer doctors have continued to practise into their eighties and nineties. In 1993, at the age of eighty-seven, Dr Kyoko Matsuyama continues her small-town practice in Kanegase, Miyagi Prefecture. She has been serving the community for half a century. Growing up in a doctorless village taught her the need for local physicians.[42]

The nursing profession is the largest occupational group composed mostly of women. In recent years low pay and very poor working conditions have driven some to leave. Nurses are paid 20 percent less than an average office worker. They work long hours, six days a week. Because of the shortage of nurses many hospitals fail to meet the minimum patient-nurse ratio

Junko Ikegawa, former president of Kōchi Women's University, now professor emerita, with the author. Morley is holding *The Phoenix Stirs: Japan 1946-51* by Camera Johnson, a diary of the Occupation years that Ikegawa edited and translated. Ikegawa was the first woman president of a national university in Japan, garnering a lot of publicity on her appointment. Though there are now a few women university presidents, they are still rare.

required by law. There are also constant violations regarding the number of night shifts per nurse per month, set at eight by the Health and Welfare Ministry. Low pay, frequent night shifts, physical and emotional strain, and lack of a childcare support system compel over 45,000 nurses to leave their jobs every year.[43]

In national universities, women have been lecturers and research assistants since the 1950s and assistant professors since the '60s. Women are now found at senior university levels but continue to experience difficulties in hiring and promotion.[44] Women writers and artists have forged an impressive record in Japan for centuries, yet modern women writers were considered a breed apart from mainstream writing until the last twenty years or so.

Yoneko Ishida, professor of history at Okayama National University, 1993. Women full professors are uncommon in Japan.

In the last decade women have been making significant inroads into politics and law. Also in recent years women have become police officers, taxi drivers, jockeys, realtors (especially in residential real estate), veterinarians, construction workers, commercial pilots, members of the Self-Defense Forces, and cabinet ministers.[45] One has even become a Supreme Court justice. Such activities seem strangely at odds with broad social patterns and expectations. The patterns, the generalities, and the exceptions are all part of the fabric of this unusual society, which has been changing slowly since 1945.

The entry of women into some of these professions is very new indeed. Hisako Takahashi's January 1994 appointment to the fifteen-member bench of the Supreme Court was termed 'tokenism' by some. Others hailed it as 'a new wind' blowing over Japan's arch-conservative judicial world. Takahashi is a former Labour Ministry bureaucrat, not a lawyer, and she has completed a four-year term. At the time of her appointment, one journalist noted that she would probably challenge assumptions that underlay 'the traditional patriarchal family structure under which marriage is seen as the main means of financial security and social status for women.'[46] The lack of subsequent media attention, however, suggests that she did not make waves. A less sanguine editorial noted the contrast between theory and reality in the Supreme Court. Established after 1945 under the influence of the United States, the Supreme Court was intended as a 'fortress for human rights.' Its conservative appointees have made the reality 'quite opposite.'[47]

Women accounted for 7 percent of judges, 6 percent of lawyers, and 3 percent of prosecutors in 1994. In the 1980s and early '90s, more women were

Dr Oishi, veterinarian, with injured dog.

turning to law because of exclusion from other career-track areas. The percentage of women who passed the highly competitive national bar examination topped 10 percent for the first time in 1980 and reached a record 19.8 percent (125 women) in 1992. A television drama series featuring a law office with seven women lawyers began in 1990. A pioneer who began her legal practice in 1951 noted that women pay attention to detail and are able to sympathize with suffering people.[48] The Ministry of Justice appointed Shoko Hashimoto in 1993 as the first woman probation office chief.[49]

The qualities that have long made women popular in the service industries are helping them to enter new fields. Women cab drivers are appreciated because they are generally friendly and cheerful. Male Japanese cabbies tend to be impassive, and many make no attempt to assist passengers with baggage. Women cabbies have been on the road for the last decade but their numbers have been rising rapidly in recent years. Hours are flexible, and the pay for men and women is the same. This means a much higher income than that earned by a female clerk.

Local governments are attracting women university graduates, and municipalities are making changes to employment tests to encourage women to apply. These include dropping law and economics from the list of examination subjects and raising the age limit for applicants to thirty. Promotion opportunities are lower in this field, but decentralized locations may reduce 'commuting hell.'[50] Some municipal offices are staffed solely by women. They handle family registers, counselling, and assistance in coping with administrative policies. These offices are proving popular with both sexes

For the more ambitious, the federal bureaucracy has offered career-track jobs for women since the 1970s. A very few pioneers entered the Women and Minors Bureau of the ministries of Education and Labour between 1950 and 1975. Government departments, including the prestigious Ministry of International Trade and Industry, began to employ female bureaucrats with career ambitions in 1976.[52]

Government advisory panels under guidelines to increase female representation to 15 percent by 1995 have created a demand for women bureaucrats. In the past male bureaucrats have seen nothing incongruous in all-male panels discussing, for example, housing standards. The requirements for eligibility to sit on these panels make it unlikely, however, that quotas for female members will be met until other changes occur in Japanese economic and political structures.[53]

Some token women police officers entered the National Police Agency in 1976, but substantial participation would take another decade to accomplish. In the 1990s, the police and the Self-Defense Agency have been increasingly popular with women. The first woman to head a police station was appointed in 1994, and the Metropolitan Police Department was planning at that time to increase the number of female officers by about 300 over the next five years. The first women helicopter pilots in the Tokyo Metropolitan Police received their licences in 1992.[54]

Some seventy women entered the four-year program of the National Defense Academy in 1992, the first since it opened in 1952.[55] However, rumoured cuts in the Self-Defense Forces caused by the end of Cold War tension may put their future at risk. The five-day work week for police officers and members of the SDF are attractive to new officers. Special services and educational opportunities such as the National Defense Medical College, the Meteorological Agency, and the Aeronautical Safety College have also attracted women in the 1990s, a period when the SDF began to train women as transport pilots.[56] In 1994, after two years of flight training, Hiroko Miyamoto became the first woman airforce pilot to receive her wings.

Modern women who are setting records include astronauts, mountain climbers, and Olympic athletes. Chiaki Mukai, Japan's first woman astronaut, took part in a fourteen-day mission in July 1994, on the US space shuttle Columbia.[57] A Japanese alpinist became in 1992 the world's first woman to reach the highest mountain peaks of seven continents. Junko Tabei was fifty-two at the time of her 'seven summits' challenge, and her achievement ⸗ shared by only four male alpinists.[58] Also in 1992, Akiko Kato became the ⸗t Japanese woman ever selected to do research in Antarctica as a member of a joint international project.[59] By 1993, women were joining in the previously all-male practices of *yamabushi*, ascetics who scale mountains and stand under ice-cold waterfalls, seeking through such extreme austerities to re-establish fundamental ties with nature and fellow humans.[60]

Down on solid ground, women are moving mountains rather than climbing them. Since the late 1980s, they have been choosing construction jobs and work in skilled building trades. Most postwar Japanese have tried to avoid '3K' jobs until recently, preferring to leave to others work that is *kitsui* (physically difficult), *kitanai* (dirty), and *kiken* (dangerous). Yet modern women are putting on their gloves, driving heavy machinery, and climbing scaffolding. They are working as electricians, plumbers, plasterers, and engineers. And enjoying it.[61]

Until the labour shortage of the late 1980s, most female workers at construction sites were part-time cleaners. Although they are still a small minority in construction, the change since 1987 is startling. A survey of twenty-nine companies in October 1991 revealed a 650 percent increase over the four previous years.[62] The construction industry was hit harder than any other sector by the shortage of skilled labour in 1990. Women are choosing construction jobs for a variety of reasons including better pay, outdoor work, and relief from office stress. They agree that the work is interesting. Various legal barriers are outstanding, including a regulation that forbids women from working late at night.

An amusing irony lay behind one construction company's move to hire women for jobs on site, beginning in 1986. The original intention of its president, Yoshio Sato of Sato Komuten, was to assist his male employees who had neither time nor opportunity to socialize to find brides. 'Lady Task,' his innovative policy, received media attention that resulted in a hefty increase in job seekers of both sexes.[63] The unexpected twist is indicative. The diversity of jobs being tackled by the second postwar generation of Japanese women, along with startling moves into new areas in the last decade, suggests that the pace of change for women is quickening. Employment practices can only be changed by stronger pressures from women themselves, both in the workplace and at the political level. And this is happening.

They also have allies in unexpected places. Ichiro Ozawa, a senior and influential member of the Diet, spoke out in 1994 against discriminatory work practices for women and the sharp distinction in pay and benefits for part- and full-time workers. Given the aging population, falling birth rate, and declining supply of labour, he may have been spurred less by idealism than by a clear-sighted view of necessity: 'Japan's labour mark still shaped by the uniform assumption that men go outside to work while women maintain the home. The permanent employment system hinders women, as it hinders senior citizens, from entering the work force.'[64] He admits that conditions are changing but sees the pace as much too slow. Ozawa calls for companies to strengthen maternity and childcare leave options and for men to take a share in the work of the house. A 1991 survey found that only one working man in thirty did any housework at all on weekdays. As for Sundays, even those married to women with full-time jobs spent an average of twenty-six minutes on housework and twelve minutes playing with their children.[65] Ozawa states unequivocally that the nation cannot afford, either economically or socially, for capable career women to be forced to leave their jobs in their peak working years.[66]

Aided by national necessity, those women who wish to combine employment with homemaking may find it easier in years to come.

CHAPTER 7

THE TWILIGHT YEARS: CARING FOR THE ELDERLY

No home will admit someone like that because they're terribly short-staffed ... There's really no solution to this problem. It tears many families apart. The wife simply has to cope.

Men are so helpless, thought Akiko, clicking her tongue in irritation ... She was extremely agitated performing this unpleasant task while Nobutoshi and Satoshi stood stiffly by, mistakenly assuming that Akiko was accustomed to performing this ritual.

SAWAKO ARIYOSHI, *The Twilight Years*

SAWAKO ARIYOSHI'S POWERFUL NOVEL, *The Twilight Years*, vividly dramatizes the hardships and the horrors that growing old may impose on both the elderly and their families. She shows that in Japan the burden of such care is carried almost exclusively by women, not always out of choice. And she suggests that, if Japanese men become senile, they may bear some personal responsibility for their fate due to their postretirement withdrawal from activity and effort.[1]

These themes are built up with sensitivity and a mordant gift for black humour through the story of the Tachibana family: husband Nobutoshi, wife Akiko, their eighteen-year-old son Satoshi, and Nobutoshi's eighty-four-year-old father Shigezoh. The latter's steady slide into senility after the sudden death of his wife and Akiko's attempts to deal with the worsening situation shape the novel's action. Ariyoshi gives a stark warning: we are responsible, at least in part, for our own physical and mental health. Shigezoh 'had only himself to blame for his wretched condition' (p. 84).

The early chapters sketch a portrait of Shigezoh as an arrogant man of the Meiji era, pampered and overindulged by women for a lifetime, hypochondriacal, and utterly selfish. When he meets his daughter-in-law on th street laden with heavy bags of groceries, he offers no help as they walk towards home, although he is still physically strong. The family knows that his deceased wife, 'a true Meiji woman,' had stoically devoted her entire life to a man who was almost impossible to please: 'Mother was a slave to father' (p. 35).

With the death of his wife, Shigezoh's focus is transferred to his daughter-in-law. The elderly couple had been living in a cottage adjacent to their son's house. Now the old man, who cannot be left alone, begins to sleep in his son's living room, and it soon proves necessary for Akiko to sleep beside him. Shigezoh becomes unable to recognize his son, mistaking him for a burglar. Satoshi concludes that his grandfather is an animal who instinctively recognizes only the person who is absolutely necessary for his survival: his daughter-in-law.

Nobutoshi has neither the will nor the wish to help care for his father, whose senile state confronts him with his own future. In this family's winter of discontent, Nobutoshi regularly goes drinking after work and returns home late. He refuses to help his father urinate in the night. He works a six-day week and sleeps till noon on Sundays. He even refuses to help wash his father's genitals, a task that Akiko finds very distasteful. Returning home one night at two in the morning, he rings his doorbell although he has a key. Akiko reflects that 'men always tried their utmost to avoid the troublesome details of running a household' (p. 88).

Akiko has held a job with a legal firm for most of her married years. Her income has helped to reduce the mortgage on the family home and to build a cottage for her in-laws, but Nobutoshi has never recognized these facts and has put the houses in his name alone. Akiko enjoys her work and is reluctant to lose it. Faced with the care of her father-in-law, her first allies are a flirtatious widow who lives nearby and the Community Centre for Seniors.

Before long, the widow has lost patience, and the number of nighttime disturbances have risen from one to four. Exhausted and desperate, Akiko obtains tranquilizers for Shigezoh. However, they lead to incontinence, a regime of diapers, and his occasional disappearances in the night. Akiko appeals for help one night, but Nobutoshi excuses himself on pretence of 'a busy day tomorrow' and returns to bed. Furious, she finds him irresponsible and insensitive: 'Like father, like son, thought Akiko' (p. 151).

The Tachibanas, however, are depicted as having a happy marriage and a basically good relationship. In Ariyoshi's portrait, male insensitivity is culturally induced, bred in the bone through male arrogance and female indulgence. This holds true as much for men such as Nobutoshi, born in the 1920s, as for those born in the Meiji era.

Akiko now embarks on a serious effort to inform herself about social services and nursing care available to seniors, only to find that Shigezoh, difficult as he is to care for, is considered to be in better health than many others his age and to be very lucky to have a caring family. Some of the features of his senility that make caring for him so onerous also make him ineligible for a nursing home. These include his long runaway walks through the city. 'The wife simply has to cope as courageously as she can,' a social worker advises Akiko, who now understands 'that the current welfare system for the elderly in Japan was appallingly backward and that the official policy had so far failed to take account of the increase of old people in the population' (p. 161).

By this time, Nobutoshi has been informed by his workmates that the percentage of senior citizens had increased dramatically in Japan in recent years and that very few measures had been taken to deal with the aged even in the West: 'He had also heard that by about the year 2000, there were likely to be more than thirty million people over sixty in Japan; the Japanese would be a nation of senior citizens ... Still echoing in his ears was his son's fervent plea: "Mum, Dad, please don't live this long!"' (p. 167).

Shigezoh falls ill with pneumonia, recovers, and enters a relatively benign phase of second childhood. Akiko has taken a leave of absence from her job and now knows many other women in similar situations. Later still, aided by a college student, she manages to work a three-day week, sharing the job with another woman. Shigezoh is found smearing his excrement over himself and the tatami. Eventually, as he is about to be admitted to a nursing home, he dies quietly. No one sheds a tear, and the officiating priest, who has a bedridden father, tells the bereaved family that he envies them.

The bleakness of this portrait is relieved by the increasing sympathy and understanding that the situation induces in the wife and teenaged son and by Ariyoshi's gift for irony and humour. Her harshest criticism is reserved for the men who contribute to their own demise and for the culture that encourages them in these patterns of behaviour. The disenchanted neighbourhood widow lectures Akiko, comparing Shigezoh with other seniors at the centre who remained alert at ninety-two: 'They all say that Mr Tachibana became senile because he didn't exercise his mind or body. They also say that he was probably lazy. A man can slow down the ageing process by keeping mentally and physically active. Mr Tachibana must have made his wife work like a slave while he did absolutely nothing ... Women rarely become senile, because they have to use their brains – whether they're sewing or doing the laundry' (p. 104).

Left alone, Akiko reflects on Shigezoh's lifelong habits of self-indulgence and complaint, on his lack of friends and disinterest in hobbies. The socia worker tells her that the majority of those who become senile are men: 'They're so used to working that they don't know what to do with themselves when they retire' (p. 168). *The Twilight Years* depicts a man who is largely responsible for his own selfishness and senile dementia, and the women who find themselves forced to care for him.

This fictional portrait was first published a generation ago, in 1972. Since then the number of seniors has rapidly increased, as the novelist forecast and, compounded by other social changes, problems with care for the elderly have multiplied explosively. Japanese life expectancy in 1990 was the highest in the world at 81.81 for women and 75.86 for men, according to reports by the Ministry of Health and Welfare and the United Nations World Health Organization (WHO). The growing numbers of elderly Japanese constitute a women's issue, because women make up 60 percent of the elderly and a very large percentage of the care givers.

Japan's demographics are unusual and conceal alarming possibilities.

Perhaps most startling is that the number of people over sixty-five will move from 10 percent of the population in 1985 to 20 percent in 2007 and that this doubling will require only twenty-two years, the shortest period for any country in the world. By comparison, Sweden's population will require sixty-six years to double, between 1947 and 2013. More recent statistics show 14.1 percent of the population over sixty-five in 1994, with 21.4 percent anticipated by 2011 and 25.9 percent by 2025.[2]

At the request of the Japan Medical Association, the Nihon University Population Research Institute (NUPRI) compiled estimates on the population, economy, and social welfare system from 1990 to 2025 based on the 1985 national census. In 2025, at roughly 26 percent, Japan's seniors will constitute a bigger portion of the population than in any other country. Japan will enter 'an era of aged women,' with 19.18 million elderly women, 4.5 million more than the number of elderly men.[3]

The same institute predicts that women not working outside the home will bear heavier and heavier responsibility for the aged: 'Among women in their forties, one out of every fifteen were likely to be caring for either a bedridden or senile elderly person in 1990. In 2025, one out of every two women in their forties are likely to be performing such tasks.' The family support ratio, or number of adults available to support a parent, 0.76 in 1990, will be cut in half by 2010, making it the world's lowest. Savings, as a percentage of the nation's gross national product, will decrease sharply over the same period: an aging society will save less, creating a smaller financial base from which to provide increased care for the elderly.

In short, ministry reports depict Japan as a nation in crisis whose

Takako Tani of Sapporo practising *kyudoh*, Japanese-style archery, in preparation for the annual national sports competition for seniors. The presence of women in this sport is a break with tradition.

demographic patterns are changing faster than those of any other country in the world. Small wonder that in the summer of 1993 Keigo Ouchi, Democratic Socialist Party chair and Health and Welfare minister, spoke of the urgent need to build a 'welfare state' to cope with the aging society.[4] Not all the issues raised by an aging society are negative. Indeed fresh initiatives such as the concept of lifelong learning and other quality-of-life issues suggest that the presence of substantial numbers of elderly people might prove a wholesome leaven in Japanese society.

The heavy burden laid primarily on women as care givers to the elderly continues to preoccupy many writers and is frequently addressed in the popular press. A 1989 survey showed that most Japanese of both sexes continue to believe that care for the elderly is a woman's duty and that bedridden parents should be cared for by a daughter or daughter-in-law, even if this means that the woman must quit a full-time job. Sawako Ariyoshi's perceptions are confirmed by this indication that men become even more dependent on women as they age.[5]

One journalist writes of three women whose lives had been dominated by the need to care for parents. Each knew many other women with similar stories, and each could not help but wonder why they were expected to shoulder the burden alone. Yuriko gave up her hopes of a career as a librarian and a marriage prospect to devote more than a decade to parental care, only to be beaten by her father in his last years. He was unable to express his frustrations in any other way. Tomoko, who cared for two ailing parents for twenty years, would have liked to marry and have a family but found no man mentally equipped to help shoulder her burden. Nobuko nursed a disabled, alcoholic father and a psychotic mother for seven years. Each woman had a brother, and each brother declined to help.[6]

Obviously these women and others like them who sacrificed marriage chances to care for parents, along with those who choose a career over marriage, may face their last years alone. And since women live on average six years longer than men, many will inevitably find themselves in need of help at some point near the end of their lives. By the year 2000 there will be 3.34 million more elderly women than men, and the percentage of women over sixty-five living alone will rise from 1.47 percent of the total population in 1990 to 19.5 percent in 2010. The percentage of women aged eighty-five or older will grow more rapidly in the next three decades than any other age group among the elderly.[7]

In my own interviews I learned of elderly women, currently fit, who dreaded the thought of living for many more years and becoming senile; and of widows whose husbands had died suddenly in their seventies and whose friends had told them they were 'lucky.' One young woman, an only child, was in love with a man who was also an only child, and both sets of parents had forbidden the marriage. All four parents were in their late fifties or early sixties and in the best of health, but each was ready to block their child's happiness because of the distant spectre of a dependent old age and the prospect of only one care giver for four seniors.

Japanese women are very conscious of this spectre, more so than their counterparts in the West, where institutional care is more common. Many women in Japan plot what one sociologist calls 'strategies of aging' throughout a substantial portion of their lives. The situation was very different before the Pacific War. Until fifty years ago, Japanese inheritance law gave the eldest son the largest share of the estate along with the responsibility to care for parents and siblings. The latter were relatively free of such responsibilities. Legal changes under the Occupation gave each child an equal share of the inheritance.

Abolishing the *ie* (the 'stem' or extended family of the male line) as a legal entity undermined structural support for the older generation's *right* to the gratitude and long-term care of

A woman in her eighties exercises regularly in a small town hospital's fitness centre for seniors. As a society, Japan is doing more than North America to encourage seniors to exercise.

the younger generation, but custom continued to support the old ways for several generations. Even today, Japanese society honours parental responsibility, and many still consider it irresponsible and unkind to send parents to an old people's home.

The availability of such homes is another matter, and Ariyoshi's parable shows the scarcity that prevailed in the 1970s. Conditions have worsened since then. Other changes such as the increase in working women, geographic mobility, and life expectancy of the general population compound the problems of aging and leave women uncertain whether the daughter-in-law who would have cared for them forty or fifty years ago would still do so today. One result is that Japanese women currently prefer to depend on

This farmer in Shinjo, Okayama-ken,
manages two large rice paddies and two
prized black cattle. Her husband is a
full-time salaryman. Her grandmother,
aged ninety, weeds the ancestral graves
on a nearby hillside.

their own daughters. Moreover, postwar education and custom, especially in recent years, allows a little more room for the value of individual choice in type of care. The high rate of suicide among elderly Japanese women shows the anxiety and uncertainties that they confront.[8]

Talking with thirty-five elderly women in a small city in Japan in the 1970s, Takie Sugiyama Lebra found that they tended to remain silent about their expectations for care in the final phase of aging. Each woman stressed that she would do anything to avoid being a burden and that care, if needed, should be voluntary. They hoped to die *pokkuri* (abruptly). Many informants identified themselves as belonging to a loser generation squeezed between two demanding winner generations, their autocratic mothers-in-law and their independent children.

Each woman seemed to be exploring other alternatives. These included economic self-sufficiency; inner self-sufficiency through involvement in hobbies or some *ikigai* (purpose of life); and commitment to maintaining good health through exercise and mental activity. Ariyoshi's novel – whose Japanese title, 'A Man of Ecstasy,' refers to senile psychosis – was well known and often quoted by these women. Another strategy for some elderly women was to help their daughters, often by caring for grandchildren, in order to accumulate further credit or indebtedness. Alternatively, they might attempt to intensify identification with the ancestors enshrined in the household altar, in part by maintaining the gift-giving obligations to the houses into which several generations of the family's women had married. The custodial women hoped that the ancestors would bestow a *pokkuri* death on the worshippers and that the custodian of the family altar was moving towards her own enshrinement. Custodial care of the dead was considered vital to the continuity of the *ie* in prewar Japan. Finally, a grandmother could bond with a grandchild in order to build indebtedness. In Ariyoshi's novel, one of Akiko's co-workers is working to help support a bedridden grandmother.

The continuity of these women's lives was apparent in neighbourhood groups that facilitated cultural programs and social exchange. A woman who may have belonged to the PTA when her children were in school typically graduated to the Women's Association in her mid-forties and to the Old People's Association at sixty-five. Association leaders emphasized educational goals rather than mere entertainment.

Alumnae reunions are popular as women age, and occupational ties lead to group activities. Groups are spawned around shared interests by anyone with leadership ability. Lebra observes that in associations with both male and female members leadership roles were taken by men save during periods of recreation and entertainment, when women dominated. Women with activities outside the house tended to be teased as *dezuki-baasan* (outgoer granny) by family members.

Group travel with peers is enjoyed by elderly women and seems to release lifelong inhibitions. Lebra observes: 'The absence of males indeed emancipates these female co-travellers from the codes of conduct pertaining to their routine life, and allows them to entertain one another with scatological jokes of extraordinary magnitude. But as soon as the bus stopped at a celebrated spot for sight-seeing, all the bus riders rushed to souvenir shops to buy gifts for their families ... Even the most uninhibited joker was transformed into a straight, humourless housewife during the shopping intervals' (p. 350). The Japan Travel Bureau organizes 'Ripe-age Overseas Tours.' Planners continue to be surprised by the eagerness of the elderly to study while travelling abroad. Since the number of elderly women with independent incomes continues to grow, the 'silver market' is becoming, in Japan as in the West, the target of many entrepreneurs.

Age can mean freedom as well as dependency. Some Japanese initiatives are building on this premise, as lifespans are being prolonged at a rate never before experienced in Japan or any other country. Surveys from the 1970s show that whereas seniors of that era enjoyed having unhurried time with family and friends, only a small minority spent time on sports, hobbies, learning activities, or volunteer service. Attitudes began to change in the late 1970s, when ideas of sports participation for seniors and lifelong learning gained ground.[9] These trends continued through the 1980s and '90s, as the concept of education broadened to include a wide-ranging enrichment of life.

By the late 1980s, Japanese ministries had begun to herald the twenty-first century as a 'New Silver Era.' Since 1989, the Ministry of Health and Welfare has been promoting the establishment of 'universities for the elderly' throughout the country. By March 1992, thirty-three prefectures had created some such institution and were offering courses in a variety of subjects, including pottery, horticulture, health and welfare, culture, computer use, and English conversation.[10] The radical nature of this breakthrough is apparent when we remember that the Japanese have always been very conscious of age and of hierarchical relationships based partly on age. I was startled to be told by a man in his fifties that he could not imagine students of widely differing ages studying together or being friends.

Old taboos, such as a prejudice against romance for seniors are slowly giving way. Many widows have no desire to remarry, but some elderly couples are having relationships while continuing to live separately. This variation on a common-law relation allows widows to retain their survivors' pensions and offspring to worry less about inheritances. Others are taking the plunge and marrying again in middle or old age. Matchmaking parties and dances are newly popular. An upward trend in second marriages among those of riper years points to changing attitudes.[11]

There has even been, since April 1992, a matchmaking television program for singles aged fifty-five and over. Based in Tokyo, this live variety show invites three men and three women each week to take part in a game of asking questions to members of the opposite sex. In the program's first six months, some sixty men and sixty women appeared on the show, and roughly 60 percent of them became couples.

A specialist on mental health for the aged observes that old people seek 'spiritual exchange and intimate human relationships.'[12] Siblings can fill this role as well as partners of the opposite sex. The popular centenarian twin sisters Kin Narita and Gin Kanie, whose first names mean gold and silver, made their television debut in 1991 and have since become national idols, role models for an aging society. The sisters are 'cute' and full of life, but few confuse their ideal image with the realities of aging.

The stress of retirement on both spouses, when husbands often become an unwelcome presence in the home, are reflected in new idioms. The terms *sodai gomi* (giant garbage) and *nureba* (wet, fallen leaves) were coined in the 1980s by wives to describe husbands whom they found underfoot and unwanted. Japanese garbage is sorted into three categories, and *sodai gomi* refers to large objects such as broken appliances and furniture. (By 1987 younger women were adopting the term to complain that pre-retirement husbands refused to help in the house during the few hours they spent there.) A heated discussion of the term was carried on in the letters to the editor of the *Mainichi* newspaper in 1984, as Kittredge Cherry notes. Letters to the editor in Japanese newspapers record blackly comic tales of women driven to distraction by retired husbands who attempt to participate in housework only to turn the kitchen into a disaster area, buying unwanted groceries that happened to be on sale, putting too much detergent in the washing machine, and allowing the laundry to drip on the floor. Others sit and expect constant service. Another insulting term is *raberu no nai kanzume* (unlabelled canned goods). Husbands define themselves in terms of their jobs, and a retiree has been stripped of the company name that provided identity.[13]

Husbands naturally try to forestall the evil day as long as possible, and customarily take a second job after retiring at fifty-five or sixty.[14] Major employers help in finding this second position, which is often with a related firm. During the recession years of the early 1990s, jobs became scarcer and two contradictory trends received media coverage. Those conscious of the rapidly worsening ratio of workers to pensioners urged that the retirement age be raised, while a depressed economy was forcing some employers to retire workers at an earlier age.

Young and even middle-aged workers fear that a public pension system, planned to begin in 1994 to cover self-employed and small-firm workers, will be bankrupt before they become eligible for benefits. One pensioner was being supported by 6.5 workers in 1992, but the number is expected to drop to 2.1 by 2020.[15] In the late 1980s, businesses started to employ more female and elderly workers to cope with a labour shortage, but this trend was halted by the recession of the early '90s.

Pre-retirement illnesses, tied to the prospect of quitting work, have been documented by several Tokyo neurologists. Symptoms include dizziness, severe headaches, stomachaches, diarrhoea, and sleeplessness. Dr Toru Sekiya notes that retirees, once deprived of their business cards and corporate titles, must face the fact that they are simply aging men. Dr Takashi Sumioka underlines the contrast between the sexes at this point in their lives: 'Diversified values have turned housewives to finding meaning in such activities as attending classes at culture centres, doing volunteer or regular work. The gap between their husbands, for whom work was the only thing worth living for, is causing the tragedy.'[16]

The greater flexibility that women need over a lifetime, and the emotional commitments to family and friends that most develop from early childhood, serve them well as they age and doubtless contribute to their longer life expectancy. With each phase of life – marriage, motherhood, menopause, and the empty nest – women must re-invent themselves. This contrasts with the single-minded career focus of most men.

Perhaps men are beginning to change. Pressured by job shortages or influenced by changing social attitudes and government initiatives, some Japanese men are becoming care workers and learning to make the emotional connections vital to care giving. Women still form a large majority of such workers at homes for the aged, but statistics point to a striking change: in October 1991, only 3.9 percent of all such care workers were male; in March 1993, men formed 22.5 percent of aspiring care workers about to graduate from vocational schools and welfare colleges. One instructor considers it better to have workers of both sexes in every kind of occupation: 'To have the opposite sex gives zest to the workers as well as to the recipients of their services.'[17]

Care workers remain in short supply. The Ministry of Health and Welfare hopes to triple the number by 1999. One woman worker, speaking for many others, observes that helpers see their job as 'a striking learning experience.' Eiji Yoshida, an official with a private homecare company in Saitama Prefecture, notes that 'not just anyone' is capable of this demanding work. He finds that job applicants are either women in their twenties resolved to do social welfare work or married women in their forties and fifties seeking fulfilment. Homecare is *kitsui, kitanai,* and *kiken* (difficult, dirty, and dangerous) – 3K work. Yoshida notes that social awareness about its importance must be raised, along with raises in pay and job status, if the labour shortage in the field is to be resolved.[18] One solution to homecare that many Westerners find attractive, namely hiring women from underdeveloped nations to help care for children or the elderly, is still unacceptable to most Japanese.

In the West, the state has been active since the 1980s and earlier in providing help to the elderly in their own homes. In Japan, this help was still minimal by 1992 and was often hampered by bureaucratic regulations. Frequently, home helpers were sent more than a month after a request had been filed. Numerous regulations, such as one limiting help to only once or twice a week and another giving low priority to those living with family members, restricted the usefulness of the system.

Early in 1992, the Health and Welfare Ministry published *A Guideline for Home Help Work,* a manual for officials in prefectural governments. The ministry raised the standard remuneration significantly, to over ¥3,000,000 per year. Half the costs are to be borne directly by the national government and one-quarter by prefectural governments, with some of the balance offset by grants from the central government to municipalities.[19]

The guidelines put assistance ahead of regulations, with practical suggestions such as despatching workers first and doing the paperwork later. Initiatives include shortening the training courses for home helpers and dividing them into three levels. In the 1980s helpers underwent 360 hours of training to qualify for a licence. By 1991, a first-level certificate for part timers took forty hours of study over fifteen days.[20]

Meanwhile, housewives in many areas of Japan were organizing themselves in self-defence. The 600-member Life-Care Association in Kōbe began to provide home help in 1982. They assisted 1,000 households over the course of their first ten years. Members also took turns helping one another in various crises. This group has called attention to the number of housewives who fall ill or die from overwork in caring for the bedridden. Many women's groups once concerned with childcare, education, or women's full participation in society have turned their attention to helping the elderly, with projects such as delivering dinner twice a week.[21]

Co-operative movements, a variation on volunteer activities, are increasing. One such, begun in 1985 in Takamatsu City by eight housewives and social workers to supplement the limited governmental welfare services provided to the elderly in their homes, became a nationwide network in 1991. It is now called the Japan Care System Association. Members provide limited nursing care and help with household chores in exchange for points. These can be used later for the same kind of service free of charge in their own homes in time of need. Most of the co-op members are housewives in their forties and fifties. A very small number are men.[22]

More and more elderly have begun to live alone over the last twenty years. They are often semi-independent, in two-family or adjacent homes, as Ariyoshi depicts. Demand for duplex houses rose sharply in the early 1990s. Many are built on the parents' land after an older house has been torn down. Some look like separate houses; in others, the two generations share some facilities while maintaining various degrees of individual space. One young wife, who enjoyed her job and was reluctant to live with her husband's parents, pointed out that the new house allowed them 'to pursue different lifestyles.'[23] This wife anticipated receiving help with her child, when she had one, and giving help to her in-laws in later years, the kind of reciprocity examined by Lebra in the late 1970s. Only the duplex is new.

'Senior houses' offer another type of semi-independence. Apartment buildings exclusively for the elderly began in Nagoya in 1985 and soon spread to Osaka, Tokyo, and other areas. They are divided into two types, one for those who want independence and another for those who need varying degrees of care. Run by local residents, senior houses are usually very costly.

A welcome variation on housing combined with care is offered by the Koseikai (Kosei Association) in Tokyo. Created by Isao Hiromasu to allow seniors to lead their own lives, the Koseikai respects members' privacy and provides help through sixteen workers who live on the premises and hold other jobs, half of them within the seven buildings of the Koseikai complex. The workers make friendly visits to keep channels of communication open and provide further help when needed. In return they get a considerable discount on their rent. The seniors pay ¥10,000,000 to join and a very low monthly management fee. By contrast, nursing homes built by large insurance companies charge an initial fee from ¥30,000,000 up.[24]

Above all, the aging of Japan means change. Repercussions have already been felt in politics and the economy, including the changing job market. Currently, Japan has no universal government pension plan for seniors. Its social spending in 1986 represented only 15 percent of gross domestic product, the lowest percentage of all OECD countries. By 2010, spending in this area is expected to reach 26 percent of GDP, and care for the elderly will consume 41 percent of total health care spending. By 1993, an entire industry embracing medical care, meal distribution, house cleaning, and many other services had emerged. By 1997 there were more people over sixty-five than under fifteen. By 2010, Japan will have the highest ratio of seniors to workers in the world. Associations of seniors have sprung up in Japan and will doubtless become a significant political force, as they are in the West.

Meanwhile, the elderly (variously defined as people over sixty-five or over seventy) pay only 3 percent of national medical costs. Can the nation avoid making business bear this increasing burden? Up until 1993, as Philippe Pons notes, 'companies in Japan ... contributed much less to financing social welfare programs than their counterparts elsewhere.' The so-called economic miracle of the 1960s was fuelled by a young and energetic population. Greater numbers of seniors mean smaller savings, diminished pension funds, and general financial constraint on the nation.[25]

Japanese public space has not been hospitable to the elderly. Many subway stations lack escalators, and public building codes do not insist on wheelchair accessibility. It is to be hoped that this will be corrected. Changing demographics will also affect traditional features of Japanese society such as lifetime employment and higher wages for seniority. Labour shortages seem certain.

Japan has untapped resources in women, many of them currently underemployed. If more daycare were to be made available, along with a change in social attitudes towards women's roles, women could become a major source of much needed labour. How will these possibilities be harmonized with the forecast that by the year 2025 one out of every two women will be involved in caring for senile or bedridden seniors?

CHAPTER 8

SEXUAL POLITICS

Too many women's jobs in our country call for a cringing nonperson. Whatever
I do, I want to be respected for doing well. Do you see?

TOYOKO YAMASAKI, *Bonchi*

FOR CENTURIES, Japanese men have chosen to think that Japanese
women come in two different models: mothers and whores. This harsh view
of Japanese society finds support among scholars, journalists, and Japanese
women themselves. It helps to explain the pornographic culture found in
postwar *manga*, mainstream magazines, videos, television, controlled prostitution, and sex tours. Abuse of women, subtle or blatant, is endemic. In
language as in life, the basic presumption is that males are more important
than females.

These attitudes have survived for centuries because women, having
few options and little power, have been forced to accommodate them.
Moreover, cultural conditioning has taught both sexes to think that the
treatment of women was 'normal' and ethically correct. Women have
adapted to male expectations or subverted them as best they could. For
more than a century women reformers and writers have fought the system
openly. In recent years a new militancy prevails among women, yet during
the same period their exploitation remains entrenched.

Kazue Morisaki, in a contemporary Japanese-language study of women
in the Fukuoka area, points to the comfortable male logic that has sustained
a social system in which men have had free access to both types of women.
A reviewer writes: 'In [Morisaki's] view, women in modern Japanese history
can be divided into two basic categories: child-bearers, essential to the family system to provide progenitors to carry on the family name, and whores,
deployed under the system of licensed prostitution to satisfy the sexual
needs of men.'[1] The age-old division, Morisaki argues, continues to be the
basis of sexual discrimination throughout the modern age.

A similar observation is found in a sympathetic study of the lives of one prewar geisha and one postwar streetwalker in mid-twentieth-century Japan. American journalist Sara Harris introduces her paired biographies by linking mothers and prostitutes: 'This is a book about geisha, *pan-pans* or streetwalkers, and wives and mothers who, because of the Japanese disregard for women are, curiously, associated with them.' Harris sees her subject as providing insight into the 'maleficent' side of the Japanese man, a man 'hedged in always by demands of group responsibility, heir to a thousand lifetime frustrations growing out of constant repression of human feelings.'[2]

Reviewing Harris's study in the early 1960s, Canadian novelist Hugh MacLennan was struck by the spirit of self-sacrifice that governed the life of a woman born in 1915, sold as a *shikoni*, or child geisha-in-training, in 1922, and bought by an aristocratic 'protector' in 1933. MacLennan found her dedication and discipline very similar to that of a nun. The novelist may have known little about geisha save for the insight provided by Harris, but he knew a great deal about Christianity. I find the comparison apt, and helpful in understanding the Japanese mentality.

Both nuns and geisha learn to discipline the body and personal desires and to subject them to a higher ideal. For the geisha in Harris's study, the absolute was *duty*, the core of her life: duty to her substitute parent or foster mother, the madam who had bought her from her parents when famine left them little choice; and duty to her protector, the count who had also bought her and thus acquired her obligation. Like Fumiko Enchi's long-suffering heroine in *The Waiting Years*, the geisha has internalized the moral code learned in youth: 'I would not know how to live except by the doctrines of my ancestors.'[3]

When the count was imprisoned in 1945 as a war criminal, his wife commiserated with his mistress. The two women thought it hard for him because, unlike women, men did not know how to live without power. Earlier, the wife had allayed the touch of guilt felt by the geisha towards her by saying that a geisha was a 'business wife.' If she helped her master to prosper by flattering his associates, then his wife and children (read *sons*) would be the richer. The geisha felt pity for the wife, deprived of all social intercourse with men. The wife pitied the geisha, sold at the age of seven and sold again at eighteen. Both women knew that they depended utterly on men.

At the time of the sale, the madam had asked the count to put a house in the geisha's name. He considered this ridiculous. Property meant self-determination, enfranchisement. Brought up on Confucian principles, he knew that 'the gods did not preorder a world where women were men's equals.' Women depended, rather, on men to take care of them (p. 79).

Volunteers dressed as geisha await the start of Kyoto's annual Jidai Matsuri, a parade commemorating hundreds of years of history. The elaborate make-up and costume can take about an hour to put on and restrict movement quite severely.

To the geisha, the division of women into mothers and whores seemed natural and right. In her eyes, the primary obligation of both men and women was to their parents, who had the right to choose a child's spouse. If a man married for love, he might be tempted to neglect his duty to his parents. Both would lose face. Moreover society *expected* a man to take a mistress, if he could afford one. And while he had only minor duties to his wife, he had, in this geisha's view, little or none to his mistress (p. 95).[4]

Men, she believed, should be flattered and pitied. They were like children: witness their behaviour when drunk. If men were skilfully managed, as mothers manage small boys, both mistress and mother would reap rewards in time. Please his vanity and have nothing to fear: 'Men's childlike hearts demand that women walk behind them' (pp. 104-5). The geisha termed herself 'libertine and bondswoman. Seductress and drudge. Workhorse and inamorata. And a fine artist besides!' She still held these views in 1960 as she surveyed the changing times and the very different attitudes of her own daughters, whose devotion to duty, she feared, was weaker than her own.

A bolder view of prewar geisha and the balance of power between the sexes is found in a novel written in roughly the same period, the late 1950s. Toyoko Yamasaki's *Bonchi* is an epic story of a very traditional merchant family in prewar Osaka, and of the five women loved by the head of the firm. Five? Kikuji comes to see his womanizing as an attempt to escape from a household of powerful women. For several generations in this merchant dynasty a single daughter had been born, and each had married a man adopted into the family. The pride in the family name or *ie*, inseparable from the business, is the duty that drives Kikuji's mother and grandmother. Law and custom barred women in the family from the male world of business, leaving them 'vigorous, restless and unfulfilled.'[5] They are forced to wield power indirectly, until the death of Kikuji's father makes him the head of the firm.

Kikuji, forced into romantic entanglements by his effort to escape from mother and grandmother, is both masterly and weak. The name *bonchi*, master, catches this paradox, punning on his family nickname *Kiku-bon* and *bon-bon*, French for *sweet*. His wife, discarded soon after the marriage by her mother-in-law, denounces him as a 'Semba bon-bon.' Semba is the famed Osaka business district and the novel's setting. The translators observe that Yamasaki has described the traditional Osaka woman as having, beneath an amiable and courteous facade, 'the strength and endurance of one who will, if necessary, pull an ox-cart to market.'[6]

The women in Kikuji's life have very different personalities yet each requires a life of her own. Seventeen-year-old Ponta, proud of her dancing, wishes to continue this art after Kikuji has bought her freedom from a geisha house: 'I cannot take pride in introducing myself by saying "I am someone's mistress" ... I cannot, Master, really I cannot – be – just a mistress' (p. 146). O-Fuku is equally determined to retain her work and her identity. She is proud of being the best head waitress in Osaka, a vantage point from which she sees the whole human comedy: 'Only a little, tiny bit of me is free, but, oh, Master, how I treasure that little tiny bit!' (p. 228). She wishes to continue working until she has a baby, and again after it is born. She cannot spend her time 'filed away in a house' waiting for Kikuji; she must, she tells him, be busy and sociable (pp. 300-1). Similarly Ikuko, whose desire to be 'respected for doing well' forms the epigraph for this chapter, has 'professional pride' in establishing and maintaining her identity (p. 155). Hisako, a bar hostess, extends Kikuji's view of the world.

In 1946, as the novel ends in a rural temple where the four surviving women have sheltered from bombings, Kikuji prepares to bid them goodbye. He realizes that although they have relied on him, 'in a much more essential way' he has relied on them (p. 378). Kikuji discerns that they are all 'perfectly capable of managing their own affairs' (p. 397). The interdependence of the sexes is one of Yamasaki's themes.

An even stronger theme and a point made repeatedly is women's desire, and need, for independence: for their own work and public recognition of their individual talents. Financial security is not enough, nor is love, nor the fulfilment of duty. Born in 1924 and influenced, doubtless, by postwar events as well as by the extensive research that underpins this novel, Yamasaki is a thoroughly modern woman. The voices of prewar and postwar Japanese women sound together in this powerful and popular fiction, which is also a prophecy of social change.

The one-sided idealization of women as mothers, combined with a disturbing silence towards abuse and discrimination, continues today. In 1990, then-Prime Minister Toshiki Kaifu's keynote address at the United Nations World Summit for Children was received even in Japan as discriminatory, sexist, and one-sided after he said that the education of girls was important because they are 'the mothers of the future.'[7]

Prostitution was legal in Japan until 1958, when the Anti-Prostitution Law for which women's groups had long fought took effect. The law, never intended by male legislators to be taken seriously, simply changed the name of the game for some 500,000 prostitutes and their clients. Brothels became 'soaplands' or 'massage parlours,' and continued to flourish in what one journalist called 'a relatively hospitable atmosphere.'[8] Prior to privatization in 1958, the Japanese government had been officially regulating prostitution for 800 years. As early as 1193, in Kamakura, girls from impoverished families were indentured by their parents on contracts for ten or twenty years. Society pitied rather than condemned the girls, since filial piety was regarded more highly than personal chastity.[9] More recently, when the northern island of Hokkaido was opened in the late nineteenth century to settlers from Honshū, Kyūshū, and Shikoku, the government made prostitutes available to the pioneering men.[10]

During the feudal or Edo period, 'playgirls' (*yujo*) were confined to twenty-five officially licensed quarters. The Yoshiwara, in Tokyo, was the most famous of these red-light districts. In the nineteenth century, the Yoshiwara included Jokan-ji temple, nicknamed *nage-komi tera*, or 'throw them in the ground.' The temple has since burned down, but a monument erected in 1958 commemorates the more than 20,000 women buried there who died of illness, mistreatment, suicide, or accidents.[11] Arranged like a fortress, the Yoshiwara was surrounded by a moat and high walls with guarded gates. Obviously the government thought that segregated quarters would make it easier to maintain

Sukiyaki waitress, Kyoto, early 1990s. This skilled service in an expensive restaurant earns a living wage, and allows for conversation with the diners.

order. Legend has it that the famines of the late eighteenth and early nineteenth centuries forced many women into prostitution. The Yoshiwara alone held more than 10,000. In 1952, about 18,000 licensed brothels in 618 locations were operating, according to Ministry of Labour statistics.[12]

Postwar attitudes to women continue to be affected by the samurai culture that prevailed from 1603 to 1868. It fostered male bonding and relegated wives to a lowly position. Sociologist Chie Nakane sees the postwar persistence of samurai influence in the exceptional popularity of the tale of the forty-seven *ronin*, or masterless samurai, who sacrificed their lives to avenge their lord. The incident took place between 1701 and 1703. Their master had been forced to commit suicide after drawing his sword in the castle grounds of Edo, a serious crime. After his death, the *ronin* waited two years until the time was right, then decapitated their lord's old enemy. Nakane observes that such an all-consuming relationship leaves little room for wife or sweetheart. In traditional morality, she writes, the ideal man should not be involved with a woman: 'His emotions would be completely expended in his devotion to his master. I suspect this was the real nature of *samurai* mentality, and to a certain extent the same may be true of the modern Japanese man.'[13]

Since 1945, male loyalty has been transferred to the company, and modern male workers are commonly called corporate warriors. This loyalty is nurtured by a culture of after-hours drinking with male colleagues and flattering, subservient bar hostesses. *Yakuza*, mobsters involved in extortion and prostitution, also see themselves as latter-day samurai warriors. There is a link between samurai ideals and a contemporary culture 'awash' with violent sexual images, one that shocks many male foreigners.[14]

Bushido, variously called 'the soul of Japan' and the way of the warrior, was the unwritten code of laws based on feudalism and Confucian ethics that governed the conduct of the nobility from 1603 to 1868. Inazo Nitobe's famous analysis of this ethical code includes a chapter on the training and position of women. A samurai woman, Nitobe writes, annihilated herself for her husband so that he might annihilate himself for his master and that master, in turn, 'might obey Heaven.'[15] Similarly, a Confucian precept advised women to approach their husbands 'as Heaven itself.'

Nitobe acknowledges the parallel with the Christian ideal of service and self-sacrifice but fails to confront the difference openly, namely that the object of woman's total abnegation and veneration in the samurai code is – a man. A human male. Admitting that *bushido* sets woman's status and value well below that of man, Nitobe calls the code *binomial:* as a sociopolitical unit a woman counted 'not much, while as wife and mother she received highest respect and deepest affection' (p. 153).

Such a code, combined with the view that men have two different kinds of women available to serve them, goes far to explain the schizophrenic combination of prudery and pornography that marks modern Japan. In former centuries, Japanese women were exported to other Asian countries and later to the United States as prostitutes.[16] Legalized prostitution was encouraged in sixteenth-century Japan because it was considered unethical for a married couple to enjoy sexual pleasure together. Adrian Waller sees this as the beginning of a 'prostitution culture.' Coupled with Confucian sexist and patriarchal views that a woman must obey, in turn, father, husband, and eldest son, it established the view that women were lesser beings: 'From this grew a disquieting male logic that infiltrates every segment of daily living today. Men think that women are fair game for sexual abuse and discrimination because of their "prostitute-like nature."'[17]

In the 1950s, the same decade in which some 18,000 licensed brothels flourished in Japan, the translation into Japanese of D.H. Lawrence's *Lady Chatterley's Lover* led to litigation and the eventual banning of the novel by the Supreme Court. Even today, passages are deleted from the Japanese translation.[18] In 1957 Japan's highest court deemed it obscene 'to damage one's sense of shame; to cause excitement and stimulation of sexual desire; and to be contrary to standards of good sexual morality.' The editor of a major newspaper observed in 1994 that Japanese laws and regulations concerning pornography are tougher than those in Europe and the United States, yet Japanese bookstores were full of pornographic images and television was sending 'raw images' into homes. 'What,' asks the editor, 'are we to think of this gap?'[19]

What indeed? Japan's sex-related industries are not only a release for overworked and repressed salarymen, as Sara Harris suggests. They are also big business. The market for pornographic videos, films, and telephone services has grown rapidly in recent years. By the early 1990s it formed a market of over ¥4 trillion. It takes two to generate this kind of money: a creator and a willing consumer.

One researcher, noting the conflicting quality of male Japanese attitudes to sex, believes that the subject is regarded as 'secret' in Japan and hence men need pornographic videos and 'love hotels,' things separate from everyday life, in order to have sex. Not all commentators agree with the secrecy theory. James Fallows was disturbed by the openness of the pornographic material that commonly formed the reading material of salarymen on commuter trains. Sports papers carried spreads of nude women. Adult comics ran to hard-core pornography. Fallows observed that American men rarely read skin magazines in front of women, but Japanese men are far less inhibited, perhaps because of the anonymity of crowded trains.[20]

Another Western journalist is surprised by the gap between a façade of propriety and the apparently insatiable appetite of the Japanese male for pornography and prostitution. There is no showing of affection within the family. Kissing in public is taboo, and it is rare to see couples holding hands. Derek Sidenius writes that the salaryman in his dark suit has 'a sexless quality' and a face empty of emotion, 'but beneath the facade lurk all-too-human fantasies.'[21] Sidenius sees two possible causes for 'love hotels' and pornography: the intensely crowded living conditions and general lack of privacy at home, and the inordinately strong work ethic that puts a man's job first and his family a distant second.

Advertisements for pornographic telephone services are common in phone booths, shopping malls, and residential areas. In 1989, Nippon Telegraph and Telephone Corporation (NT&T) began the 'Dial Q2' service. Within two years it was offering over 7,000 programs with sexy female voices and messages. Male users pay a fee; women are not charged. The company claims that it is merely a carrier that leases lines and cannot control content. This excuse was rejected in 1993 when a district court ruled that an irate father was not responsible for a bill of ¥500,000 for his teenage son's use of the adult information line.

This pornographic poster advertising sexual services includes telephone numbers and is placed in downtown Okayama City. Courtesy of Dr Mary McCrimmon.

The posted advertisements have led to a battle between the suppliers of telephone pornography (often crime syndicates) and the public. NT&T officials travel in pairs, for safety, to remove ads, which are promptly replaced. Some creative distributors have dropped them in the bicycle baskets of college students. Flyers ('Are you lonely? Bored?') offer 'a different angel each time you call,' 'a love telephone for two,' or ask, 'How many lovers can you have? If you're trendy, you already know about this.' In 1990-1 alone, NT&T earned ¥28 billion in commissions and circuit fees for such services.[22]

Women's groups are fighting back. Deluged with sex ads throughout their neighbourhoods, citizens in some cities are posting paintings by children on telephone poles and in phone booths. This strategy has proven effective in Ōita, Nakatsu, and Beppu, where children's art has significantly reduced the number of pornographic ads and graffiti.[23] Volunteers belonging to the New Japan Women's Association are organizing boycotts and legal suits, demanding that NT&T cut back on pornographic services. They maintain that women's rights are being violated and children harmed.

Pornography flourishes in many countries, but the Japanese version has disturbing characteristics. Voyeurism, paedophilia, and pornography distinguished by what James Fallows calls 'graphic nastiness' are particularly popular in Japan. Advertisements often show women being peeped at from under manhole covers. Youth, innocence, and school uniforms are popular turn ons: 'The *kawaii* [cute] look is dominant on television advertising, giving the impression that Japanese masculinity consists primarily of yearning for a cute little thing about fifteen years old.'[24]

For forty years Japanese society has been saturated with violent, pornographic images. Witness the extraordinary popularity of *manga*, comics read by children and well-dressed businessmen alike. Their dramatic images and strong but simplistic storylines had reached unprecedented popularity by the 1980s. In the 1950s, the content was relatively innocuous. Even today, the market targets different audiences and not all *manga* are violent or pornographic. After 1960, however, subjects previously considered taboo such as sex, extreme violence, and scatology were introduced. Prewar adventure comics depicted violence in a restrained style, but from 1959 *manga* for the pay-library comic market showed heads rolling, eyes gouged out, and showers of blood. Magazines in the '60s stressed graphic sexual violence, and one student of the genre, Frederik Schodt, describes 'horribly well behaved Japanese children' reading scenes that would shock adults from 'more liberal' cultures.[25]

Schodt suggests that fantasies he describes as sadistic and wanton may be rooted in the comic eroticism and nudity of woodblock prints in earlier centuries. He believes that they have not harmed Japanese youth, however, and to bolster his theories points to what he calls a 'remarkably unviolent society' with a pacifist constitution, strict gun control, and low crime statistics, including the figures for sexual crimes.[26]

By the 1990s it is clear that such views are wishful thinking. Rape continues to be under-reported and typically uninvestigated. A 1988 'White Paper on Police' treats rape as little more than a minor inconvenience. Investigators called the rape statistics in this report 'a ludicrous underestimate.' Most Japanese women, knowing that police do not take this crime seriously, fail to report it. In an article prompted by the abduction, torture, and killing of a seventeen-year-old Japanese girl in 1988 by four youths, a Western journalist blames freely available and sadistic pornography for desensitizing many Japanese men. Why, asks Peter Hadfield, do the police not take rape more seriously? 'It could be because policemen read the same newspapers, comics and magazines, and watch the same movies, videos and TV programs as the rest of us. In these media, the most gruesome and tortuous rapes are seen as a common and normal form of male activity, and not something that should be open to scrutiny.'[27]

In the early 1990s some attempt was made to regulate the pornographic content of children's comics without touching adult *manga*. Japanese police are only just beginning to connect sexually violent comics, read by 69 percent of all high school seniors, with sexual crimes committed by juveniles.[28] 'Adult' *manga* enjoy a weekly circulation of over 4,000,000 copies. Colin Nickerson describes the plots as revolving around sex, brutality, or both: 'Rape scenes abound, as do panels depicting men with whips looming over skimpily clad women in chains.' Such misogynous adventures are read openly by young and middle-aged men alike.[29]

For the sake of research, a British journalist located an evening of sadomasochistic 'entertainment' offered in 1991 in a private home in Tokyo for an admission fee of ¥30,000 (CDN$350). The main event consisted of the opportunity to torture willing subjects. Kate Berridge describes the preliminary to live torture as a porn video of women being tortured while hanging upside down.[30]

Sex tours abroad and prostitution at home are a socially accepted part of Japanese culture. Foreign tours are arranged by companies, the government, and occupational associations of many kinds. Both the male participants and their Japanese wives risk being infected with AIDS, a danger that attracted little media attention until recently. I was told of one wife who had objected strongly to her husband going on a sex tour organized by his agricultural co-operative. His response? He would 'lose face' if he failed to go with his group. This in the 1990s.

Travel agents organize all-inclusive sex-tour packages for men only that include a flight, hotel room, meals, sightseeing, and the services of young prostitutes who meet clients at the airport. Government studies show that 3,000,000 Japanese men travel abroad, alone, as soon as they get one of their semi-annual company bonuses. Most go to Bangkok or Manila.

Japanese men consider prostitution a socially necessary service. Obviously the 'water trade' is considered an essential part of conducting other business in a suitable atmosphere. Many firms offer women to their clients. The manager of one club whose services include prostitution admitted to police that his club billed companies directly.[31] In Japan it is not illegal to buy sex, but it is against the law to sell it: an interesting example of blame-the-victim mentality.

Prostitution itself is big business, a multibillion-dollar industry in Japan and Southeast Asia. And the women providing this service in Japan are often non-Japanese. A spokeswoman for the Asian Women's Shelter, formed by Japanese women in 1977 to help foreign prostitutes, claims that Japan 'had not only raped its neighbours militarily but was now sending plane-loads of men to neighbouring countries to do it sexually.'[32]

On the supply side, the trade is fed by poverty – poverty, and the shortage of other types of work for women. Just as earlier generations of Japanese farm daughters had sacrificed themselves for their families, so Thai and Filipina women hope to help their impoverished relatives back home. Other jobs are few and poorly paid. Steven Herman writes that as long as a huge imbalance exists in living standards between Japan and the rest of Asia, the attitude of *sho ga nai* (it can't be helped) will prevail, and local pimps will continue to sell women to the *yakuza*.[33] Most of the foreign women speak little or no Japanese, but *sho ga nai* is quickly learned.

The young Southeast Asian women who began pouring into Japan's sex industry in the 1980s are called *japayuki-san*, a term derived from *karayuki-san*, the name given to tens of thousands of Japanese women who left Japan at the turn of the century to become prostitutes in Southeast Asia and the United States. *Japayuki-san* refers to 'those who go to Japan.'[34] Many of the women brought to Japan by *yakuza* syndicates expect to work as hostesses, waiters, or entertainers. Once there, they are told they have incurred debts of some ¥4,000,000 for travel, papers (often forged), and other questionable expenses. Locked up, lacking formal papers, and unable to speak Japanese, they are forced to work as prostitutes without pay until the inflated debt is repaid.

Rebellious young women are easily disposed of, and police have generally taken very little interest unless events and the media force their hand. An American researcher writes: 'In the words of one of the many *japayuki-san* brokers and production company bosses working in Manila and Osaka, "This is a business, and in this business those girls are merchandise. If we thought of them as human beings, there's no way we could run these operations."'[35]

These women are victimized by what one writer calls 'Japan's endemic chauvinism and xenophobia' as well as by the organized criminals who exploit them. Some are being helped by a women's organization called the Asian Women's Shelter, also known as HELP (Help in Emergency of Love and Peace). Director Mizuho Matsuda drew attention to discrimination against women, especially Asian women, and to the shortage of legitimate types of work for immigrant women. Matsuda spoke of the violation of many human rights in contemporary Japanese society, looking forward to changes that would eliminate discrimination.[36]

A dark chapter of Japanese history came to light in the early 1990s when Asian women who had been forced into prostitution by the Japanese military before and during the Second World War brought forward their charges. At first, in 1990-1, the media spoke of 'allegations' and 'comfort women,' a literal translation of the Japanese term used in the 1930s and '40s. As the issue heated up more women came forward, a few former soldiers spoke out, and documents were uncovered that demolished the government's claim that the brothels had been privately organized. Media terminology gradually became blunter. This was sexual slavery on a grand scale, one that, by the estimate of many historians, involved some 200,000 women, principally in Korea, Taiwan, and the Philippines. A large majority were Korean.

In the early 1930s, the Japanese government had decided that enslaved women were necessary for troop morale and public order in occupied territories. The first such army brothels were set up in China, partly to avoid the mass rapes committed earlier by Japanese troops in conquered areas. Ironically, a system of sexual slavery was viewed as a way of preventing conduct that might further tarnish the nation's image. Japan had signed conventions aimed at stopping international trafficking in women, yet it flouted these treaties in its colonies of Korea and Taiwan.[37]

The women's struggle for recognition and compensation was fought through litigation, the media, and public pressure. It took some time before the Japanese government was forced to admit that it had been directly involved. By late 1994, bowing to pressures from inside and outside the country, the government announced that a billion-dollar fund would be used to compensate the women symbolically by establishing a foundation to build and operate youth centres in a number of Asian countries to promote exchanges and collect historical materials. A separate, *privately* financed plan to make direct payments to victims was also under consideration. The government remained frightened of setting a precedent in the case of compensation to individuals.

These announcements, designed to launch a year-long period of self-reflection leading up to the fiftieth anniversary of Japan's defeat, marked a reversal of decades of postwar diplomatic efforts to avoid accepting responsibility for acts in China in the 1930s and during the Pacific War. Japan had always maintained that the San Francisco Peace Treaty of 1951 and other pacts signed with its wartime enemies, except for Russia and North Korea, had legally settled all reparation issues with the countries concerned. No responsibility towards individuals had been admitted. The grants promised in 1994 would be labelled gifts of atonement, not compensation.

It is difficult to imagine the horrors experienced by the girls and women involved in this sexual slavery. Some are documented in international reports that began to come out in 1992. The women testified that they were forced to have sex with soldiers day after day without rest; that those who resisted were tortured; and that those who became too ill or weak to serve were killed. Survivors have suffered for a lifetime not only from physical diseases but also from deep emotional scars and often family rejection.[38] Many did not survive. They died of disease, abuse, suicide, or were shot as the troops withdrew.[39] The Korean respect for female chastity that had led Japanese officers to target Korean women made it very difficult for survivors to fit back into their society after the war.[40]

Soldiers of many nations have committed atrocities in war, but the story of these women has a shocking difference. The enslavement was an official activity ordered by the highest authority in Japan. Everything went through proper channels, from the Cabinet to the Army Ministry and then to local governors and on to soldiers like Seiji Yoshida, whose job was to go on field trips to Korea, accompanied by subordinates and police officers, hunting for women to imprison in Imperial Army brothels. The result was a system of nationalized sexual slavery unique in modern times. Once again, women were regarded simply as commodities.

Yoshida, a director of mobilization for Yamaguchi Prefecture during the war, spoke out in 1991 and published a book about the events. He had been only one of thousands of employees of the Patriotic Labour Association involved in conscripting labourers and sex slaves in the colonies.[41] After speaking out, Yoshida was denounced by veterans' associations and became the target of death threats.

By now there is massive, well-documented evidence that before and during the Pacific War 200,000 women in countries adjacent to Japan suffered state-organized mass rape. It is difficult to avoid a comparison with the contemporary situation of enforced prostitution inside Japan, where large numbers of foreign women, the *japayuki-san*, are forcibly detained for sexual service by private entrepreneurs. That *yakuza* organizers see their trade as a business and women as subhuman 'merchandise' must surely owe something to entrenched male attitudes in Japan and to a culture that continues to devalue women. Harsh words, admittedly. And strong evidence.

Even in the milder form of sexual harassment, sexual abuse is a power play. It is much less about sex than about power. This home truth is not lost on contemporary Japanese women. Nor is the companion truism, that pornography is based on contempt for women. Japanese women regularly face pornographic public advertisements, office calendars, and games. Sexist ads include one by a men's clothing manufacturer featuring a naked woman in a man's raincoat lying barefoot on the ground, hair dishevelled, soiled hands tied behind her back: a rape scene. One full-page newspaper ad by Toyota used a naked pregnant woman to launch a new wide-bodied car.[42] A senior bureaucrat reports that 'girlie calendars are everywhere, on desktops and walls, sending an unmistakable message about how women are viewed. Basically, the ministries are male-chauvinist institutions.'[43] Major Japanese toy companies promote pornographic games such as 'Human Trash,' in which players buy and sell women labelled with numbers representing how many men they have slept with. Analysts of both sexes see products like these as indicative of general male attitudes in Japan. The use of all such pornography is hotly contested by women's groups. Ayako Yamaguchi, chair of a women's organization that has mounted international protests against pornographic games, believes that they reveal 'the Japanese mentality,' including deep male sexual biases that extend into all aspects of life.[44]

Although it is ordinary women who bear the brunt of sexual harassment, the new prominence of a few women politicians in recent years has made them the butt of sexist attacks. Extensive American studies have shown that the more nontraditional the job for a woman, the more sexual harassment she attracts.[45] It appears that Japanese men are reluctant to admit women to power-sharing positions and consciously or subconsciously use harassment as a way of making women employees or colleagues feel vulnerable and of keeping them 'in their place.' Harassment is a control mechanism.

The shocking case of Kyūshū assemblywoman Kazuko Kitaguchi may represent only the tip of the iceberg. Kitaguchi had campaigned in Kumamoto in 1991 on the issue of women's rights. Even before being elected she had been subjected to a series of insulting and threatening telephone calls deriding her as a woman trying to enter the 'man's world' of politics. At a dinner for local politicians held after the election, a senior member of the governing Liberal Democratic Party (LDP) had struck her breasts, then grabbed and bruised one. Mitsunori Baba is reported to have said, 'This is what you deserve.'

After he refused to apologize, Kitaguchi took legal action against him. Baba was found guilty but given no penalty. Incredibly, Kitaguchi was ordered to apologize to him for speaking out and bringing suit. The demand for her apology was withdrawn only after she collapsed and was rushed to hospital, suffering from stress. Ever since her initial complaint against Baba, she had been subjected to threatening anonymous telephone calls and verbal abuse from loudspeakers outside her home. By 1993, Kitaguchi, not a woman easily intimidated, had won assembly approval for a telephone counselling service for women suffering from harassment and was receiving more respect both inside and outside the assembly.[46]

A similar case surfaced in Tokyo in 1993, when Assemblywoman Mariko Mitsui publicly resigned from the Social Democratic Party of Japan (SDPJ) after charging that she had been sexually harassed, both verbally and physically, by fellow Assembly members. She was serving her second term and, like Kitaguchi, had been active in trying to improve the position of women in Japan. Assemblymen had told her that they supported the custom of treating women as inferior to men. She was finding it impossible to work under such conditions. Informed of her resignation, the secretary general of the Tokyo SDPJ group said, with a shrug, that he doubted her capacity for 'consistent political thought.'[47]

Until the late 1980s, the very concept of sexual harassment was so foreign to the country that the Japanese found it necessary to borrow English words to produce the term *seku hara*. In 1989 the Tokyo Bar Association opened a one-day hotline to accept telephone calls from women who had been victimized by sexual harassment in the workplace. There were 138 calls. This led to the drafting of a bill designed to prevent such harassment. The association presented its draft to the Ministry of Labour in 1991 but little action followed. Many Japanese men find the notion of legal punishment for sexual harassment unthinkable, but some costly suits brought against employees of Japanese companies in America are gradually changing attitudes among those working abroad.

Media reports of university professors suspended for harassment or of police officers warned to be respectful to women journalists continue to surface. In 1991 separate subway cars for women were proposed as the answer for *chikan*, gropers who take advantage of crowded rush hour conditions. This idea died on the vine, but more women are gradually daring to object rather than suffering in silence.

Also encouraging are occasional editorials such as a 1991 *Japan Times* one prompted by the Senate judiciary hearings in the United States following Anita Hill's accusations of sexual harassment against Clarence Thomas. Thomas had been nominated to the Supreme Court. The writer recognized a continuum between the graphic depictions of sadomasochistic bondage and rape commonly found in Japanese *manga* and the 'milder' form of sexual oppression known as sexual harassment. This continuum, the editor stressed, 'perpetuates the view of women as largely brainless creatures incapable of assuming responsibility,' whose function is to serve and please men.[48]

The semi-official Japanese response to the fracas that consumed America that fall was made by Chief Cabinet Secretary Misoji Sakamoto, who unconsciously revealed an attitude common to many Japanese men by telling reporters that sexual harassment was not a problem in Japan. The editorial writer went on to give results of recent Japanese polls showing that large numbers of women were complaining of sexual harassment in the workplace, and that 95 percent of women in a Tokyo-area survey would prefer to work full time and long term provided that systems of childcare leave and leave to care for the elderly were adopted or improved by their companies. The latter runs counter to the prevailing myth favoured by employers, that women *like* to retire when they marry and to work part time in later years. With relentless logic, the writer concluded that the prevailing system of cutting women out from full-time work after marriage and thus denying them both benefits and careers was really 'sexual harassment of a most persistent and insidious kind.'

One suspects that the number of Japanese men who share this view, which is tantamount to calling their workplace structurally sexist, is very small. Ninety-five percent is a massive vote for the option of full-time work, which relatively few Japanese women are enabled to pursue. Are Japanese men and women still talking to one another? Are they *listening*?

CHAPTER 9

OUR LITTLE NOAH'S ARK PLANET: EMPOWERMENT THROUGH WORKING TOGETHER

This little planet begins to have a headache
Since humans occupied it and took it out of God's hand ...
Meanwhile killers get high on the God of Science and cheer the big Arms race on ...
Will anyone witness our little Noah's Ark planet drown in the universe?

KAZUKO SHIRAISHI, *Little Planet*

IN THE 1970s, large numbers of Japanese women began moving out of the relative isolation of their homes into community activism and volunteer groups. A broad focus was provided by women's desire to help with environmental problems and to ensure peace. Eco-feminism understands not only that war and the destruction of the environment are the world's most serious problems but that such problems involve spirituality and power relationships. They are, in short, political. This chapter deals with women in politics and with volunteering, especially in the areas of pacifism and environmental concerns.

The crass exploitation of the earth parallels the exploitation of women and the failure to value community and human relationships. Pollution in Japan has also offended, among other faiths, the traditional folk belief in the sanctity of ancestral land, the animistic faith of Pure Land Sect Buddhism.[1] Sociologist and writer Kazuko Tsurumi, a professor emerita at Sophia University in Tokyo, links the destruction caused by industrial pollution to that caused by nuclear and chemical weapons. She notes that Minamata disease has been as deadly to the unborn babies of poisoned mothers as radiation was to babies in the wombs of mothers victimized by the atomic bombs in 1945: 'By destroying nature, men ... destroy themselves.'[2]

Environmental issues have escalated in Japan, as elsewhere, since the 1960s. Rural Japanese women have long co-operated with farm tasks as needed, but the large-scale and often national voluntary co-operation of urban women has greatly increased in recent decades.

Conditions favouring activism in the 1970s included the United Nations' International Decade for Women, which generated energy and higher self-awareness for women, and trends towards higher education, longer life, fewer children, and greater technological efficiency in the home. These led to gradually increasing freedom for housewives, while the restrictions placed on women in the paid work force held firm. Shorter work hours and very limited career opportunities meant that part-time jobs were not consuming all of their energy and talents.

Public eagerness to help victims of the Great Hanshin Earthquake of 17 January 1995 in Kōbe indicates the degree to which the concept of volunteerism, led by women, has taken root in Japan over the last twenty-five years. Within six weeks of the quake, approximately 34,000 had registered for volunteer work at the Hyōgo Prefectural office, and many more were involved unofficially. Reverend Ken'ichi Kusachi, a co-ordinator for local NGOs and volunteer workers, said that Japanese were accustomed to the government taking the lead in social activities: 'The administration has always regarded volunteers as supplemental to its work such that it has been almost impossible for volunteer activities to take root in Japan ... For the first time the administration appears to have recognized the swell of volunteers as an independent and self-disciplined force.'[3]

Writing in 1977 of the role of women throughout Japanese history, Professor Tsurumi noted that both male and female scholars had acknowledged that women were the most powerful agents in consumer movements, antinuclear-weapon peace movements, and antipollution movements: 'A political scientist in Tokyo called housewives the full-time citizens in citizens' movements, implying that men are only part-time participants.'[4] One of Tsurumi's illustrations is the case of three young female employees of the Shōwa Electric Appliance Factory who publicly and with considerable personal risk accused their company of discharging toxic effluent into the nearby river, thereby causing the Second Minamata Disease.

Women have always been witnesses and recorders as well as activists. The observation, narration and transmission of historical events, *kataribe*, was originally the function of women shamans in ancient Japan, and prominent critics have emphasized the persistence of the shamanistic quality in Japanese women even in the highly industrialized stage.

Modern women write personal columns in Japan's major newspapers and stinging letters to the editor. More and more, ordinary women are writing their observations for their children and their communities. Tsurumi calls such women 'small shamans' at the grassroots level, both anonymous and famous, and believes that their eye-witness records of contemporary historical events have inspired and sustained consumer and citizens' movements for peace and environmental protection.

I was fortunate to hear one such 'shaman' in Okayama Prefecture in October 1993. Dr Itoko Ikubo (b. 1936), a local physician speaking at a community centre on the topic, 'Okayama Women's Progress [literally, 'women's walk'] after the War,' urged her all-female audience to reflect on history and on their personal experience in order to understand and influence the future: 'Each of us should start with our own body, our own experience.' Oral history, she emphasized, had special importance and should be recorded. She spoke of her own experience during and after the war; of her mother's diary and its effect on herself; of democracy in Japan 'going backwards' after the start of the Cold War and the Korean War; of farm wives becoming active to improve their lives co-operatively; of the ongoing destruction of the environment and the increasing frequency of cancer in her own hospital; and of her group, whose members study old newspapers on microfiche and have discovered that 'we too can write.'

To write 'true things' from their own experience, Dr Ikubo told her listeners, was their 'homework for life.' This talk was powerful, and empowering. To find a comparison in the contemporary West one would have to turn to an evangelical preacher. This Japanese woman spoke of both spiritual and practical things with no creed save a strong belief in the value of the individual and in the need to protect the good earth that sustains us.

Women gained legal political rights in 1945, but the hard economic times of the 1940s and '50s, along with rapid urbanization, the government-sponsored image of the 'professional housewife,' and cultural emphasis on gender roles isolated urban women inside the home and lessened their confidence outside it. Confidence has been a problem for many women as they cope with rapid change in the second half of the twentieth century. In Japan, this problem concerns the National Women's Education Centre (NWEC), founded in 1977 by the Ministry of Education, Science and Culture. In 1989, the editor of the centre's newsletter noted what she called a common belief, that a Japanese woman has 'a strong sense of guilt which leads in turn [to] a lack of confidence in herself.' The centre had been founded, the editor implied, partly because the typical Japanese woman needed to realize 'that the root cause of her lack of identity lies in the social norms – particularly sex roles – imposed on her.'[5]

I think of the many Japanese women who introduced themselves to me in the 1980s and '90s by adding 'I'm just a housewife' to their names. Ironically, most of them were involved in self-study groups and various volunteer activities. They wore many hats. What had damaged their self-confidence? Husbands typically used the same phrase to describe their wives. These individuals spoke English fluently and must have known the meaning of 'just.' The Japanese penchant for modesty when speaking of oneself and one's relatives does not, to my mind, apply to this situation. No Japanese man would introduce himself as 'just a husband,' or 'just a farmer.'

Many of the centre's activities in the 1980s focused on the theory and practice of self-discovery, with titles such as 'Self-Discovery for Ability Development.' The relative isolation of Japanese women in the early post-war decades (as we saw dramatized in Ayako Sono's story, 'Fuji') and their lack of exposure to other cultures before a vigorous economy made foreign travel economically feasible meant that Japanese women had little awareness of the power of cultural conditioning in their lives. They had few bases for comparison.

The dramatic effects of overseas travel on young Japanese housewives from Iidate, Fukushima Prefecture, showed up when a group of women who had been sent abroad for two weeks as part of a plan to stimulate the local economy returned with new confidence. They subsequently petitioned local authorities to reconsider a proposal to build an off-track office for betting on horse races. One of the petitioners said that young women had felt silenced in their male-dominated farming society: 'The two-week overseas trip we made in 1989 gave us the strength to express our opinions about village life in Iidate.'[6]

In recent decades, women in Japan and many other countries are recognizing their increasing importance in a rapidly changing world. They see, too, the need for women to take responsibility for their communities and their countries, not merely for their own families. At a 1989 international conference of women students in higher education, delegate Yuko Matsuda spoke with restrained anger of the illogicality of a society in which women are encouraged to study at postsecondary levels and then denied access to career positions. Matsuda considered this situation to be 'a pattern of life for Japanese women.'[7] On the same occasion, editorial writer Dr Michio Nagai said that in co-operation with men, women would 'determine the future course of human history to a far greater extent than they have done in the past.'

Why have political activism and volunteer activity been slower to develop in Japan than in the West? Considering the close co-operation common in prewar rural communities it seems paradoxical until we remember the cultural legacy of autocratic, centralized rule. Japan's bureaucratic structure is very resistant to change and to individual initiative. And the bureaucracy had other priorities. Before the Second World War, Japan sought territorial expansion and military power, and women were co-opted to serve male goals. After the war, the country concentrated on rebuilding its shattered economy. Unfortunately the pro-development Ministry of Construction has a budget 100 times bigger than that of the Environment Agency. Moreover, environmentalism became tarred with a socialist brush since reform parties tended to support campaigns against polluting companies. Business and the ruling Liberal Democratic Party stood aloof.[8]

Writing on Japan's environmental movement, Maggie Suzuki finds it generally fractionalized and weak, although stronger than similar movements in neighbouring countries: 'It is not as socially acceptable, and usually not as effective, to challenge authority in Japan as it is, for example, in the United States. People are reluctant to express strong dissent, and those who support environmental issues are almost automatically considered out of the mainstream as soon as they advocate something different from what the authorities are promulgating.'[9]

After decades of work at the grassroots level by millions of women, the country is becoming more conscious of environmental and political issues. Suzuki believes that local activists are now building national networks that may help them to change laws and regulations. Women's networks, unlike hierarchical governmental organizations, are typically concentric and egalitarian.

In the interest of promoting its international image in connection with environmental protection, the Ministry of Foreign Affairs published three glossy magazines on the topic in 1992. They feature male writers, male scientists such as Noritaka Ichida, and large-scale projects, some overseas. The work of women, termed 'housewives,' is given one sentence each in two of the three substantial brochures. Ichida, an ornithologist and committed environmentalist, is the director of the Wild Bird Society. He joined the society in 1970 and is praised in the Ministry publication for being the first 'to offer support for the grassroots environmental movements beginning to take shape in local areas throughout Japan.' The phrasing is misleading or unconsciously ironic, since many members of a citizens' group of local housewives were already strong environmentalists long before the ornithologist added his efforts to theirs. Ichida, who encouraged the women activists with lectures and advice, is presumably the group's first male, or first scientist, or both.[10] The publications' failure to give credit where credit is due seems to be a case of cultural blindness by the patriarchy towards the major part being played by women in environmental work and contemporary Japanese society in general, despite the restrictions laid on them.

I find it surprising, for example, that substantial government publications, with titles such as *Japan's Environmental Endeavours* and *The Forefront of the Environmental Movement in Japan*, ignore the significant work being carried out by members of the Hokkaido Fisheries Association Women's Auxiliary, who have been planting trees in the coastal mountains of Hokkaido every spring for seven years in order to restore health to coastal waters. Logging near rivers causes silt to run off the denuded land and down the rivers, forming a destructive 'red tide' that harms marine life in the coastal waters.

Since November 1994 the International Center for the Environmental Management of Enclosed Coastal Seas has been functioning in Kōbe, but the Hokkaido women were aware of the problem in the 1980s and have been actively working with farmers and fishers for many years to improve the environment: 'We want to leave something better to our children,' says Fuyo Honda, chair of the Women's Auxiliary.[11] This group, along with many other women's co-operatives in Japan, has been working to improve the environment for over thirty-five years. It seems as if women are in some strange way invisible to many male bureaucrats and politicians once they step outside their designated role as housewives.

Environmental problems plague every nation today, and business interests tend to be universally resistant to mending their polluting practices. Japan, with its large population and relative scarcity of natural resources within a limited land area, faces severe problems. Natural hazards include high humidity, earthquakes, and typhoons. Historically, the Japanese have shown a special affinity with nature, and the system of irrigated rice paddies has functioned well for maintaining topsoil and nutrients.

During the high-growth postwar years, industry was a heavy consumer of oil and coal, and vast amounts of pollutants spewed out into air and water. The construction of dams on most of Japan's rivers created as many problems as they solved. Wasteful construction practices such as discarding wooden forms after a single use have helped to deplete the tropical forests of neighbouring countries.[12]

Shin'ichi Sano contrasts today's high-speed consumption with conditions thirty years ago, 'when thrift and recycling were just common sense and things would be used until they were barely recognizable.'[13] This male writer documents waste in twelve categories, including automobiles, paper, office automation equipment, medical care, and nuclear waste, leaving the

Workers at a small town festival in northern Okayama-ken provide delicious food and a joyous atmosphere. This type of volunteer work, with its focus on the local community, has a long tradition among Japanese women.

These volunteers offer the tea ceremony to tourists in an historic samurai house in Katsuyama, northern Okayama-ken. Funds raised maintain the building, promote local traditions and, like so many volunteer activities by women, encourage community spirit.

reviewer to share his 'profound sense of despair.' Many women volunteers, however, are choosing action over despondency.

Environmental problems may be aggravated by an *uchi/soto* (inside/outside) complex. Japanese have enormous responsibilities to an in-group, related by blood or circumstance, but none at all, by traditional cultural attitudes, to outsiders.[14] The Western concept of volunteering to help those outside a personal circle has not been widespread in Japan until the last quarter-century, although a Japanese branch of the Red Cross Society dates from the late nineteenth century. Japan had, instead, a tradition of rural neighbourhood co-operation for rice planting, festivals, funerals, and other activities. Industrialization and urbanization began to affect these traditions as the business world lost touch with communities.[15] In recent decades, Japanese women have been reversing modern trends by extending their understanding of the local and personal to include the nation and the world.

Since the 1960s, citizen groups consisting largely of housewives have grown steadily. Many began as small collective purchasing co-operatives. By the 1970s, their concerns embraced the use of synthetic soaps and detergents and by the 1980s, the disposal of used cooking oil. One 'soap movement' was launched in Kawasaki in 1974 by a group of housewives who noticed cracked skin on their hands and irritation on their babies' skin. They suspected synthetic soaps, which contain a fluorescent bleaching agent believed to be carcinogenic, and the detergents whose foam had polluted the rivers. The need for an environmentally friendly washing product was the greater because houses in many towns and provincial cities empty their washing water directly into a network of small canals. House lots are typically too small to accommodate the large weeping-tile beds that serve the septic tanks of rural areas in North America.

The Kawasaki volunteers belonged to the Seikatsu Club, which began as a purchasing co-op in Tokyo in 1965. By 1990, there were 650 such co-ops in Japan with a membership of 195,000 nationwide, 63,000 in Kanagawa alone. The Seikatsu lobbies for environmental and health measures. Over fifteen years, members found a single solution for two pressing problems, the manufacture of pure soap and the disposal of used cooking oil. In 1989, the Kawasaki branch launched the Kawasaki Shimin Sekken Puranto (Kawasaki Citizens' Soap Plant) with ¥23,000,000 raised by members. Their products are environmentally friendly soap and soap powder made from used cooking oil collected from the homes of Seikatsu members, restaurants, and company dormitories. Their soap bears the Eco-mark, an ecology seal awarded by the Japan Environmental Association.

Several such plants already existed in Japan, but the Kawasaki plant is unique in being operated entirely by six housewives, assisted by Hiroko Nakamura, a staff member from the Seikatsu Club. In 1989, the Seikatsu was awarded Sweden's Right Livelihood Award, sometimes called the 'Alternative Nobel Prize.'[16]

The women's movement to recycle paper containers for milk and juice is almost as widespread as the one for used cooking oil. The thick containers are made from 100 percent virgin coniferous pulp laminated with polyethylene. Paper containers appeared on the market in the 1960s, and by 1990 were used for 80 to 90 percent of milk sold. The movement to recycle the containers began in 1984 through the grassroots action of a group of mothers in Ōtsuki, Yamanashi Prefecture. Hatsumi Hirai, one of the founders and by 1990 the head of the nationwide movement, says that she and other women began collecting the containers 'as a way to show our children, who live in a throwaway age, that resources must be valued.'[17]

According to the national campaign office, the 3.2 billion paper containers produced in Japan each year consume 1.7 million twenty- to thirty-year-old trees. By 1990, only about 0.1 percent were being recycled, although women had collected 60 million containers in the first five years of the movement. Their initial efforts had been rebuffed, but eventually six paper mills agreed to accept the used containers and recycle them into toilet paper. The polyethylene layer, initially a reason for a mill's rejection of the women's proposal, is turned into combustible gas.

The project is economically feasible only because of the women's volunteer work. Containers are washed, cut open, and packed 200 to a cardboard box. Thirty containers weigh one kilogram, and once a minimum of 60,000 containers have been collected they are sold to agents for ¥5 to ¥7 per kilogram. Individual homes serve as collecting stations. A Tokyo group used their profits to donate three cherry trees to a park.

Seikatsu Club staff member Hiroko Nakamura describes housewives as 'people who are not tainted by the values of industrialism.' Or power, one might add. Some, however, have recently been finding ways to influence the bureaucracy. Miyoko Matsuda of Saitama Prefecture is the leader of an all-woman advisory group to the Ministry of Health and Welfare on garbage reduction. Matsuda travels nationally to lecture women on the careful management of refuse disposal. She describes herself as 'just a housewife' who is putting garbage reduction ideas into practice: 'That makes it easier for average citizens to listen to me because I can't and don't try to describe complex theories.'[18]

Matsuda also leads a bottle and can collection drive in her home city of Kawaguchi. Proposals made by her all-women's Committee for Discussing

Garbage Reduction include the placing of 'post boxes' for empty bottles at train and subway stations and for milk cartons in supermarkets, and the imposition of taxes on excessive packaging and throwaway products. The latter proposal is particularly important in Japan, where the packaging is often considered as important as the item being packaged.

In contrast to the environmental consciousness of many women, a typical response from a male official in the Tokyo city government to the ever-increasing piles of garbage is: *build more incinerators.*[19]

The idea of volunteering is growing slowly in Japan, mainly among women and young adults, and volunteer work by women has many targets in addition to the environment.[20] Company attitudes are also changing, again slowly, as corporate citizenship programs are introduced to allow employees to take short leaves for volunteer work. In 1995, a large advertisement appeared in the *Asahi Shimbun*, a respected daily newspaper, headed 'You can be a volunteer along with your job if you work for these companies.' The names of several dozen companies were listed along with their volunteer activities. These included making large-letter books for students with weak eyes (Fuji Xerox); preserving a section of each factory's grounds as a bird sanctuary open to the public (Suntory); inspecting vehicles for welfare institutions (Toyota); making Braille translations (Matsushita Electric); and permitting workers to go abroad with the Peace Corps. The idealism of volunteer work is changing Japanese society.[21]

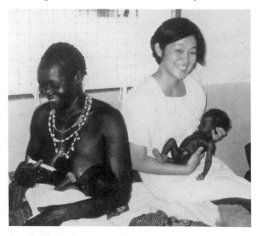

Many volunteer associations have an international focus. Yukiko Sohma founded the Association to Aid Indochinese Refugees (later the AAR) in 1979. At that time, as she told a journalist in 1995, 'volunteering was an uncommon practice in Japan.'[22] The AAR has helped refugees to settle in Japan and given aid to those abroad, from medical care and food to job training and well digging. At

Many staff members of the Japan Red Cross are sent abroad each year. Here Naomi Imamura of Kumamoto Red Cross Hospital is working in an international Red Cross hospital in Kenya. Courtesy of Japanese Red Cross Society.

the age of eighty-three, Sohma is the current president of the AAR. She was impressed by the number of volunteers who helped people after the Kōbe earthquake and believes that young people are increasingly drawn to volunteering. Many now work abroad with the AAR and other private groups. Sohma believes that the world is getting smaller and borderless, with universally acceptable values increasing.

Hatsuko Kawanaka with Watongwe boys. In 1997, Kawanaka and her husband, Kenji, established the Watoto Foundation to support school children living in and around Mahale Mountains National Park, Western Tanzania. Many Japanese women do volunteer work abroad. Courtesy of Yukiko Nakamura.

Other charitable organizations with an international focus run by women include the International Ladies Benevolent Society, the International Women's Club, and the Asian Ladies Friendship Society. Many conduct annual bazaars with handmade goods to raise funds. Médecins sans frontières (MSF), which sends emergency medical teams to crisis areas, now has some sixty Japanese volunteers of both sexes and roughly 1,000 contributors.[23]

Family planning and education are two of the oldest areas to concern Japanese women activists over the last 100 years. Since 1989, the Japanese Organization for International Cooperation in Family Planning has collected and repaired 11,000 abandoned bicycles and sent them to thirty countries to improve the mobility of health workers in family planning programs.[24]

Some groups are small, and many were started by a single enthusiast. Eiko Kakizawa launched a campaign in the 1990s to urge people to have their eyes checked regularly because with early discovery glaucoma can be cured. Her current goal is to establish an ophthalmic hospital and reduce the number of people who go blind.[25]

Women are helping themselves as well as others. Female entrepreneurs have special difficulty obtaining bank loans and often succeed only with the aid of a male relative as guarantor. This world-wide problem for businesswomen has been addressed since 1979 by the Women's World Banking (WWB), a New York-based institution with fifty branches, mainly in developing countries. Banks have traditionally been reluctant to deal with women because they lacked credit history or collateral or legal standing. A citizens' group that operates twenty *Daisansekai* (Third World) shops in Japan invited the WWB to the country and was successful in bringing a branch to Tokyo in November 1990. Called the Citizens' Bank, the branch

Okayama City Charity Bazaar, where the
International Angel Association raises money
for children's education and care in Bangla-
desh. Courtesy of Dr Mary McCrimmon.

initially offered only advice and contacts or networking with lawyers and accountants, but now extends loans for grassroots projects such as catering services for senior citizens and natural food restaurants. Another branch office opened in Itami, Hyōgo Prefecture, in 1991 and holds two-day seminars to stimulate entrepreneurial ventures.

Small businesses targeting niche markets have thus spun off from women's activism. By 1991, more than 100 of the women who attended the initial WWB seminars in Tokyo, Sapporo, Fukui, and Kitakyūshū had started environmentally friendly businesses such as natural food restaurants, boxed-lunch shops using organically grown vegetables, and bakeries that sell additive-free bread and pastries.[26] The energy of freshly coined empowerment runs through these ventures.

Vancouver-born poet Kazuko Shiraishi (b. 1931) has become an international voice for the anger and anxiety felt by many women concerning environmental degradation and rearmament. She pictures the earth as 'our little Noah's ark planet,' drowning in the universe.[27] A long poem entitled 'Seasons of the Sacred Lecher' resonates with indignation and energy:

> Too many people
> Too many cars
> People produce words, use them, it's time to
> Get rid of the garbage ...[28]

Shiraishi has been called 'the outstanding poetic voice of her generation of disengagement in Japan' (p. v). Translator and editor Kenneth Rexroth sees her as the last, the youngest 'and one of the best' of a line of protest that began with the Beat generation in the United States and the Angry Young Men of England. Her chosen topic is modern Tokyo in the third quarter of our century, shown as the international megalopolis pushed to the extreme: 'Shiraishi's Tokyo is straight out of Dante' (p. vi). She finds a stifling authoritarianism in Japan in the 1980s. As she puts it, 'In Tokyo, life forces people to be part of the machine. Everyone in some way has sickness, nerve sickness. It is hard to appreciate culture when poison has made you sick. Japanese life makes me think of this life's future.'[29] Shiraishi's rage, her concern for peace and for the environment, are shared by hundreds of thousands of Japanese women who may lack her creative flair and talent for performance art but who share her determination and vision. When Shiraishi reads aloud in Japan people cry, she says, because her work is 'so spiritual.'

Taeko Kōno (b. 1926), in a prose fiction that is less flamboyant but equally effective, maps the appalling emotional and spiritual losses of the Pacific War for women and men and for the living as well as the dead. The youth of

Kōno's generation (like that of Shizuko Gō, whose novel *Requiem* was discussed in Chapter 2) was spent in factories, not schools. It would take years for these women writers to fully comprehend their personal experiences of war.

The protagonist of Kōno's short story 'Iron Fish' (Tetsu no uo, 1976) struggles to understand the monstrous experience of her first husband, who was killed while serving as a human torpedo. Translator Yukiko Tanaka notes that during the Second World War the Japanese Imperial Navy made large torpedoes that carried a man inside, 'an aquatic version of the kamikaze pilot.'[30] Kōno's protagonist goes with a friend to visit a shrine that honours the servicemen of the war. She harbours a secret plan and by hiding at closing time manages to be left alone in the museum. She spends the night in and beside a rusted torpedo like the one in which her husband died. She imagines his claustrophobia: the cylinder is only four feet in diameter. She reads the display sign mounted by the government, a voice from wartime propaganda – 'Neither debt nor guilt nor any tie to women need I feel' (p. 357) – then climbs into the iron fish: 'Had he not wanted to see the brightness of the sun again, to breath the fragrant air, to stretch his arms towards the sky?' (p. 359).

Meanwhile, outside the museum, the friend who had accompanied her knows that she is there alone overnight. Sleepless, the friend is haunted by three images: of a monk enduring some particularly arduous discipline or trial; of a criminal; and of an accident victim (p. 352). With delicacy and power, Kōno, like Shizuko Gō, catches the mixed feelings of the Japanese towards this trial by fire and water, the precious quality of the life lost, and the appalling waste.

Similar feelings and reflections are caught in a poem by Makoto Ōoka, translated by Janine Beichman. In the wind of zelkova trees and the sound of temple bells, Ōoka hears the whispers of thousands of souls lost in war.[31]

Women in Japan and many other countries have worked actively for peace since the nineteenth century.[32] As the fiftieth anniversary of the Second World War approached, the literal interpretation of Article 9 of the Constitution was challenged in the media, both in Japan and abroad. Article 9 states that Japan renounces the threat or use of force 'as a means of settling international disputes' and abandons the right to maintain all forms of 'war potential.' In the interpretation handed down by the government in power at the time the Constitution was established in 1946, Japan had forever renounced war, including defensive war, as a sovereign right. This interpretation was subsequently modified to allow a military force on a scale deemed necessary for the nation's self-defence and to provide a cloak of constitutionality for the nation's Self-Defense Force (SDF), which flourished and expanded during the Cold War years.

Japan became a member of the United Nations over forty years ago, in 1956. Various international crises of the 1990s, including the Gulf War, have posed the question whether SDF forces can be sent overseas under the name of 'international co-operation.'[33] Japan's large financial contribution to the allied side during the Gulf War was termed 'checkbook diplomacy,' and it was accused of *heiwa boke* (peace euphoria), or being out of touch with the real world after more than forty-five years of peace.

Most Japanese women have stood firm against any military involvement under the guise of 'international co-operation.' Urged on by prominent politicians such as Morihiro Hosokawa and Ichiro Ozawa, however, the nation now seems to be considering the kind of involvement urged by its allies. The editor of a leading newspaper called 'blanket' pacifism irresponsible, a stance that might 'serve as bait for an aggressor.' Meanwhile, since the spring of 1993, textbooks approved for junior high school by the Ministry of Education state flatly that an independent nation has a right to self-defence and that the SDF does not constitute the war potential prohibited by Article 9.[34]

Undaunted, Takako Doi continues to be the spokeswoman for many women voters who want a strict interpretation of Article 9. Her party, the Japan Socialist Party, or JSP, stands alone in calling for an unarmed neutral Japan and in opposing both the US-Japan Security Treaty and Japan's Self-Defense Forces.

Japan's most prominent woman politician is a constitutional scholar and former law professor. Doi is the first woman to lead a major party in the Diet. She served as chair of the JSP from 1986 to 1991. In the dramatic Upper House election of July 1989, the socialists gained twenty-four seats thanks largely to the women's vote. Many women candidates campaigned as 'ordinary housewives,' and Doi attracted crowds of women who came wearing pink scarves to hear her speak about restoring faith in politics. In the most devastating setback of its thirty-four year reign, the LDP won only thirty-six of the 126 seats at stake, while the JSP took forty-six. This election gave the combined opposition parties control of the Upper House for the first time. When she learned the results of the vote, an exultant Doi said that she 'truly felt the mountains moving.'[35]

After the equally explosive general election of July 1993, which ousted the LDP from its thirty-eight-year majority rule, Doi became the first woman speaker of the House of Representatives. An impressive figure by any standard, Doi believes that women are more effective as politicians than men because they are less concerned with status and power and more concerned with serving the public's needs.[36] Women politicians were noticeably missing from the Diet until recent years. The significant gains they made in the 1989 Upper House elections were lost a few years later, possibly because the surge of energy inspired by Doi's successes had ebbed. Women politicians say that they are still not taken seriously in Japanese politics, which are generally seen as 'a male thing.'[37] In politics, as in *kabuki* theatre, the key roles are often passed down from father to son. In 1989, agriculture minister Hisao Horinouchi had the gall to call women 'useless in politics,' while Takayoshi Miyagawa, a male political analyst who admired Doi's forceful style, attempted a compliment by saying 'I call her a man.'

Compliments and brickbats aside, Doi believes that being a woman is an advantage in Japanese politics rather than a handicap: 'You have no fame,' she said, 'no social status, no special connections to worry about, so you can be clean.'[38] Since the late 1980s, the ranks of the JSP have been swelling with reformers of both sexes from a wide variety of backgrounds. The elected members and their supporters may not be socialists, but they believe that this party will protect women's interests. Women are also making modest gains within the LDP.

Mitsuyo Sawa, elected mayor of Zushi in November 1992, is another woman who strives for peace and the environment. Sawa is only the second woman to serve as mayor in postwar Japan.[39] A stubborn fighter, she campaigned on an issue that local citizens' groups had been battling for more than a decade: the prospect of a large housing development in an environmentally sensitive area south of Yokohama. The Ikego Hills consist of 290 hectares of biologically diverse forest, the only such area left in the metropolitan area. It also contains important archeological artifacts dating from the Jomon period and giant white clam fossils preserved for 3,000,000 years.

The Diet had concurred with a request from the US Navy to build 854 housing units for its personnel on the Ikego Hills. Sawa's sensible counterproposal was that US Navy families should be given subsidies to rent homes within the Japanese community, thus fostering communication between the two groups. She also pointed out that there was empty military housing in the Yokohama area and vowed to oppose the project 'until the citizens of Zushi win back the Ikego forest.'[40]

Sawa's criticism of the Ikego Hills housing plan early in 1993 extended to the Diet itself: 'This world of money, power and compromise was thought to be beyond the comprehension of women. Today, the outcome of all this is that beyond being incomprehensible, the world of Japanese politics, particularly at the national level, has become plutocratic and corrupted ... It has become a world remote and invisible to the general public.'[41] She expects that many more women will follow her into politics.

To a woman journalist Sawa said that the goal of politics should be the improvement of daily life. Greater participation by women in politics would change the current 'power-and-money' system, since women 'are generally more sensitive to their daily lives.'[42] One example was the priority given by her municipal government to welfare for the aged. Zushi's mild climate and natural setting have attracted many elderly people. Sawa noted that a woman's viewpoint was helpful in this area, since women traditionally shoulder the work of caring for the elderly. She stressed that it was work such as this, 'enhancing people's living standards and promoting peace,' that constituted real politics, 'unlike the money-power politics of Nagatacho [the Diet].'[43]

Sawa's criticism of the male-dominated Diet was echoed the following month by Morihiro Hosokawa, just after he was swept into power as prime minister in July 1993. As governor of Kuramoto province in Kyūshū, Hosokawa had discovered the power of Tokyo bureaucrats when he had tried to move a bus stop a few hundred metres and had been forced to send a delegation to Tokyo: 'In Japan, you can't tie your own shoes without official permission.' Hosokawa believes that Japan's political system has grown moribund and that its legislators, fattened by wealth and complacency, are out of touch 'with the realities of the rest of the world' and 'mere tools of government agencies,' devoted to reflecting the ideas of bureaucrats in party policy and decisions. Hosokawa pronounced the central government to be 'even more reactionary and absolutist than the premodern, feudalistic system of the shoguns.'[44] Strong words. Unfortunately Hosokawa himself would soon be tarred by scandal.

It requires an insider to fully understand what Hosokawa calls the 'reactionary and absolutist' workings of the Diet and of the so-called 'iron triangle' of politicians, bureaucrats, and businessmen. Any citizen, however, can be aware of the endless scandals that feed media reports. Women, increasingly, are fed up with what one professor called 'the unprecedented degree of corruption' in Japanese politics and are working for change and greater openness.[45]

A member of a women's collective in Kyoto sees 1989 as a landmark year for women's participation in politics. By then, the ruling LDP had held power for thirty-four years. In June, a by-election in the Upper House was won by a woman backed by the opposition Social Democratic Party, sending shock waves through Japan.[46] In rapid succession, women proceeded to win seats in the Tokyo Metropolitan Assembly (moving from 7 to 13 percent) and in the House of Councillors (moving from 8.7 to 13 percent). Following this, the House of Councillors nominated Takako Doi for prime minister, while the House of Representatives nominated Toshiko Kaifu. Kaifu won, but Doi had the honour of being Japan's first woman candidate for prime minister.

During the late 1980s female candidates began using a new campaign tactic. Many of their campaigners were housewives, which doubtless helped to capture women's votes. Responding to the new atmosphere and the widespread popularity of Takako Doi, Kaifu appointed two female ministers to his cabinet in August 1989. Mayumi Moriyama, the new chief cabinet secretary, took the highest government post ever held by a woman in this male-dominated society. In a direct appeal to women voters, Kaifu described Moriyama as a housewife as well as a bureaucrat, one who could contribute 'the people's perspective.'[47]

The NWEC newsletter reported enthusiastically, 'It is like magma starting to blow and erupt. Men's last fort, politics, is giving way.'[48] By 1992, the magma was cooling and there were no women in the Miyazawa cabinet, but women's representation in 1991 elections to local assemblies increased, reaching 3.1 percent in political bodies outside the national Diet.[49] Concludes Hisako Okamura, 'Women are obviously beginning to take a more active part in politics.'

Representation and visibility were well served at the local level in 1992 by Mariko Mitsui, a member of the Tokyo Municipal Assembly and of the Social Democratic Party. Mitsui is an outspoken supporter of women's rights and co-founder of the Alliance of Feminist Representatives. The alliance, inspired by a political model in Norway, hopes to raise the number of women elected to the Diet to 30 percent.[50] Mitsui's 1992 study of women politicians, *Momo-iro no kenryoku* (The political power of pink), contrasts Japan with Norway, where a 1988 legislated quota system requires a minimum of 40 percent for both male and female representatives in parliament and in all policy deliberation bodies. In Japan, 'pink-collar' work means jobs typically filled by women, usually low paid and often involving poor working conditions.

The increase of women members of the Diet remains slow, since some women politicians prefer working within their communities and many lack the financial support needed for election. Change continues, nonetheless. The Fusae Ichikawa Memorial Association offers classes on politics to women candidates and crash courses in campaigning without bribery or other illicit influences.[51] A one-year political school for women opened by the Japan New Party in February 1993 has met with an enthusiastic response. Most important, women are now aware of their power as voters, and polls show that they are exercising that right in increasing numbers.

Doi continues to work towards her goal of making all of Northeast Asia a nuclear-free zone. She believes that building the future should begin with acknowledging the past and urges Japan's leaders to issue an unambiguous apology to her neighbours for wartime aggression: 'We must stop avoiding our past and acknowledge – to ourselves – our sins as a nation and take responsibility for our history.'[52] By June of 1945 the government was still choking on the word 'aggression' and still unable to issue an apology that would satisfy Japan's neighbours.

Volunteer women's groups devoted to the cause of peace are legion and have been active ever since the Second World War. The Women's Democratic Club was formed early in 1946 to oppose nuclear weapons and power plants and to promote environmental conservation and antipollution practices. Writer Ineko Sata was one of the founders. Part of the group's original mandate was also to raise the social status of women. Since August 1946 the club has published the *Women's Democratic Journal*, a weekly with more than 60,000 subscribers by 1991.[53] Another national women's organization is the Japan Women's Council, established in 1962 to fight for world peace and 'the full liberation of women.' The JWC, described in its literature as 'a network of women who deeply appreciate the importance of peace,' supports a strict interpretation of Japan's Constitution and of Article 9.[54]

Groups with similar aims include the Red Dragonfly Society, the Hiroshima Women's Group for Peace, the Nara Coop Peace Association, and the Hiroshima-Kure-Iwakuni Peace Link.[55] The last of these opposes the entry into Japanese waters and air space of US warships and planes carrying nuclear weapons. Typical of the grassroots nature of many group actions was a 'die-in' for peace in 1991, staged in front of the Atomic Bomb Dome in Hiroshima by seventy-seven housewives from all over the country, all members of various co-operative societies.

One antinuclear group has linked up with a group in northern England to oppose the transfer of Japan's plutonium and radioactive waste to that area. Headed by Yurika Ayukawa, director of international relations for the Citizens' Nuclear Information Center in Tokyo, the 'Save Peter Rabbit's Homeland' campaign opposes reprocessing of spent Japanese nuclear fuel at the Sellafield nuclear power plant near the town of Seascale in Cumbria, England.[56] Spent Japanese nuclear fuel cooling in ponds while awaiting reprocessing has seeped radiation into local rivers and lakes and even contaminated the Irish Sea. The leukaemia rate among Seascale children is fourteen times the national average. Ayukawa calls the widespread ignorance of the issue in Japan 'shameful.' Her group is calling for a halt to the entire nuclear power industry.

Many women activists believe that women understand the value of life better than men do. Clearly the thesis admits exceptions. Husband and wife painters Iri and Toshi Maruki have spent much of their lives creating a visual testament to the atom bomb experience in Hiroshima. The painters arrived in Hiroshima a few days after the bomb dropped and stayed for one month to help the injured. Their work, painted between 1950 and 1982, consists of fifteen enormous murals. The paintings have been exhibited in Britain and the United States, where a critic called them 'perhaps even more emotionally charged than Picasso's Guernica.' In a book reproducing the murals in colour, Iri Maruki calls them paintings of hell. Toshi adds: 'Of course, those who cause pain and suffering end up in hell. But we also painted ourselves falling into hell, because we do not have the strength to stop war.'[57]

Reiko Okada, another woman painter, has published a book of paintings about a poison gas factory in Okuno Island, Hiroshima Prefecture, where she worked as a student during the Second World War. This artist's credo, that international friendship is possible through public confessions of past history, has been verified.[58]

The vigour of political activism among women is impressive, given the sex-typed role expectations that continue to prevail in Japan. The 1946 Constitution guaranteed legal equality in political rights for men and women. In practice, however, and until relatively recently this has meant only an equal right to vote. A study of Japanese women's search for a place in political life published in the early 1980s revealed the range of feelings experienced by women in this regard and the stress laid on them by role restrictions.[59]

Susan Pharr relied on lengthy interviews conducted in Japanese with 100 women volunteers, selected from over fifty groups ranging from political parties, through protest movements, to feminist groups: a full range of political activism. She divided her subjects into three types in terms of the role ideologies they themselves expressed: 'neotraditionalists,' 20 percent who accepted the wife-mother role as primary; 'new women,' 60 percent who represented the middle ground; and 'radical equalitarians,' 20 percent who rejected the role expected of them by society. All three types of political women faced role strain. The techniques they used to cope ranged from compliance to open defiance, and all three types used a full range of techniques in varying situations.

Recalling Shizue Ishimoto Katō at ninety-three – raising her fist in a parting salute as I left her living room and saying, 'You tell them we are *not* going to have more babies!' – I am not surprised by Pharr's 1982 prediction that women's participation in politics would increase in the 1980s and '90s. What is surprising, given the strength of gender and political socialization, is the long, determined struggle by women since the late nineteenth century to take on a significant role in managing the affairs of their nation and their own communities. Since 1989, this political struggle for empowerment at many levels has seemed to be moving into a new phase.

CHAPTER 10

FIREWORDS: EMPOWERMENT THROUGH WRITING

If women saw life in the same way as men, then it would be pointless to write.
SEIKO TANABE, interview, 3 July 1986

I believe the system of bartering used by the mountain men and the villagers
was called 'silent trade.' I am coming to understand that there was nothing
extraordinary in striking such a silent bargain for survival. People trying to
survive – myself, my mother, and my children, for example – can take some
comfort in living beside a wood. We toss various things in there and tell ourselves that we haven't thrown them away, we've set them free ... Meanwhile
the creatures multiplying there gaze stealthily at the human world outside ...
Some sort of silent trade is taking place.
YUKO TSUSHIMA, 'The Silent Traders,' *Shōwa Anthology*

Ability knows no gender, but theme and vision are of
course influenced by experience and opportunity, as are critical reactions.
In the West, for example, 'virile' was a term of high praise for painters in the
1910s and '20s, and many women painters, such as Emily Carr, were
excluded from critical notice. So, too, the biases of a male-dominated critical tradition meant that the writers presumed to be best were almost exclusively male. Jane Austen and Virginia Woolf were the exceptions, the token
females admitted to the club until women's studies programs and feminist
scholars began to open doors in the 1970s.

A similar movement was taking place in Japan in the late 1960s and
the '70s on a much smaller scale. More women writers were finding pub-
lishers and winning literary awards. The lack of translations was becoming
obvious. Beginning in the early 1980s, publication of a number of anthologies of short fiction by Japanese women served to introduce these writers to
an international audience.[1] Most have substantial introductions that present

Sculptor Kyoko Asakura at home in her studio in Sendagi, Tokyo, 1991. Asakura's subjects are typically women. Her bronze sculptures are moving and poetic, with a striking intensity.

Two Women/Futari (1983), Asakura's life-sized sculpture of two young women on a long bench. She writes: 'The work's title is derived from the notion that one person resides in two and two in one ... I would like the work to give voice to the moment.'

modern and contemporary Japanese women's writing as hitherto neglected. Earlier, and continuing through the 1980s, mainstream anthologies of Japanese stories in translation tended to represent male writers exclusively.

For Japanese women and women writers, the power of social expectations and the pressure to conform can be illustrated by a story written by Shugorō Yamamoto during the 1940s or '50s. In 'The Peach-tree by the Well,' set in the feudal period before the Meiji Restoration but with, one suspects, self-consciously contemporary implications, the female protagonist invented by this male writer is a plain girl who has loved reading and writing from early childhood and who becomes, as a young women, a talented *tanka* poet.

Koto intends to remain single in order to devote her life to poetry. An elderly woman advises her that she can never understand life completely until she has a husband and children. Without such experience her verse may show 'a certain facility' but will

Painter Tamako Kataoka in her home. Born in Sapporo in 1905, Kataoka left home at eighteen against her parents' wishes to study art in Tokyo. Her early work focused on children and the family. Later she turned to passionate and dynamic landscapes and to portraits of famous Edo artists in which she strove to reflect the character and thoughts of her subjects. Her work stands with the best Japanese art in this century.

never stir the soul. Marriage, the mentor adds, is every woman's dream. Behind this view lies the Japanese expression for an unmarried woman, *han-nin*, or half-person, an epithet once hurled at Takako Doi by a male member of the Diet.

Convinced, Koto marries a widower and becomes stepmother to his sons. She is now too busy to write poetry, but she is happy with her housewife's life since 'it clearly reflects the shifting lights and shadows of her soul.'[2] She has come to understand that being a homemaker 'is no mechanical job, but one every bit as creative as writing poetry' (p. 185). Years later, looking back on her life, she sees the great difference between the poet she might have been and the woman she has become, and she 'would choose to be born a woman every time' (p. 189).

So much for female literary ambition. The *bushido* ideal of self-sacrifice was alive and well in postwar Japan. For women it spelled hearth and home, while salarymen were urged to be 'samurai warriors.'

In Heian Japan (AD 794-1185) women wrote phonetically in a system known today as *hiragana* (one of two *kana* syllabaries), involving some fifty symbols learned in childhood. This was called 'female lettering,' while male lettering involved thousands of *kanji*, or Chinese ideograms, and extensive study. *The Tale of Genji*, known as the world's first novel, was written in women's letters by Lady Shikibu Murasaki in the eleventh century. Court poetry also used the phonetic system of *kana* to express daily life in the native tongue.

Lithographer and sculptor Yuriko Oido depicts life in Hokkaido's small towns and villages, typically focusing on women. At our first meeting she said she tires of always hearing about male artists and subjects, and strives to catch 'the smell of women' in her work. Courtesy of Yuriko Oido.

From this ancient beginning came the recognition of *joryu*, or 'female-school' literature as a separate category of writing. Modern writers, whatever their sex, use the same written language, a mixture of *kanji* and *kana*, yet only recently has writing by women been accepted into the mainstream of Japanese literature.[3]

During the feudal period (1603-1867), women were confined to the home as wives and mothers. They ceased to write. Women's voices were lost to literature for nearly 300 years. This gap is one reason why the work of Meiji poet and essayist Akiko Yosano (1878-1942) is so impressive, and so essentially contemporary. Her biographer, Janine Beichman, calls Yosano a 'poet of modern Japan.' Leading contemporary writers such as Fumiko Enchi, Seiko Tanabe, and Harumi Setouchi have all written of their debt to her as a woman and a writer. And for many ordinary Japanese women, as Beichman observes, Yosano's writing and the example of her life were 'part of the underground canon ... something they held close to their hearts.'[4] Takako Doi is one admirer. It was Yosano's image from the feminist poem 'Yama no Ugoku Hi' (The day when the mountains move), published in the first issue of *Seitō* in 1911, that Doi paraphrased to express her exhilaration in the wake of the 1989 election.[5]

For a decade before the feminist journal burst on the scene in 1911,

Yosano had been a highly respected and prolific writer. In 1901 Hō Shō (Akiko was a pen name) left her home in a provincial town near Osaka to marry Hiroshi Yosano, founder of the New Poetry Society and editor of *Myōjō*, an influential literary magazine. In the same year she published *Midaregami* (Tangled hair), *tanka* that revitalized an ancient verse form languishing in the hands of effete court poets.

Her *tanka* showed women at home and in the fields, in streets and inns, temples and cities. The translators of a modern edition write: 'Hers was a poetry of protest, of love, of emancipation for women, of the glorification of the flesh. She sympathized with the downtrodden – the lonely prostitute, the woman kept waiting, the isolated traveller ... She was the first to glorify the female body.'[6]

From this imposing beginning, Akiko went on to produce twenty volumes of prose and verse over the next forty years, along with eleven children. Her relationship with the mercurial Hiroshi was emotionally charged and always difficult. In later years Akiko came to believe that he was *two* men, and only the one she loved was 'real': his anger, his neglect came from a sick doppelgänger. Beichman calls Yosano's marriage one long lesson in pain and forbearance, prime evidence of the enormous strength of will that was one of her central characteristics.[7]

Myōjō, Hiroshi's magazine, stopped publication in 1908. His earnings from writing had always been small, and at this point they became less. Throughout their marriage Akiko was the chief wage earner. In the wide-ranging essays and verse that supported her large family, Akiko tackled substantial issues from a woman's point of view. In 'Watakushi to Shukyō' (Myself and religion), an essay written in 1937 two years after Hiroshi's death, she wrote that all women of her age, 'no matter how uneducated and ignorant, have attained a degree of enlightenment which no man can begin to grasp, even if he sits in meditation on a chilly platform. A woman's austerities take 20, 30 or 40 years ... Women have no need of Zen meditation.'[8]

In mid-life, Yosano spoke of having 'returned to the female,' although the strength and breadth of her themes made her an androgynous social critic. In essays and *tanka* she wrote of birth and labour, asserting that because women were capable of this great deed they were equal to men, different but complementary. She compared the birth giver to a warrior and described birthing as an act of cleansing, not impurity. Towards the end of a long series of *tanka* on giving birth, she writes: 'as if lashed / by the whip / until it ran with blood / but still unrepentant, / I have returned to life.'[9] Small wonder that this impressive writer has been an inspiration to Japanese women in succeeding generations.

At Kawasaki Medical Welfare University in 1993, women students asked to translate into English and comment on Yosano's poem, 'The Mountain Is Moving' or 'The Day When the Mountains Move' found it 'encouraging,' 'moving' and 'a big problem.' One wrote, 'This story melted my heart.' Other comments included, 'Women should move more'; 'I will get into society three years from now and I will, as the poem says, awake and move'; 'We young generations must make the wonderful women's society, little by little'; and 'Now women's position becomes higher than before ... Still there is much room for improvement.'

The next generation of women writers, such as Fumiko Enchi (1905-86), would straddle the watershed years of the Second World War. They would experience not only the sociopolitical conditions that Yosano did in her last decades but also the new winds of the postwar years. Critic Mark A. Harbison has written that before the defeat there was no legitimate concept of the individual in Japanese society and that this single fact is Enchi's central theme. Certainly the legitimacy of individual rights and especially of women's rights *is* a strong theme in Enchi's fiction, but that legitimacy remains, fifty years after the war, an embattled concept within a culture still built around the group.

In 1986, I was fortunate in being able to talk with some of the major

Writer Fumiko Enchi in her home in Tokyo with translator Mayumi Kurokawa, July, 1986. Enchi died the following October.

Japanese women writers whose fiction I had been reading in translation. Enchi met me in her Tokyo home only a few months before her death. The July heat was blistering, the humidity almost unbearable. Enchi received me in blue cotton pyjamas and beige socks, rebuffing her maid's repeated offering of a robe. She was already too hot; why add more clothing? Here was an unconventional woman who clearly knew her own mind. At eighty-one Enchi was frail and unable to walk alone. Her demeanour was simplicity itself, but her aura projected power and self-possession. Portions of our talk follow:

MORLEY Are you very conscious of being a woman in a society run by men?
ENCHI That has always been the way our society is run.
MORLEY Do you think your perceptions are different from those of a man?

ENCHI I think so. I was born some years ago in the Meiji era ... [Gradually] such aspects as women's rights and freedom have been more and more recognized ... The model of the heroine in *The Waiting Years* is my grandmother, on my mother's side. [A male secretary interjected that the real feelings of her grandmother were secretly told to her mother, and through her to the author. Enchi added that she was fifteen when her grandmother died.] ...

MORLEY One thing that fascinates me in your fiction, your point of view, is the combination of admiration for the characters and yet anger. You are angry at what they endure, and yet you admire them.

ENCHI Exactly, I meant it that way ...

MORLEY This double point of view comes out very well in 'Boxcar of Chrysanthemums' (Kikuguruma).

ENCHI I was aware of it when I wrote the story ...

MORLEY Women's lives are changing in Japan as in the West, but change is much faster in the West.

ENCHI Yes. These days it's the women not men who ask for a divorce.[10]

When we met, physical frailty masked the wit and intellect of this woman. These qualities are much in evidence in *Masks*, a novel in which the female protagonist accomplishes her goals through secrecy and subversion.[11] In a curious and symbolic way, *Masks*, written just as the serialized version of *The Waiting Years* was nearing completion, is a sequel to Tomo Shirakawa's story. Both women are secretive, but the inner submission that marked much of Tomo's life is replaced by Mieko's fiery independence and bold stratagems.

In *Masks*, Mieko Toganō is a woman in her fifties who lives in Tokyo with her son's widow. Yasuko helps her mother-in-law to edit a poetry magazine, and both women are interested in the study of spirit possession in the Heian era. Two professional men, Tsuneo Ibuki and Toyoki Mikame, belong to their study group, and both admire Yasuko. The fifth character essential to the intricate plot is Harume, twin sister to Mieko's dead son Akio. Beautiful but brain-damaged, Harume has been brought up separately but now lives with Mieko and Yasuko.

Mieko is a woman with a grievance, who is patiently working out her revenge. Before the war, at the start of her marriage to a wealthy landowner, she had discovered that one of her husband's maids was his mistress and had twice been forced to abort her child. Angry at the bride, the maid caused an accident so that Mieko miscarried. As in *The Waiting Years*, the writer sympathizes with both women: with the maid who 'desperately' wanted to bear children but had no choice save to obey her master; and with the bride, who unwittingly stumbled upon betrayal, hatred, and injury, and who lost her unborn child.

As the two men from the study group discuss the old story learned from a friend of Mikame's father, they at first call Mieko's husband 'the real villain,' and then absolve him as simply the creature of his society. Finally, Mikame and Ibuki agree that outspoken, 'aggressive' women are unattractive: one of Enchi's little jokes.

Enchi's chief device to mask her message is a long essay, written by the fictional Mieko in 1937 for a little magazine and rediscovered in an old bookstore. 'An Account of the Shrine in the Fields' purports to be an analysis of the Rokujō lady in *The Tale of Genji*, another betrayed woman whose feelings Mieko uses to reveal her own. Mieko describes the lady as an example of 'women's extreme ego suppression' (p. 75) and as a negative archetype of man's fear of women. Her essay profiles a character who is her own double: strong, forceful, highly intelligent, and vengeful when scorned. Mieko writes that she feels intense sympathy for this character, whose lively intensity could not be fully surrendered to any man (p. 50). Discouraged from a life of action, the Rokujō lady turns first to spirit possession as an outlet for her strong will and then to writing. She discovers literary creation as 'the ideal means of exercising her powers' (p. 55). As did Enchi herself. Enchi pushes her double entendres to the limit as Mieko's fictional literary criticism becomes the means for a statement on women's inner strength and their need for independence (pp. 55-6).

To her daughter-in-law Yasuko, Mieko admits that the essay 'unmasks' her, and that it had been written for the lover who was the father of her twins, Yasuko's dead husband Akio and his twin sister Harume. Mieko's husband, Toganō, who believed the twins to be his, actually died without heirs. Not only taking a lover but also passing her children off as her husband's heirs are twin acts of vengeance for Mieko.

Her bizarre revenge is far from over. She encourages Ibuki, a married man, to become Yasuko's lover, and through drunkenness and darkness the two women ensure that he impregnates not Yasuko but Harume, who bears a son and dies in childbirth. Mieko thus gains a grandchild and extends her own line, though not her husband's.

Harume, a pitiful figure who resembles the *nō* mask *Masugami*, has suffered brain damage from the pressure of her brother's feet inside the womb. Damaged by a male even before she was born, the beautiful Harume lives with a mind 'malformed and incapable of growth,' 'destined forever to be a little girl' (pp. 70, 71) yet sensuous and seductive.

The source of Harume's injury makes her an ingenious symbol for the kind of woman many Japanese men *think* they desire: physically beautiful, childish, and unintelligent. (This fantasy also existed in the West in earlier centuries.) Ibuki, who learns what has happened and who later sees Harume at a distance, is preoccupied with 'the endless pathos of Harume's beautiful, detached face and of her high round belly' (p. 136). One is reminded of Ume Tsuda's 'Poor, poor women' upon her return to Japan in 1882.

The novel has three parts, each named for a *nō* mask and together composing a complex symbol of Japanese women past and present. The mask of *Ryō no onna* represents the strong-willed Rokujō lady, forced to sublimate her abilities through men. *Masugami* represents 'a young woman in a state of frenzy' (p. 61), a passionate character with a woman's body and a child's mind. *Fukai*, the mask that gives its name to the novel's third and final part, symbolizes a 'deep well' or 'deep woman,' a woman mature in both years and understanding.

Black humour and irony control the tone of *Masks* and keep the fiction, with its forceful intellectual themes, from becoming didactic. In our talk, Enchi expressed pleasure at my reference to her humour and said that this quality was not generally noted by Japanese critics. She was puzzled, however, by the term 'black humour,' and asked for an extended explanation.[12] The joke played on Professor Ibuki, who is tricked into impregnating a woman he does not know and who then suffers the indignity of finding that his wife Sadako has hired a detective to shadow his movements, is a sample of Enchi's dark humour.

The male friends agree that Sadako's action is outrageous and that sudden crises 'did, in fact, seem to bring out the least attractive side of a woman' (p. 118). Clearly, humour is based on gender as well as culture. To the reader following the intricate workings of Mieko's plan, the two men appear at times like puppets or sophisticated cartoon characters. When Ibuki is ushered out from the Toganō home late one night by Mieko and Yasuko, for example, 'he felt like a man being escorted by two prostitutes down the hall of a brothel some long-ago time' (p. 79). Mieko's plot neatly inverts the feudal Japanese notion of a 'borrowed womb' – one that belittles the importance of women in bearing children – into borrowed sperm.

Ethically, Mieko is as complex a character as Shakespeare's Iago. Enchi understands the power of hatred, and uses the figure of the Rokujō lady to comment indirectly on the unfairness of 'women's extreme ego suppression.' The Rokujō lady writes that a woman who is a favourite with the protagonist of *The Tale of Genji* still incurs his displeasure when 'her irrepressible selfhood comes out in unbecoming ways' (p. 55). One of the themes of *Masks*, that a woman is 'a vastly superior opponent' to a man (p. 133), is comically placed in the mouth of Mikame, who goes on to conclude that jealousy is a great aphrodisiac. In neo-Confucian teaching, jealousy was one of woman's cardinal sins. In Enchi's inversion it is experienced most strongly by men.

Taken together, the three women – Mieko, Yasuko, and Harume – provide an image of Japanese womanhood. The *nō* masks that give their names to the novella's three parts embody the women's experience of love, hate, madness, suffering, and suppression. A friend who gives the *Fukai* mask to Mieko says that it represents a woman mature in both experience and understanding. She adds that her father, a *nō* master, liked to think of this mask as a metaphor comparing the heart of an older woman to the depths of a bottomless well (p. 138). Mieko thinks, 'The mask seemed to know all the intensity of her grief at the loss of Akio and Harume – as well as the bitter woman's vengeance that she had planned so long, hiding it deep within her' (p. 141).[13] Like the Rokujō lady and the novelist herself, Mieko had found writing the ideal means of exercising her powers.

From here, Enchi moves neatly to the comedy of the dead Harume's wailing baby and its two adoring foster mothers, Mieko and Yasuko, who plan to move to Kamakura where the environment will be healthier. In *Masks*, the womb becomes an instrument of power, a symbol of women taking control of their own lives. It thus foreshadows the pattern of a declining birth rate that has marked the last twenty years in Japan. Enchi's manifesto of women's independence is shrewdly prophetic.

Writing is always a means of exercising both personal and social power, and Yūko Tsushima's fictional portraits of the loneliness, frustration, courage, and growing strength of single women cannot help but have a powerful effect on readers. When I met her in the summer of 1986 she was thirty-nine but looked much younger in a pink cotton T-shirt, pink lipstick, and casual skirt. She stroked a black cat while we talked. A prolific writer, Tsushima had published nearly a score of novels, novellas, and story collections in the first two decades of her prestigious career. She had married in her early twenties, obtained a divorce after six years, and was raising two children as a single mother.

This experience, which made her an outsider to social conventions, underlies much of her writing and has shaped her archetypal protagonist, a single mother supporting herself and a child while trying to come to terms with independence. Of *Child of Fortune*, critic Christine Chapman writes, 'The novel rubs painfully against the Japanese grain as it describes a woman who is self-indulgent and temperamental, neither patient nor submissive, open about sexual relationships and disdainful of her family. Unsure of herself but ultimately courageous, she is a new heroine in a disapproving society.'[14] Tsushima's father, novelist Dazai Osamu, committed suicide when she was one year old. Her beloved mentally retarded brother died when she was twelve. Tsushima's early introduction to pain and emptiness has added depth and maturity to her work. Portions of our talk follow:

MORLEY What are your recurring themes?

TSUSHIMA Because I'm a woman, I naturally write about women. Also about human solitude, which I try to convey implicitly. Isolation, helplessness – people experience these in subtle ways. 'Solitude' sounds abstract, but my work often deals with the difficulties of communication, and people's strong desire to communicate.

MORLEY The desire to communicate is also a central theme in the work of Canadian writer Margaret Laurence. I'm interested in your image of women as outsiders. You were quoted in a recent article as saying that Japanese women have more room than men to manoeuvre in society, 'because women are already, simply by being women, outside – or rather, they're not central to society. So women have greater range or breadth, both in their way of thinking and in their way of living.'[15] Since writers are also outsiders, a woman writer is doubly so.

TSUSHIMA Yes, I think so too.

MORLEY Are you conscious that as a woman your perceptions of human life are different from those of men?

TSUSHIMA Yes, I think I've been uneasily conscious of this since I was a girl ...

MORLEY We were talking of humour, and its importance in your work. I was pleasantly surprised to find a great deal of humour and irony in writings by modern Japanese women. Are these qualities typical of Japanese women writers?

TSUSHIMA Yes, I think so. Women live their lives as outsiders, and as a result they see differently, and with irony.

MORLEY The Canadian population is small, and this may have nurtured a sense of irony in Canadians. Many of our best writers in the last thirty-five years have been women, and many have been divorced women. I think this has given them an understanding that affects their point of view as writers.

TSUSHIMA Yes, many Japanese women writers are also divorced and in similar situations ...

MORLEY What writers have influenced you?

TSUSHIMA At first, William Faulkner. Tennessee Williams. I studied

English literature at college. And Virginia Woolf! I was surprised, and shocked by her work. I think I was greatly influenced by her.

MORLEY Because there were no women novelists with a strong women's viewpoint in Japan before the war?

TSUSHIMA That's right.

MORLEY How old were you when you read Woolf?

TSUSHIMA I was twenty. I also liked Emily Brontë's *Wuthering Heights* very much. I still do.[16]

We went on to talk of Tsushima's prize-winning translator, Geraldine Harcourt, and Harcourt's conviction that the majority of Japanese women

Geraldine Harcourt, winner of the Wheatland Prize for Translation, is a New Zealander whose published translations include Yūko Tsushima's *Child of Fortune* and *Woman Running in the Mountains*, Michiko Yamamoto's *Betty-san*, and Shizuko Gō's *Requiem*.

whose writing had been translated by 1986 had been upper class and thus not representative of the whole field. Tsushima said that her own background might be called upper class, as she had been sent to prestigious schools and had been able to take a variety of lessons. I spoke of the 'feminization of poverty' for women in North America over the last thirty years, a phenomenon that has accompanied the steady increase in the divorce rate. Young single mothers and women who found themselves suddenly divorced in their forties and fifties had experienced sharp changes in income and sometimes in status.

Tsushima said that she had found herself in just such a situation and that the class structure in modern Japan was becoming more mixed, 'especially for divorced women.' The divorce rate in Japan in 1986 was a low 20 percent, yet it had doubled since the early 1970s. Tsushima noted that there was still a social stigma against divorced women and their children; that attitudes were changing, but very slowly.

Her recent novel in English translation, *Woman Running in the Mountains* (1991) features a pregnant, unmarried young Japanese woman at war with convention. The protagonist's personal coming of age seems to symbolize the coming of age of Japanese women. In that same year, however, a news story of a pregnant and unmarried teacher who had made two hard decisions reveals current attitudes in Japan towards unwed mothers. The woman had decided to carry her baby to term and to give it up for adoption. She told the interviewer that if she lived in America she would keep the child but that in Japan it would suffer severe social stigma. She herself was considered 'irresponsible' for not aborting the foetus.[17] The incident shows just how far Japanese society still is from allowing single women and especially single mothers to play a full part in the social fabric.

The 'silent bargain for survival' dramatized in Yūko Tsushima's 'The Silent Traders' offers a wealth of psychological parallels.[18] Two, however, stand out. In the story, a single mother lives with her widowed mother and two children in a city apartment near a walled garden. The first analogue is explicit. The narrator, watching her children set out food for a wild cat that comes from the park at night, believes that they are seeking a father substitute. She regrets that she has been unable to give them 'the experience of a father.' An afternoon outing with their biological father is black comedy, proving only his indifference. From the cat who comes at night, the children take the illusion of interest and concern: 'In their dreams, the children are hugged to their cat-father's breast' (p. 41).

This story also symbolizes the lonely life of a writer and her 'silent trade' with readers. Fiction is a time capsule, like the messages stuffed into a bottle and buried in the park by the narrator as a teenager. Literary images and implications may be as secretive as the densely wooded park at night. A story, silent and alive with possibilities, is a writer's 'silent bargain for survival' with society. Reward, recognition, even comprehension is tenuous and uncertain, yet the silent trade goes on.

Writer Yūko Tsushima in her home in Tokyo, 1986.

Humour is an essential ingredient in the work of Seiko Tanabe. Author of over 100 books and countless newspaper articles, Tanabe is less well known abroad than Enchi, Tsushima, or Sawako Ariyoshi (1931-84) because only two of her stories had been translated into English by 1994.

Her use of Kansai dialect in some fiction poses special difficulties for translators. By combining a strong literary talent and a scholarly knowledge of the classics with warmth, humour, and vernacular language, Tanabe has become a highly popular writer in Japan.

Ironically, the humour in Tanabe's story 'Sentimental Journey,' for which she won her first big literary prize, the 1964 Akutagawa Award, made some judges uncomfortable. Was the theme (a very brief love affair) and its treatment too frivolous for this high honour? One judge defended the frivolity by comparing Tanabe's story with the jarring sounds of modern jazz music, which he deemed 'appropriate for expressing new modern life.'[19]

Writer Seiko Tanabe in her rose garden, 1986.

In a 1975 essay on humour, 'Yuumoa ni tsuite,' Tanabe explains that she uses humour to express gentleness and understanding. Humour is a social skill that allows her characters to preserve 'face' and to interact well.[20]

When we talked in her home near Osaka in 1986, I found a friendly, gracious, and lively woman in a white lace dress who later enjoyed showing her guests her rose garden, terrarium, and collection of antique dolls. Some of her curios are as whimsical and intriguing as her imagination. Tanabe expressed a keen interest in women's issues, an area in which Japan, in her opinion, lagged far behind the West. She uses humour as a device to draw attention to women's concerns. Portions of our talk follow:

TANABE Men are not interested in reading about women's issues, so I try to include humour and some criticism in my work. I wrap it in humour, and sex, so that even hard-headed conservative men may want to read it.

MORLEY In the West, men sometimes say, What do women want? Some men feel unsure of themselves. Is it so in Japan?

TANABE Yes, exactly. I often write about what men want, and miss, and lack. And I write critically about women if necessary ... I try to write from a woman's point of view, and a middle-aged woman's point of view. I also write as a person who experienced the war. It's important to combine these· three viewpoints. I was seventeen when the war ended ...

MORLEY Do your readers write to you?

TANABE Yes. I get many letters from women, from people of all ages, and from retired men who have nothing to do.

MORLEY Older men like your work?

TANABE They say my work is 'delicious,' *oishii,* 'wrapped in humour.' I was happy to read this. I would rather be delicious than useful ...

MORLEY Some laws intended to help women in the workplace have been passed, but custom seems stronger than law.

TANABE I think women themselves just can't get out of their customary ways. They are naïve. They worry too much about men's feelings, and not enough about their own.

MORLEY Are things changing in the '80s?

TANABE Yes, but still slowly. For example, some young wives are working today, but these women always rush home to turn on the lights and prepare a meal. They say they are relieved when they get home first. It's a common attitude.[21]

One of Tanabe's popular publications, serialized for years in a weekly magazine, is *Onna no chunen karuta* (Cards for middle-aged women). The *karuta,* or cards, consist of poems, aphorisms, and drawings: art with a social message. Examples include 'Women come to understand the real world for the first time after a divorce' and 'There is no retirement for women.' The latter quip is reminiscent of Akiko Yosano's aphorism half a century earlier: 'Women have no need of Zen meditation.'

Tanabe's two stories in English translation demonstrate her gentle mocking of the foibles of both sexes. In 'How to Win a Woman Writer,' a lonely widower in his mid-forties is intrigued by a new next-door neighbour, an attractive woman with a self-confident voice. He discusses her with a younger colleague, who discovers that the woman is a well-known writer. Taketa has never bought a book, save for technical manuals, and has rather a low opinion of wives: 'There's wives and there's women. Talking to your wife isn't like a conversation between adults.' Nevertheless, he perseveres in wooing the writer, totting up the principles that advance his suit. These include not being frightened, telling the truth, and praising her work from a new and unexpected angle. Along the way, Tanabe makes good-humoured fun of all her characters as she crafts an off-beat romance without a hint of sentimentality.[22]

'How to Seduce Miyamoto Musashi' is a witty parody of a well-known samurai epic. In a 1930s version by a male writer, Musashi is a famous swordsman who disdains women and the ties of emotion, like the Western frontier hero. In Tanabe's 'deliciously' comic pastiche, the young giant lacks common sense and needs someone to look after him. That someone turns out to be the widow Osugi, an energetic woman delegated by her village clan to find Musashi and punish him for local crimes. Musashi calls her 'granny,' but Osugi considers herself to be 'in the prime of life and the bloom of womanhood.' She winds up as his companion and thoroughly enjoys her chance to travel the world and see the sights.[23]

Tanabe's targets include her own writing and an idealized young woman who is also pursuing Musashi, along with all the stock characters and situations of an epic melodrama. The all-too-human hero is nearly caught by the pure young woman as he munches a jam bun in a teahouse, and he gets a stitch in his side during his narrow escape from her snares. Tanabe transforms a macho hero and an old crone into amusing travelling companions, one idealistic but wildly impractical, the other shrewd but kind. The combination is reminiscent of Cervantes' Don Quixote and Sancho Panza.

Like Tanabe, Minako Ōba (b. 1930) skilfully employs parody and satire to depict relationships between men and women. Ōba's images and tone, however, can be darker, sometimes acidic.[24] Both writers were teenagers during the war and can never forget the air raids and the human devastation. In 1944, Ōba's family moved to Seijō City, near Hiroshima. Ōba and her schoolmates were mobilized to work eleven hours a day in their school-turned-uniform-factory, where students were evacuated into nearby wheat fields during air raids. Unlike the other students, Ōba never forgot to take a book to read in the field. She saw the mushroom cloud rise over Hiroshima and formed part of a student rescue squad to help survivors, the living dead. Much later she described this experience in an essay, 'Hell's Service' (1973).[25]

Ōba graduated from Tsuda College, married in 1955, and spent eleven years in Sitka, Alaska, with her engineer husband. They have one daughter. Ever since the family returned to Japan in 1970, travels abroad have remained an important part of Ōba's life. Exposure to other cultures was for her the beginning of a deeper understanding of her Japanese society.

She wore a beautiful blue kimono when we talked in her home in 1986:

Writer Minako Ōba in her home in Tokyo, 1986.

MORLEY At what age did you begin to write?

ŌBA Around the age of twelve. But I was simply writing for myself. My work was not published for more than twenty years. I was in my mid-thirties when my first book came out.

MORLEY I've read that, before you married, you made your future husband promise you could continue to write.

ŌBA Yes, he promised.

MORLEY That's good. Are you very conscious of being a woman in a society run by men?

ŌBA Well, perhaps half conscious and half unconscious.

MORLEY Is it easier now, in the '80s, to be a woman writer, compared with, say, thirty years ago?

ŌBA That's a difficult question. Men appear to have power and to control society, but women control the inner life. They wield power indirectly. And that situation hasn't changed for thousands of years ... However, I'm an individualist. Every person has her own way of thinking. I try not to generalize.

MORLEY I'm an individualist too. It took me some years to become aware of the power of social conditioning in my own culture. And then exposure to Japan gave me a fresh understanding of how strongly a culture presses on each individual within it. Did your experience in America deepen your understanding of Japanese life?

ŌBA Yes. In a foreign country, a foreign culture, you are shocked by that culture and yet at the same time you discover yourself. Not others but yourself.

MORLEY Canadian novelist Margaret Laurence had seven years in Somalia as a young adult. She said that the strangest thing you come upon while travelling is yourself.

ŌBA I really think so. In the States I rediscovered Japan and myself. Until I went to Alaska I had never been outside Japan and had never really known Japan.

MORLEY So it was lucky that you went to the States.

ŌBA Yes.

MORLEY And after you came back, you had new eyes for Japan?

ŌBA I think so. I had found other ways of living. Many Japanese women never think that there are other ways besides their traditional one.

MORLEY Is Japan changing recently?

ŌBA Yes. Many cultures are fusing.

MORLEY And does your writing show changes coming in women's lives?

ŌBA Perhaps. But this is not in my consciousness. I don't consciously write for social-scientific reasons, nor to analyze society. If you write with such conscious purposes, it won't be good literary work.

MORLEY You don't want to be didactic, but your intentions, your ideas, do show indirectly?

ŌBA Right. I'm not a social scientist, I express my feelings spontaneously.

MORLEY Is humour important in your work?

ŌBA Yes, certainly. Without humour it would not be first-class writing.

MORLEY I had thought Japanese writing was more romantic, sentimental, or tragic. I've been pleasantly surprised to find so much humour in Japanese women writers ... In your first prize-winning story, 'The Three Crabs,' the characters' lives seem empty. Are you satirizing modern society?

ŌBA Of course. I don't expect the characters to be admired. I write to show their thoughts. I am puzzled too.

MORLEY You are puzzled by your own characters?

ŌBA Yes, yes. Probably I am puzzled by myself, and also by phenomena around me. When you can see other people, you find yourself.

MORLEY So daily life can be like foreign travel. Every other person is a strange country?

ŌBA I think so.[26]

Ōba's feeling for the importance of the individual shows in a 1974 essay, 'Double Suicide: A Japanese Phenomenon.'[27] She finds this Japanese custom of ill-fated lovers puzzling and disturbing, because 'the couple chooses to die rather than seek a possible, though perhaps difficult, solution to their problems.' In Meiji times, an illicit love affair could have led to the death of both parties, but certainly to the death of the woman. Modern attitudes are less severe but still censorious, driven, Ōba writes, by the family system and rooted in agricultural practice, which requires co-operation for survival. These two structures stifle individuality: 'When the social structure becomes so rigid that the individual chooses death rather than existence within the system, then that system has lost its original function' (p. 347). The double suicide is an act of inverse rebellion, a protest – and a curse – against society.

Ōba examines the close relation between oppressor and oppressed, locating the killing pressure placed on lovers in the heavy responsibility held by the male head of family and the inferior status of women that accompanies this male prerogative: 'He bears the burden of "protecting" women, as they are not expected to live an equal, independent existence. A system that requires one to destroy his own individuality also tends to sanction destruction of the individuality of others' (p. 348).

In the continuance of double love suicides in Japan, Ōba sees evidence of 'the silent pressure that the system exerts on the consciousness of the Japanese people, continuing to smother the growth of individuality ... The old concepts remain deeply embedded in the hearts of the people, who continue to identify themselves with family and group' (p. 349). She concludes that the values of a society that necessitate such a desperate mode of self-expression 'should be of deep public concern.' Ōba's hard-hitting polemic against unwarranted social pressure on the individual is as direct as her fiction is subtle.

Award-winning novelist, biographer, and essayist Harumi Setouchi (b. 1922) was born to a progressive mother who admired Margaret Sanger, practised birth control in her own family, and believed that women should be economically independent. Her father was a tolerant man, and despite the opposition of relatives she entered Tokyo Women's University in 1940. This was the only university open to women before 1945. Like Ōba, Setouchi was exposed to foreign culture as a young adult, when she married and joined her husband in Beijing during the last three years of the war. The couple returned to Japan in 1945 and the marriage fell apart, ending in a divorce in 1950. Setouchi was forced to leave their only child with her former husband to be raised by another woman. An early and precocious reader and a prolific writer, by 1987 Setouchi had written more than thirty full-length novels, fifty short stories, and numerous essays.

In 1973 she startled her readers by taking Buddhist vows, and now lives in Kyoto as a Tendai-sect nun while continuing to write.[28] Jakucho, her Buddhist name, means 'listen deeply to stillness.' Despite taking the tonsure proper to a Buddhist nun or priest and wearing a habit, Jakucho wears no coif, unlike a Western nun. The effect is startling. With her bright eyes, wide smile, confident expression, and lively manner, Jakucho strongly projects vitality and youthfulness.

I saw her first seated at the front of her own small temple adjoining her home. The temple's single large room was filled with women students seated on tatami at low desks. The women were copying the sutras, Buddhist scriptures, as an avenue to psychological and spiritual peace. Jakucho later told me that she wrote *with* the students, to encourage them. Some were troubled, some were considering becoming nuns. Jakucho provides counselling. She herself had entered religious life in order to understand the problems of her society and, especially, the problems of women within it. She said she was disturbed by her society's refusal to understand that men and women are of equal value.

We began by talking of *Seitō*, the journal that gave voice to the first Japanese women's movement for liberation and one that interests Jakucho strongly.[29] Her biography of Toshiko Tamura (b. 1884), a member of the Seitōsha and contributor to *Seitō*, is also a history of this group, which Jakucho believes has been central to women's progress in Japan. Tamura was the first Japanese professional writer, the first to be able to earn her living by writing, and thus, to Jakucho, an important role model. She also admires, and quoted to me, Haruko Hiratsuka, better known as Raichō, the woman whose famous manifesto begins, 'In the Beginning Woman was the Sun.'[30] I moved on to my usual question put to Japanese women writers:

MORLEY   Are you very conscious of being a woman in a male-dominated society?

JAKUCHO   There is no distinction between men and women; we are all humans. However, as Simone de Beauvoir said, she was born as a human being but raised as a woman. I was born female into Japanese society in 1922, and this meant having a large handicap when compared with men, even though I have self-confidence. Even today, which is called the age of women writers, you can open any magazine and see how few women writers are included.

MORLEY   And very few have been translated.

JAKUCHO   Yes, only a few ...

MORLEY   Do your perceptions differ from a man's?

JAKUCHO   Yes. Women are more sensitive. As an example, just look at the sensitive perceptions made by Shikibu Murasaki in *The Tale of Genji* ...

MORLEY   What are your recurring themes? And have they changed since you entered the religious life?

JAKUCHO   A hard question. In today's Japan, and in my lifespan, women have experienced many restrictions. I felt these contradictions strongly. Further, I think that what humans desire most is freedom. It can be a freedom of spirit or mind ... Everything is futile without love. Buddhism teaches that there is *katsu ai* (thirst love) and *jihi* (mercy, compassionate love). They correspond to eros and agape in Christianity. Thirst love causes suffering, but enables us to move towards compassion. I write about this ... After entering the religious life I realized that we exist under some superior Being outside ourselves ... Novels are about human beings. If we think about humans hard enough, we end up in religion ...

MORLEY One critic wrote that Japanese women have a tendency towards masochism. Do you think so?

JAKUCHO No. Not masochism. In the past Japanese women were put in miserable situations, but they did not choose to suffer.[31]

Jakucho, or Setouchi, is known as a feminist writer, although her writings address a broad range of problems and situations. She has written many biographical novels about prominent figures in the Japanese women's liberation movement, along with a few auto-biographical novels, a popular genre. Setouchi's more recent works draw on the lives of famous Buddhist monks. With her spiritual passion, emotional depth, and strong concern for women's welfare, Setouchi is a powerful voice in contemporary Japanese writing.

Unlike several of the women writers examined here, Ayako Sono (b. 1931) does not see herself as an outsider. Born into a wealthy, cultured family and having married into a similar atmosphere, Sono is an insider to Tokyo's social and intellectual elite.[32] At the start of her career in the early 1950s, Sono was called 'a mademoiselle writer,' meaning an attractive young woman of fashionable appearance who seemed to 'have everything.' Her early story, 'The Guests from Afar,' was nominated for the Akutagawa Literary Award in 1954. It did not win but earned her the reputation of

Writer Ayako Sono at her home in Tokyo, 1986.

being the first young woman writer to appear in the literary world after the war.

Behind the elegant façade lay a Catholic faith, a keen interest in spiritual matters, and perhaps an experience of emotional insecurity that allowed her to empathize with the tragic figure of Marilyn Monroe. Sono uses the American actor's life story to portray the fictional experience and problems of an insomniac Japanese woman actor.[33]

Like Ōba, Sono married a man who readily agreed that she should have time to write. She told me that when they married he said to her, 'First read the book. Then, if there's time, clean the room. Reading comes first.' She enjoys what she calls 'a perfectly equal relationship,' and is *not* conscious of seeing through women's eyes: 'I am conscious only of my individuality,' she said. Much of our talk was conducted in English.[34] Sono emphasized that she was free to travel, and 'quite free' in all matters. Her extensive travels have played a prominent part in her writing.

When asked if she wrote for others or for herself, Sono replied 'For others' but then added, 'We Japanese writers write for ourselves, because we don't *know* our readers.' Sono has not been influenced by women writers but acknowledges the influence of Osamu Dazai, Graham Greene, Oscar Wilde, and Somerset Maugham. In general, her writing is anomalous within the body of writing by Japanese women, yet in the story 'Fuji' her portrait of the lonely and resentful young wife is strong and memorable, while the novel that draws on the experience of Marilyn Monroe skilfully reveals, in the words of one critic, 'the throes of a woman who cannot balance what her physical beauty brings with her inner needs.'[35]

Yasuko Harada (b. 1928) represents the fourth generation of the Honshū pioneers who came to settle and develop Hokkaido in the late nineteenth century. Like Ōba and Sono, Harada's husband accepted his wife's calling at the start of their relationship: 'I married him on condition that I would be allowed to write novels.' When we talked in Sapporo in 1986, Harada showed very little awareness of herself as a woman writer and no conscious concern for women's issues, yet her first novel, *Banka* (An elegy), was wildly popular with young women in their twenties and thirties and sold more than 2,000,000 copies.[36]

MORLEY When did you start writing?

HARADA I was about twenty years old.

MORLEY Are you very conscious of being a woman in a society run by men?

HARADA No. But I think that women before and after the war are different in their views. Our society has changed drastically since the war, but because I was born and grew up in Hokkaido, I don't think I really became aware of the changes and differences or aware of being a woman.

MORLEY What did you do after the war?

HARADA I was seventeen when it ended. Because of the confusion of post-war society, I couldn't go back to school or find a job right away. I helped in our house for a time, but soon I started working for a local newspaper in Kushiro [Hokkaido's third-largest city]. Working for the paper taught me a great deal about politics and economics in a male-dominated society, mainly on the local level. It was hard to be a woman working for men in a male-dominated company.

MORLEY Then I'm puzzled by your earlier answer.

HARADA When I was a reporter in a man's world, of course I was very conscious of being a woman. But now I work at home, it's a different environment. My husband is understanding and I don't need to be conscious of being a woman.

Harada offered another paradox when she said, 'The experience of working as a housewife and mother can be a very precious resource for a writer,' only to add, almost immediately, 'My life has been rather peaceful, and this may not have been helpful for my writing career.'

MORLEY What are your typical themes?

HARADA Relationships between men and women ... I also write about vulnerable people. I was physically weak myself, just like the heroine in *Banka*.

MORLEY I'm interested in your reference to vulnerability.

HARADA I've written about the shattered postwar society, people's poverty and vulnerability. Not just women. The war shattered us all. I've expressed my protest and my defiance of society in my writing. I recovered my own strength with time, and through writing ... I usually try to express my thoughts in humorous and indirect ways, full of droll expressions.[37]

Harada's bestseller features a love triangle. Reiko, the twenty-three-year-old heroine, falls in love with an architect, then becomes fascinated by his beautiful wife, a maternal figure. The wife eventually commits suicide. A critic writes: 'Behind the phenomenal popularity of *An Elegy* [Banka] in postwar Japan lies the almost fifteen hundred years of subjugation of Japanese women, which lasted till 1945. Reiko is a model "new woman" for the postwar generation. She breaks taboos on all fronts, destroys every conventional image of Japanese women so far depicted in Japanese literature.'[38]

Male readers were annoyed by the depiction of a carefree, egotistical, rather devilish young woman manipulating an established man in his late thirties and eventually refusing his offer of marriage. Harada's story 'Evening Bells,' her only other work in English, also offers a new image of a young, unmarried woman in postwar Japan.[39]

Ayako Miura (b. 1922), another northerner, is a spiritual seeker who found her rock in Protestant Christianity. In *The Wind Is Howling*, a powerful autobiography, Miura describes herself as follows: 'My emotional nature is such that I cannot live without a deep, spiritual love ... I have nurtured folly and evil and yet I cannot give up my yearning for purity. I'm a romanticist ... with great faith in mankind.'[40]

We talked in a quiet restaurant in Asahikawa City, Hokkaido, where Miura grew up and continues to live. The area is famous for its weaving,

and Miura wore a beautiful hand-woven rust-red jacket made locally. Physically frail after suffering from many illnesses over her lifetime, Miura projects spiritual calm and strength. Like other Japanese women writers, she sees men and women as 'basically equal as humans.' She also views men and women as equal emotionally, equally sinful, and equally in need of love.

Her awareness of, or interest in, the unequal treatment of women in society is negligible, perhaps because of a very happy marriage. Her husband, Mitsuyo Miura ('such a wonderful man'), has been strongly supportive. Throughout their marriage he has been her secretary and business partner, handling the large body of paperwork that arises from a very successful writing career. When she became physically unable to write, he took dictation. He helped to translate as we talked. Despite Miura's

Ayako Miura of Hokkaido is a popular and prolific writer. Well-known works include her autobiography, *The Wind Is Howling*, the story of her inner journey to Christian faith, and the novel *Shiokari Pass*. Courtesy of Ayako Miura.

disinterest in women's social conditioning, her views are inherently political and indirectly feminist, since she takes for granted that men and women are created equal. This belief, along with the companion concept that every individual is important and valuable, has been foreign to Japanese society but is strongly confirmed by its women writers.

During the war Miura, *née* Ayako Hotta, served as a primary school teacher in Asahikawa: 'I was sixteen when I started to teach. Then the war ended and there was a change, a big change. I felt so guilty about teaching in a militaristic system and became a nihilist.'[41] Miura had believed implicitly in wartime propaganda for a 'holy war' in the Pacific. After the unconditional surrender, as Miura watched her young students obediently crossing out all 'patriotic' lines in the ethics textbook, she felt that she could no longer continue teaching.

She puts it this way in her autobiography, *The Wind Is Howling*: 'Were the corrected textbooks right, or had they been right before? No one had a clear answer ... If I had been wrong, I should apologize on my knees to the children. Indeed, in the circumstances, just as soldiers committed suicide after the surrender, so we teachers should apologise to the children by taking our own lives ... I was constantly filled with shame and regret that, under the guise of being a good teacher, I might have taught error' (pp. 15-6).

Three months later Miura developed tuberculosis in the lungs, an illness that would dominate her next decade, leading her into despair and, eventually, Christian faith. Over a lifetime she has suffered from innumerable health problems and is currently fighting cancer. For over thirty years, beginning at the age of forty, she has continued to write:

MORLEY How many books have you published?
MIURA About fifty in all. Some forty novels, along with memoirs and essays.
   I began to write late. Before that I wrote love letters.
MORLEY What are your recurring themes?
MIURA Original sin, and hardships, the themes found in the Book of Job in
   the Old Testament. The problem of why we suffer. Loneliness, egotism,
   self-sacrifice ... Sometimes bitterness towards humans and their sins.

Miura suspected that the Christian elements in her work have made it less popular for translation into English. In Korea and Taiwan, where churches are strong, all of her work has been translated into local languages. Like Seiko Tanabe and Minako Ōba, Miura relies strongly on humour. She defines this quality as kindness, tenderness, 'a kind of love.'

Her best known novel is *Shiokari Pass*, based on the true story of a high-ranking railway employee, Masao Nagano, who sacrificed his own life to save the passengers on a coach with a broken coupling on a mountain pass.[42] A quotation from John 12.24 stands as epigraph to the novel: 'Unless a grain of wheat falls into the earth and dies, it remains alone; but if it dies, it bears much fruit.' Of *Shiokari Pass* Michiko Wilson writes: 'Miura tackles the now unfashionable concept of *gisei* (sacrifice) in contemporary Japanese society. The theme is a daring one – sacrifice of one's own life to save the lives of fellow countrymen. It challenges the traditional Japanese notion of ritual death, which occurs only to clear one's name or to avenge one's master. Renewal in death as in the case of Jesus Christ's sacrificial death for humankind or the idea that the old must die to make way for the new has never been dominant in Japanese culture.'[43] Miura's message of reconciliation is helping to promote understanding between the sexes in Japan.

During Japan's first two postwar decades, many women born in the late 1920s and '30s made impressive literary debuts. Women writers have again become part of mainstream Japanese literature, as they were in the classical period best known for its women diarists and Lady Murasaki's masterwork, *The Tale of Genji*. Chieko Mulhern notes that the rate of Japanese women writers' success has accelerated 'to the extent that women have won fully a half, if not more, of the leading literary awards in the last twenty years.'[44] Japanese women writers are gradually becoming known abroad, and their writings are taking their place, as well they should, among international literary works of permanent value. These writers, to borrow Tsushima's evocative image, are silent traders, masters of the art of indirection. They offer their readers shrewd and creative portraits of Japanese life that cannot be ignored.

As Minako Ōba observes, Japanese literature in the Man'yō age, over 1,000 years ago, shows that readers at that time 'preferred women with wit, a sense of humour and a touch of impetuosity, who conversed with men on an equal footing.'[45] Japanese society is coming full circle in this regard.

CHAPTER 11

BECOMING THE FLAG: THE TWENTY-FIRST CENTURY IS WOMAN'S TIME

Up on the roof
I'll stand until
I become the flag,
Knowing
Tomorrow will come.

MOTOKO MICHIURA, *A Long Rainy Season: Haiku and Tanka*

If you give birth
give birth to the world –
buds bursting
in the fresh green
woods.

EI AKITSU, *A Long Rainy Season: Haiku and Tanka*

SINCE THE RISING-SUN FLAG OF JAPAN has long been used as the archetypal symbol of the nation, Motoko Michiura's image of women *becoming* the flag is a powerful one, as resonant as Akiko Yosano's startling portrait of a sleeping mountain awakening to blaze with fire. There are no gender roles for flags. Psychological changes may be as irreversible as giving birth, or giving birth to the world, the image chosen by Ei Akitsu to suggest the power of women within global society and the environment, the planet on which we all depend. In Japan, working patterns, politics, education, family patterns, and human relationships are all in flux, as are the concepts of roles best suited to women and men.

Early in 1993, an event of great potential significance to Japan took place when Crown Prince Naruhito, the future emperor, married Masako Owada, diplomat and commoner. The prince had wooed his bride over six years. Owada's awareness of what her decision would mean was expressed in a card sent to her parents before the last Christmas they would spend together. She thanked them for raising her in a warm and happy family and added, 'Tough times are waiting for us, but I hope we get through.'[1]

The marriage, which was vastly popular, symbolized the union of two worlds, one ancient and archconservative, the other modern and international. Owada, whose father's diplomatic career had led her to attend an American high school and encouraged her to become fluent in five languages, is a graduate of Harvard, the University of Tokyo, and Oxford. Prior to her engagement she was a rising star in the prestigious North American division of the Ministry of Foreign Affairs and an active trade negotiator with the United States.

Her choice, to marry the crown prince, meant that her life would be ruled by members of the Imperial Household Agency, guardians of the imperial image that symbolizes the union of state and people. If she is not strong, says writer and intellectual Shuichi Kato, 'she will be their puppet. They will orchestrate her every move for the rest of her life.'[2] Owada may have negotiated a degree of freedom before taking the plunge. At the press conference to announce the engagement, she told reporters that the prince had told her, 'You might have fears and worries about joining the imperial household. But I will protect you for my entire life' (pp. 34-5). Such strong words suggest that Owada will have freedoms not enjoyed by previous empresses.

Her acceptance letter to the prince, in December 1992, was more forceful than it might appear to Western eyes. Along with accepting, 'humbly,' and promising him her support, Owada added that she would work not only to make him happy but also to 'be able to look back on my life and think, "It was a good life."'[3] Martha Duffy observes that Owada had dared to say in public that she sought fulfilment on her own terms, that she had legitimate expectations for her life.

Not everyone was pleased at the marriage. Some conservatives – mostly men – found Owada pushy, presumptuous, unwomanly, simply because she had spoken to the press herself instead of leaving *all* remarks to be made by the prince.[4] Older men in general remain oblivious to the career desires of younger women. Many working women were horrified and depressed, fearing that Owada had surrendered to pressure from the powerful imperial system and would be 'wasting her talent.'[5] Women noted her change in dress style (from dark suits and bright scarves to pastels with white gloves) and in body language.[6]

The more balanced and optimistic view, held by both women and men, is that as the wife of the crown prince and eventually as empress,

Owada will have a chance to help open up a closed world. As writer Yoshimi Ishikawa puts it, 'if Masako Owada can make a good bridge between the [Imperial] family and the people, maybe we can create a new era of Japanese history.'[7] While some Japanese women continue to debate whether Owada's decision was an advance or a setback for their sex, others feel certain that she will be able to hasten change.

Masako Owada remains an enigmatic and attractive figure, both powerful and sacrificial. I suspect that not even the Imperial Household Agency will be able to dampen habits of independence and participation nurtured for twenty-nine years before marriage. And why, we should ask, was the prince attracted, at the age of thirty-three, to such a modern, vigorous, and self-reliant woman? Through his choice of wife he has made his own blow for freedom from the system in which these two find themselves. I cannot help but think that the marriage bodes well for Japan and for Japanese women.

The '90s have been hard years for many Japanese, and particularly harsh for women. Difficult choices have been par for the course. By 1995, the country had faced four years of nearly zero economic growth, its longest slump since the end of the war. Amid rising unemployment, excess production capacity, and a mountain of bad debt held by Japanese banks, bureaucrats held firmly onto the web of constricting regulations that hamper business. Three major shocks – the Great Hanshin Earthquake, the poison gas attack on a Tokyo subway by members of the Aum Shinrikyō cult, and the *endaka*, or high yen – induced a general atmosphere of gloom and doom. The Japanese economy still found itself in a severe recession through 1998.

The slow advances made by Japanese women workers in the 1980s ground to a halt when 'the bubble burst.' Unrestrained real estate speculation combined with changing international conditions led to a radically different economic climate. North American companies have also been forced to lay off workers, but their cuts have generally been distributed evenly among male and female employees. Japanese employers have cut back drastically on new female recruits despite the fact that the period between the end of formal education and the beginning of marriage has traditionally been the time when women are most welcome in the work force and least likely to suffer discrimination in pay and benefits.

Employment prospects in 1994 were called glacial; women termed it an ice age. Since the situation in 1995 was 'even more difficult,' according to university job placement workers, it was termed 'super glacial.' Women were frozen out of the process at the very beginning, their requests for information and application materials frequently left unanswered. In recent years, many young women shut out from employment at the critical stage after university have been frustrated and angry.[8] Despite tough times in the economy, however, the rates for male hiring remained steady in the early 1990s. There were forty-five job openings available for every 100 women job seekers in 1995, as opposed to 133 openings for every 100 males.[9] 'In other words, sexual discrimination remains a fact of life in the job market.'[10]

The situation has evoked the standard excuses from management. A spokesperson for Osaka Gas Company said that women are more likely to quit a job early to marry or raise children. He spoke as if the company intended to place all new women employees in the career track. Akemi Nakamura exposed the hypocrisy: 'In fact, only four of the sixty female workers hired for men's jobs have quit the gas company over the past nine years.'[11] Many Japanese companies have actively encouraged female employees to quit jobs after marrying or having a child. Nakamura quotes an Osaka University senior, a member of Osaka Female Students Association Protesting the Job Shortage, as saying that companies should improve conditions so that women are able to work after marrying and having a child. The title of this undergraduate association speaks volumes.

Not only the practice of lifetime employment for men in large companies but even that of hiring pretty young women to serve tea and 'beautify' the office is being abandoned by companies eager to cut staff. A professor at the prestigious Keio University points out that clerical jobs for young women are threatened by technological changes in the workplace. Moreover, vacancies are fewer because more women are staying on after marriage: a neat irony.[12]

Keiko Fukuzawa stresses that a company decision not to hire for clerical positions (*ippan shoku*) is really a decision not to hire women. Such positions were dramatically slashed in 1994: 'While in theory the division is gender-free, clerical positions are filled almost entirely by women and management-track positions almost entirely by men with a few token women.'[13]

In Japan, job hunting has traditionally been carried on only once a year, in the months prior to graduation. Timing and procedures are strictly regulated. Hard times, however, have changed the rules of the game for many students, and some now begin their search earlier. As well, women students from less prestigious institutions are attempting to extract information from the job placement offices of more privileged and hence better informed schools.

Women are well aware of the discrimination practised against them. They know that companies are sending two entirely different application packets to men and women: 'What men get is really thick, and what women get is really thin. If this is not a violation of the law, what is?' (p. 158). A job placement officer admits that 'the recession has really pushed to the surface all those discriminations that were not so obvious before: your gender, your school, your major, and how well you are connected.'[14]

Furious with such treatment, senior women students of Tokyo University of Agriculture took to the streets with banners reading 'Don't discriminate against women students' and 'Stop sexual harassment questions.' The latter refers to personal remarks during job interviews, a common experience for Japanese women. The protest march led to the Ministry of Labour, where angry women presented their complaints to the minister.[15]

For discrimination in hiring practices it would be difficult to beat the following story, taken from a letter to the editor of a major newspaper in 1995. A group of university seniors, women who had succeeded in getting job interviews, were told by a company official that women candidates were doing 'far better' than men in the written test. As a result, 'the company set a higher pass mark for women so that male applicants could have a chance to be interviewed as well. Moreover, the official said that the women applicants had better academic records.'[16] The writer called the situation 'outrageous,' and added: 'Why is it that society still thinks that the role of women after marriage is to do household chores and care for children? We women have changed.'

Thirty or forty years earlier, a working woman's simple expectation of equal treatment was termed 'outrageous' by male bosses, and such incidents would rarely have become public. Pioneer journalist Reiko Masuda (b. 1929) has good reason for her belief that male chauvinism and patriarchy from the prewar era persist in modern Japan. After graduating from university, Masuda landed a job at the *Mainichi Shinbun* in 1953 as one of the country's first university graduate female reporters. She became the first female editorial writer at a major newspaper and the first woman to win the Japan National Press Club award. She and her husband, also a reporter, were forced to live separately for nine years due to his job transfer.[17]

When Masuda asked her editor why she was never given assignments involving business trips, he asked what she would do about her husband's meals while she was away. Another editor told her that not accompanying her husband on his transfer was 'outrageous' behaviour, and some people, 'mostly men,' told Masuda that her not having children was 'not ethical.' These were the prevailing attitudes of the 1950s and '60s. Masuda chose not to have children in order to show that a woman could fulfil a newspaper career until retirement. She notes that the 1991 Maternal Leave Law was enacted only after the so-called '1.57 shock' drew attention to the falling birth rate. She credits *gaiatsu*, or foreign pressure, with helping to improve problems of sexual discrimination.

The anger that such practices are provoking among women is stronger nowadays, and perceptions are more polarized. Many women are aware that even if they manage to obtain management-track positions, their workload will be as heavy as men's but their paycheques smaller. Yuko Suzuki, an historian specializing in the modern history of Japanese women, finds that the patriarchal thinking of prewar days, when women were 'domestic slaves' with no autonomy, is still strong in modern Japan. The system in which women work only to complement domestic finances and not as independent breadwinners remains. Suzuki views women's issues as human rights issues. The conviction that their rights are being violated has been heard increasingly in Japan in recent years as women take long, hard looks at their society and their personal aspirations.

Sociologist Yumiko Ehara, also a specialist in women's issues, locates a hardening of Japan's current discriminatory labour structure in the war years, when each sex had its own sacrificial role to play. After the war, during the period of rapid economic growth, a similar mentality was nurtured by the government: 'Men risked their lives for their companies and women were enslaved at home.' Without changes to this basic thinking, Ehara expects sexual discrimination to continue. Women who manage to enter the male-dominated business world will be forced to submit to an inhuman lifestyle, along with prejudice and limited opportunities. If they opt out, it will be used against them and other women.[18]

Mistrust of companies, as Fukuzawa notes, runs deep. Some women, knowing the hazards of corporate stress and the incompatibility of management-track work with marriage, would still prefer to be clerks. Surprisingly, a government report released in 1992 disclosed that 74.5 percent of single women claimed they did not care that they were unmarried. Even allowing for bravado and for a range of ages at the time when opinions were recorded, this is an extraordinary figure. Ambitious women are finding work overseas or enrolling for postgraduate studies.[19]

Fukuzawa sees four possible work styles for women in the future. The first is a short, labour-intensive career, probably in sales, a job they will leave to marry or have children. The second is professional work in law, medicine, or higher education. The third is a role as 'corporate warriors,' women working like men and sacrificing personal life to the job. The fourth option is 'spinout,' in which women use skills and contacts from earlier jobs to start their own businesses. Fukuzawa seems to consider the clerical work that has occupied two generations of young Japanese women between school and marriage to be a thing of the past. She believes that its loss will, out of sheer necessity, force women to change their outlook on work and to develop more long-term career prospects.[20] It is significant that this specialist in women's employment issues does not anticipate shorter work hours, which would enable Japanese women to combine management work with a family life, as Western women have been able to do.

Starting one's own business is not easy for a woman in Japan. The president of Dentsu-Eye, a subsidiary of advertising giant Dentsu, is one of a handful of the country's top female executives. Naoe Wakita describes every day as a battle for women in the Japanese working environment, where 'prejudice against women is still very apparent.'[21] Wakita, who carved out a niche market from her parent company, is a member of Leadership 111, a networking and support group of female leaders in the corporate, academic, and media sectors. She notes that male and female management and work styles differ, that women managers are likely to value the individual abilities of each person while the typical male manager is very conscious of rank and position. As well, women are more likely to give opinions based on their personal knowledge. Wakita is now sharing her experience by teaching part time at Sophia University.

Japanese women's determination to change conditions in the workplace was plain at the fourth World Conference on Women, held in Beijing in September 1995 in conjunction with the Non-Governmental Organizations (NGO) Forum. With no women in the Cabinet of Prime Minister Tomiichi Murayama after a shuffle just prior to the conference, it was not surprising that seven out of the ten Japanese delegates to this United Nations conference were men.[22] Between 5,000 and 6,000 Japanese women, however, were active participants in the parallel NGO Forum.

Just prior to the conference, the 1995 U.N. *Human Development Report* was published, with indices measuring human development, gender-related development, and women's participation in political and economic fields. Japan ranked third in income and education levels, after Canada and the United States, and eighth in gendered discrepancies in education and earnings (the number one spot having the smallest discrepancy). In the new index measuring women's participation in political and economic spheres, the country placed an embarrassing twenty-seventh.[23] In most countries, educating women is the key to economic growth. Japan is the anomaly, where women are highly educated but typically barred from making full use of their education in economic and political fields.

Also on the eve of the conference, Upper House member Mayumi Moriyama, one of the women who represented Japan at the World Conference on Women in Nairobi in 1985, spoke of the enormous gains made by women in the last decade. She called the enactment of the Equal Employment Opportunity Law in 1986 an epoch-making event that had led to 'many' women working in government and private-sector offices. When critics countered by calling the EEO Law tokenism and 'a farce,' since it lacked punitive measures for employers who disregarded it, Moriyama insisted that even the *idea* that men and women should be given equal opportunities was 'practically non-existent' before 1986. She noted that women were first admitted to the National Defense Academy only in 1992 and that women pilots, truck drivers, and crane operators were all new 'in the last ten years or so.' By 1995, she believed, the mountain had moved.

Moriyama's most convincing argument for change lay in her personal experience. As a guest at weddings in recent years, she had found that the bride almost always intended to continue to work after marriage and that her employer 'invariably asks in his speech that the husband cooperate so that she can continue to work.' Such speeches at weddings, Moriyama observed, were non-existent ten years ago.

At the NGO Forum near Beijing, the practices of the past and the spirit of the future were represented by seven women who worked for Sumitomo-affiliated companies. They spoke on behalf of many Japanese women. Kiyoko Kitagawa began to work for Sumitomo Metal in 1960. When she married in 1965, she became the first woman in company history to resist the attempt to make her resign. For some years she was frozen out of office work, but she persisted. When she had a son, her boss told her that even cats and dogs raised their own offspring and that by having her child cared for by others she was 'even beneath' these animals. Like many innovative women in the 1960s and '70s, Kitagawa and other women workers joined to create their own nursery. Since 1985 she has been in charge of training women employees, a task that has won her in-house awards.

When Kitagawa learned, however, that her male assistant, eight years her junior, was earning more than ¥2,000,000 more than she was annually, she and other women took their outrage to the United Nations. They are currently suing their employers and the government for wage discrimination and back pay totalling (for the group) nearly ¥500,000,000. Such legal action is new.

Chieko Ichino, another delegate in the Sumitomo group, told the NGO Forum that women are promoted much more slowly than men so that their incomes average half those of men. The recent legal action was prompted by the reluctance of companies and labour unions to resolve the issue. The Sumitomo group was preparing a report for the forum on how Japanese companies treat women employees.[24]

If the mountain is male resistance and patriarchal traditions, the lava of women's anger and dissatisfaction is flowing in the 1990s. The conference emphasized, more strongly than before, that women's rights are human rights.

Some Japanese men support fair treatment for women in the workplace. Norikazu Bito also attended the NGO Forum to oppose job discrimination based on age and sex rather than ability. This bank employee from Nagoya called the EEO Law of 1986 tokenism. He suggested that a few men are afraid to speak up against unfair policies for fear of damaging their career prospects but that many still believed in role divisions for men and women.[25] Bito's wife had met with the same kind of treatment encountered by the Sumitomo workers, including an attempt to force her resignation by transferring Bito to a distant branch. He noted that even women in so-called career-track jobs are required to serve tea and do other menial tasks, were not given the same training as men, and were passed over for promotion. Men – at least some men – are now finding that fair treatment for women workers is a matter of self-interest.

The 1995 World Conference on Women also drew attention to Japanese women's representation in politics. The Inter-Parliamentary Union (IPU), an international organization of legislators, put out a report just prior to the conference that showed Japan's ratio of women legislators to the total to be the lowest among the twenty-five advanced nations in the Organization for Economic Cooperation and Development (OECD).[26] Indeed, the IPU survey of 176 countries with parliaments ranked Japan 144th for its proportion of female legislators, a mere 2.7 percent.[27] The figure is as low as those in Islamic nations and has actually regressed since 1946.

An independent assembly member from Chiba Prefecture told the NGO Forum that women generally knew much more about their own cities and towns than men did and voters were becoming aware that women were appropriate to represent them. Since the LDP lost power in 1993, it has been easier for women to enter politics. They can now run as independents or in non-conservative parties such as the Social Democratic Party of Japan (SDPJ) and the Japan Communist Party, which have traditionally supported women's causes. A few widows won seats that had been held by their husbands. Constituencies are often kept in the family, usually by being handed down from father to son.

By 1995, thirty-five of the 252 members of the Diet's Upper House (13.8 percent) were women. In the more powerful Lower House there were twelve women among 500 members (2.4 percent). In prefectural, city, town, and village assemblies, women held 3.5 percent of the 64,428 seats in the country in 1994.[28] This tiny number is more than triple the 1976 figure. As

Mayo Issobe notes, the going for women in politics is slow and uneven. The statistics mock the 1985 UN target of 30 percent for women executive and legislative decision makers by 1995, a goal agreed to by Japan.

Women have seemed poised to take their place in politics during two periods in Japanese history: one just after the war, when women won suffrage and took 8.4 percent of elected seats; and one in 1989, when women won twenty-two seats in the Upper House, a record at the time. Many belonged to the SDPJ, headed by Takako Doi. Doi actively encouraged women to run as candidates, and their success in 1989 was dubbed the 'Madonna boom.'

The July 1995 elections of the Upper House saw many women running but fewer elected. When Prime Minister Murayama shuffled his Cabinet and failed to include a woman, he was roundly condemned by women assembly members.[29] Recently, the power of women has lain in provincial and local assemblies and with the increased political awareness of women voters. There have been more women candidates in recent elections and their appeal to women voters is direct, with slogans such as 'One step by women changes society.'

Given the rising political consciousness of women, the setback in the 1995 elections shows only that change is never easy in Japan. Letters to the editor in major newspapers are frequently from women, and the writing is often forceful, even passionate. The writers do not sound like women who might be easily discouraged. One thirty-four-year-old housewife wrote about the tiny percentage of women in the Diet and among high-ranking national civil servants:

> That corresponds to the kind of animated video dramas our generation was brought up on. We were accustomed to a cast of several heroes and one heroine and didn't question it. Likewise, when I was an OL, our company team would add one girl as a 'flower,' not to make the team stronger. That time has ended. My daughters are absorbed in a drama, *Sailor Moon*, in which girls are the majority and are the stronger characters. I hope that ten or twenty years from now the little girls absorbed in this program will enter a society in which men and women are about fifty/fifty.[30]

What gives this woman her quiet and impressive confidence?

Women's obvious desire to enter business and politics and take what they increasingly see as their rightful place is linked to two trends that go back to the 1970s. Women are marrying later and having fewer children. The 1990s has been called an age of marriage moratorium. The trend to later marriage began in the mid-1970s. Until 1973 the statistics were relatively stable, with women tending to marry by the age of twenty-four and men by twenty-six. In 1974, average ages increased to 24.5 for women and 26.8 for men, and kept rising thereafter. The average age for men to marry has not changed since 1990, but that of women reached twenty-six for the first time in 1992 and rose to 26.1 in 1993.[31] Japan now has the second highest figures in the world for late marriages, just behind Sweden in first place.

Politicians, sociologists, and journalists all have their favourite theories to account for the phenomenon. One is that young Japanese now wish to develop their own individuality before marrying. A feature article in a woman's magazine in 1994 called late marriage the best guarantee for a successful one. A commonly cited reason for marrying is to gain independence from parents, since young Japanese of both sexes usually live with their parents before marriage. The leading theory advanced to explain late marriage is the increased economic power of young unmarried women, who no longer need a husband for economic support.[32] Since Japanese men seem to have retained their fathers' (and grandfathers') view of marriage while women have changed rapidly, the gap in perceptions is also a factor in the trend towards late marriages.

Women no longer accept entrenched attitudes of male superiority. And by the age of twenty-six, they are aware that if they marry they may lose their jobs and will be paid less when they return to the labour force. They know that the salaryman's utter dedication of time and energy to his company is made possible by the wife acting as sole caretaker for home, children, and relatives.[33] As for living singly, modern household appliances make housekeeping easier. In a 1994 poll, a large majority of both men and women respondents chose the answer, 'There are advantages to being single.'[34]

A complicating factor is a demographic imbalance in the population. There are more men than women in all age groups below the mid-forties. Women are in demand and can afford to wait. This has encouraged a related trend, namely marriages in which the bride is older than the groom. A man of thirty-one married to a woman three years older observes that after twenty-five, 'personality becomes the most important factor.' His wife, employed in the same firm, believes that she 'can handle both work and marriage, but [is] not too sure about raising kids.' Another couple, newly married in their late twenties, considers raising children 'an awesome responsibility.'[35] Late marriages, for many reasons, tend to lower the birth rate.

Women's determination to work outside the house and to continue working after marriage is clearly a factor in the trend of older women choosing younger men. In Japan, this relationship is compared with that of an older sister and younger brother. Working women consider younger men to be more flexible, less dogmatic, and willing to share the housework and cooking. A Tokyo woman of forty-six, married to a man twelve years her junior, says, 'A younger man is devoted and hardworking in everything and is beneficial for a working woman.'[36]

A woman of thirty-two married to a man of twenty-five described older men as 'cunning' and generally convinced of their own superiority: 'For a headstrong type like myself who wants to take the initiative, a younger man is more suitable.' A marriage dating service confirmed the trend that women in their thirties are generally seeking younger men. The bureau noted that the number of men who find it burdensome to be the sole breadwinner is increasing.[37] Young men, some young men, do seem to be changing.

Diet member Ichiro Ozawa points out the loss to the nation that follows from structural impediments to women's full participation in the permanent employment system and envisages an environment in which husbands could perform high-level work at home 'if we want to enable women to work outside the home more readily.'[38] While stressing the importance of women's work in the home, he acknowledges that women have had the worst of both worlds: 'We maintain obstacles against women who want to work outside the home, and at the same time depreciate the work women do at home.' Women are proud of the work they do at home and want freedom to choose their work and their roles.

Ozawa also notes that the civil service was originally intended to reflect the composition of the citizenry but has become overwhelmingly composed of males: 'Neither the bureaucracy nor the Diet reflect the population they serve' (p. 195). Some of Ozawa's proposals, such as pensions for housewives, sound utopian, but the conviction of this senior statesman that Japan's troubled economy *needs* women's full participation in the workplace cannot be ignored. American companies are finding that the practice of taking top management almost exclusively from white males is becoming a business liability in the '90s. Diversity can be a competitive weapon, and the sectors most open to women and minority managers are typically those with the fastest growth or the ones undergoing rapid change. Japan can no longer afford to ignore its economic need for diversity and creativity.[39]

Aired in 1994, Ozawa's ideas are gradually becoming mainstream. In the fall of 1997, an annual fiscal white paper subtitled 'Working Women – in Quest of a New Social System,' summed up many discriminatory company practices that working women have struggled to change, especially in recent years. The paper linked the multiple problems faced by working women, such as unpaid maternity leave and the shortage of nurseries, to the falling birth rate and the recent tendency of women to marry later. Thanks to the serious socioeconomic consequences of a low birth rate, women's demand for changes in many areas finally has the attention of the mandarins. The paper stressed the need for better social support for working mothers and urged companies to make the necessary changes.

Change is also under way in the country's education system, doubtless the strongest single formative influence in the entire culture. The conformity and passivity engendered by the rigid examination system have led critics to describe today's youth as a generation waiting for instructions (*shiji machi sedai*). The total control exercised by the Ministry of Education includes strict censorship of all textbooks. Changes in senior high school textbooks in the 1990s reflect a more permissive attitude on the part of the censors. History texts, for example, now include the Ainu, Japan's indigenous people. They explain how their 'unique culture' developed, the restrictive nature of the still-current Meiji-era law, and the ongoing struggle for a new law that will respect Ainu culture.

Recent language texts include profiles on women with international careers and commentaries on popular comics such as those by Osamu Tezuka and Sazae-san. The texts point to changes in family customs and attitudes that are more 'democratic and modern.'[40] They also discuss modern Japanese writers, although women writers are still largely ignored. Texts for the study of English describe the achievements of famous women in Japan, including mountaineer Junko Tabei, fashion designer Hanae Mori, college founder Umeko Tsuda, and violinist Midori Goto. They also mention international women achievers such as Burma's Nobel prizewinner Aung San Suu Kyi and American environmentalist Rachel Carson.

The current debate on school uniforms reflects differing views on the degree of independence to be nurtured in a system that has traditionally taught children to be members of a group. Uniforms are expensive, but parents in favour believe that they make children feel a part of the school family. School, they say, is a place of group life.[41] Opponents argue that uniforms make children reluctant to dress even a little differently and restrict their sense of self. Some parents reason that children need to recognize diversity and respect difference. A spokesperson for the Okayama Board of Education said, 'We are working on an education for the development of children's independence.'[42]

The severe bullying that is a feature of Japanese schools and that leads to hundreds of student suicides each year is closely connected with a culture that frowns on difference. Each new suicide by a bullied child prompts a rash of factual articles in the media with little or no analysis of underlying causes. Psychiatrist Masao Miyamoto of the Ministry of Health and

Welfare is the exception. As we saw earlier, he interprets this form of persecution of those who are weak or different as 'symbolic of Japanese culture.'[43] Harsh words.

This insider's portrait of the Tokyo ministries, with its revealing foreword by writer-director Juzo Itami, explains why the central bureaucrats are the 'de facto national leaders.' Itami's historical survey charts, step by step, the ways in which bureaucrats subverted the 1946 Constitution and took back powers that its framers intended to give to local jurisdictions.[44] A few additional clauses to the Cabinet Act and the Diet Act were 'sneaked through,' and these small changes, combined with the powers of interpretation, enabled postwar central bureaucrats to retain the powers their predecessors had acquired in the push to industrialization in the late nineteenth century. Thus a centralized control that was 'virtually dictatorial' continued after 1946 to shape the state capitalism that made possible the economic miracle of the next thirty years.

Miyamoto charges that Japanese society functions like a totalitarian country because bureaucratic control of all forms of power, including the legislative role of the Diet, is 'nearly absolute,' and open expression of critical thought is not tolerated without the entire group's approval (p. 22). As for the psychology of bullying, Miyamoto connects it with a national leaning towards masochism, evidenced in the *messhi hoko* philosophy of self-sacrifice for the sake of the group.

Japanese-style bullying, he argues, 'uses the threat of ostracism to attack people's deep psychology and arouse anxiety' (p. 146). He notes that bullying is despised in the West but condoned in Japan, among adults as well as children, as a legitimate method of enforcing conformity to group behaviour and values.[45] The Japan that seems to be emerging now, one more tolerant of diversity and individualism, may have less room for bullies. And more room for women's multifaceted talents and ambitions.

The adjective typically ascribed to individualism is 'Western,' and the phrase usually carries the suggestion of selfishness. Someone exhibiting unconventional behaviour may also be branded as unpatriotic, a hangover from the thought-control era before and during the war, even though Japanese social behaviour is increasingly individualistic, especially in the cities.[46] Masakazu Yamazaki, playing devil's advocate, argues that individualistic attitudes and strong personalities have played formative roles in developing Japan's arts and culture over many centuries. His examples include architectural features such as the *tokonoma*, arts such as *ikebana* and the tea ceremony, and the drama traditions of *nō* and *kyōgen*.[47]

This professor of Japanese culture and of modern Japanese intellectual history objects to the simplistic idea that group harmony and its corporate version, the *ie* society, dominate every aspect of society. Yamazaki distinguishes the 'rugged' individualism of Western culture from the 'gentle' individualism he locates in Japanese arts and customs from 1392 to 1868. By including the arts within social history, he shows that all classes in traditional Japanese society had room to develop lifestyles of their own. The militarism of the twentieth century fostered unity and labour loyalty, conditions that continued after the war under the strict controls wielded by the central government.

Yamazaki blames modernization for the loss of Japan's traditional individualism and the current overemphasis on hard work and organizational loyalty. He argues that all cultures share certain basic values derived from common precultural principles and that every society has a potential for both individual and collective expression. Yamazaki sees a nation ripe for the rebirth of individualism, as lifespans lengthen and tastes diversify. This move towards greater diversity is actually the recovery of the Japanese heritage.

A softening of gender stereotypes in the last ten years is one striking feature of the diversity now percolating in Japanese society. Strong-minded individuals of both sexes have begun to cross over what one writer calls 'the great divide' that has traditionally separated male and female activities. What sociologist Eiko Arai finds most exciting about today's Japan is that ordinary people are beginning to question conventional values. At the same time, her research shows 'just how deeply rooted male dominance is in Japanese society.'[48] The word 'housewife' (*okusan*), with its literal meaning of 'in the house,' carries the attitudes and expectations of centuries, yet her interviewees had shed this weight.

Arai's female subjects included a dumptruck driver, a taxi driver, a pilot, and a businesswoman who prefers boxing to aerobics and works out at a gym twice a week. The truck driver found her work more interesting than sales or office work, had good relations with male colleagues, and anticipated more female truck drivers soon. (Her only complaint was the washroom facilities.) The taxi driver felt lucky to have such a good job. Changes under the EEO Law of 1986 had made it possible for her to work at night. The pilot is the first woman to enter the Ministry of Transport's Civil Aviation College. After graduating she failed to find work with a major aviation company and now flies small planes for surveying and sightseeing. Ryo Odashima objects to being regarded as a special phenomenon and points out the obvious, that Japan lags behind other advanced nations in its attitude to women.[49] The boxer enjoys the contrast between her day job and her evening workout. These women illustrate Arai's observation that this is an age when women are full of vitality.

She had more difficulty locating men working in traditionally female jobs but found a nursery school teacher, a nurse, and a househusband. The nursery school teacher believed that 'everybody' should take part in child rearing. He said that men in his profession were no longer rare and that being an optimist and having a strong interest in people were prerequisites. The househusband, a former newspaper reporter, had turned his work of caring for twins into a newspaper serial, later a book, and is freelancing. He now considers 'absurd' something he once took for granted: the idea that 'a good newspaper reporter is too busy to pay much attention to his family.'

Arai points to numerous signs that gender stereotypes are changing, including trends to marry later, have fewer children, and remain unmarried unless the right partner comes along. Domestic science is now compulsory for boys as well as girls in high school. Yet women still experience difficulty in finding work, and many still subscribe to 'the great divide.' Arai hopes that both men and women will soon be free to choose their work without traditional constraints. Her hunch is that Japanese society is moving that way: 'In ten, twenty, thirty years from now, Japan may turn out to be a pretty nice place to live!'[50]

Greater diversity is the order of the day in Japan as elsewhere, pushed inexorably by changing economic conditions, and it is being urged by both male and female critics. Mariko Sugahara, head of Women's Affairs in the Prime Minister's Office, diagnoses 'an insidious ailment – a potentially lethal disorder,' which she calls 'the Japanese disease.'[51] The country is experiencing ills common to advanced industrial societies, but they are compounded by symptoms peculiar to Japan, especially the tendency to value the organization and to neglect or exploit the individuals whose work and sacrifice have made it strong. The same attitude has made employees excessively dependent, economically and emotionally, on their corporations. She sees extreme homogeneity and conformity, bred in schools and in companies. Many male managers lack the ability to communicate with anyone 'who does not share exactly the same set of assumptions or speak the same shorthand' (p. 71). All this has led to ingrown organizations that lack vitality and are failing in basic research – ills affecting the entire country. Sugahara also, however, points to a growing antiwork ethic in Japan, a reaction against the long work hours and unpaid overtime required to satisfy company expectations of 'limitless diligence.'

Sugahara's sharpest criticism is aimed at the waste of human resources that follows from society's failure to make full use of the talents of women and seniors. Housework is no longer a full-time occupation. Intensive child rearing in families with only one or two children is over in a decade or less. What women and seniors want, Sugahara argues, is the opportunity to put their skills to use for the good of society. Their talents will quicken corporate renewal and the restoration of civic morality. The latter, she finds, has taken a back seat to corporate profits since the war.

Some analysts call the pace of change in Japan dizzying. Chizuko Ueno, a professor of sociology and gender studies at the University of Tokyo, examines the breakdown of the modern family, the 'largely illusory construct of industrial society,' and posits a model for a new, non-traditional one. She argues that the modern family is on the brink of collapse 'because women's perceptions are developing well ahead of outmoded male assumptions.'[52]

Strong forces for change are found in the breakdown of the old system of lifetime employment, the trend to shorter working hours, and a big reduction in overtime pay. Much of the competition to win entrance to prestigious universities has been predicated on the now-dying lifetime employment system that rewarded the top examination winners. Competition for market share is causing serious friction with Japan's trading partners, and the high yen is prompting Japanese companies to move overseas. The latter practice could cost 1,000,000 jobs in the closing years of the 1990s. Some Japanese men are running scared. They are being challenged, indeed forced, to rethink their basic attitudes and way of life. One male writer calls conditions 'a wake-up call' for workers.[53]

The ending of the lifetime employment system for men has enormous repercussions for women. Of course they must live with the stress affecting their husbands. In addition, lifetime employment for men meant lifetime financial security for wives. Marriage was assumed to be a form of permanent employment for women. For tenured male workers, pay and benefits rose automatically with age and seniority. This system is ending, while divorce rates have been rising slowly for some years, including a now not uncommon pattern of women initiating divorce at the time their husbands receive their retirement bonuses. Women must begin to plan for economic independence. A woman professor of social science at the University of Tokyo writes that current conditions are forcing change on both sexes. Men can no longer take a helpful wife for granted, and those who are helpless in the house are ceasing to be considered normal.[54]

As the recession forces change, some of the fathers who previously worked late and golfed with clients on weekends are rediscovering their families. New magazines are targeting both parents and illustrated manuals show fathers how to parent. One manual shows how to start a campfire, skip stones, snap fingers, make sandcastles, and fly paper planes. Fathers now in their thirties were immersed in entrance exam battles as children and had little play experience.[55]

Surveys show the increasing value set on family, private lives, and individual satisfaction. Asked in 1993 what they considered most important to them, 42 percent said their families, up from 33 percent in the previous survey. It was also the first year that more than half the survey respondents gave family-related matters a high priority. As for the sex of an only child, 36 percent would prefer to have a girl, compared with 29 percent in 1988. Only 33 percent wanted a boy in 1993. Moreover, asked what sex they would choose to be if they could be born again six out of ten women wanted to be born as girls.[56]

The *tanshin funin* system of transferring workers to distant branch offices is under increasing scrutiny by workers and lawyers. Editorials are now promoting family rather than corporate rights, and a group called the National Network to Revise Industry's Rights over Personnel for the Benefit of the Family is lobbying the Diet for legislative support.[57]

Adult education centres reflect the country's changing mood. Male white-collar workers are taking courses in psychology and self-development, traditionally filled with women and seniors. Some are seeking self-discovery as a way to reduce work-related stress. Others have been motivated by courses to change careers. And more men are learning to cook. After having been told by mothers (and sometimes wives) that men don't enter the kitchen, they are enjoying all-male cooking classes and discovering, as one man put it, 'a wider world.' Some have been pushed by family circumstances, such as a wife's illness or a job transfer. Others are simply finding that cooking, like the study of psychology, can reduce stress and foster self-discovery.[58]

Gradually, Japanese men are becoming aware that greater diversity in women's roles benefit themselves. Women's advance into the corporate world, for example, is changing working conditions for both sexes. Some women managers have had the courage to object to long hours of overtime work as wasteful and unnecessary; few men would have dared to say so. Women's objections to company transfers are making it easier for men to oppose this practice. In management studies and within companies, both men and women are urging that more consideration be paid to individuals and that more balanced work styles be adopted. Clearly pressure from women workers is fostering these trends.

Some men are realizing that victimization cuts two ways and that freeing women will also free men. A spokesperson for the Men's Lib Research

Group of Osaka says that men are often unaware of the problems they create for women and themselves: 'It's time for men to cast off the yoke of masculinity.' One member who has translated an American book on domestic violence believes that 'men become violent because that is the only way they know to express their anger,' and that they should learn to understand and express their feelings while not forgetting that 'men have victimized women.'[59] The group began a hotline telephone counselling service in 1995. Such groups have become common in North America but are still rare in Japan.

The traumatic events of 1995 – the great earthquake, the poison gas attacks, the high yen – have upset traditional trust in authority and willingness to cede responsibility to the group. These events, along with a continuing recession that is upsetting fifty-year-old employment patterns, may mark a transition for Japan. It is no longer a uniquely 'safe' and secure place. The failure of politicians and bureaucrats alike to respond promptly to the 'quake tarnished their image, perhaps permanently. Japanese are beginning to question authority and assume a more active role in society and in their own lives.[60] These changes in the national psyche are particularly prominent in women. How many hotlines, pressure groups, nationwide rallies, protest marches, and discrimination suits will it take for the male half of the country, the dominant power brokers, to perceive that women no longer accept the status quo?

Women in their twenties now have several generations of role models to provide inspiration and advice, women like internationally famous designer Hanae Mori, who began by opening a dressmaking shop in Tokyo in 1951. Almost fifty years later, Mori's energy and creativity continue unabated. She speaks for many Japanese women when she points to big global changes for women, in lifestyle and thinking as well as in clothing: 'From now on into the next century, women will play bigger roles in history and change the world.'[61] Mori also notes the internationalizing of information in the late twentieth century through travel, business networking, and television channels such as CNN.

The Internet is another powerful tool for women whose domestic responsibilities keep them at home. A Tokyo-based group is using the net to collect information on events related to women, an exciting development.[62] Women's Online Media sent three of its members to China to attend the NGO Forum linked to the United Nations World Conference on Women 1995. Japanese women are now linked with other women in their own country and abroad as they have never been before.

With ambassadorial tact, the Egyptian ambassador to Japan writes that 'Japanese women are taking an energetic but non-confrontational stance in their drive towards achieving equality.'[63] She adds that they are seeking their goal 'steadily and effectively.' With the latter verdict I have no quarrel, but the patience of at least some Japanese women is wearing thin. Journalist Kyoko Sato finds that gender equality is still 'a frontline postwar battle.' The women whom she quotes – Tatsuko Handa, Yumiko Ehara, and Reiko Masuda – believe that discrimination against women may have become more subtle but remains strong and should be fought persistently as a violation of human rights.[64]

As I reflect on the personal stories of the hundreds of Japanese women with whom I have talked, I think of a Tokyo woman whose son has been hunting for a bride for several years without success. Both mother and son would prefer what she called 'a traditional woman' who intends to stay home and care for her children herself: the mother, because she has no intention of bringing up grandchildren after spending a quarter-century bringing up her own children; and the son, because – well, Japanese men tend to be conservative, as we have seen. The search was proving difficult, and the woman exclaimed in mock despair, 'It's impossible to find a traditional woman in Japan!'

In a haiku, Kimiko Itami (b. 1925) catches a wonderful forked image suggestive of women:

Twilight at a port of call –
smell of daffodils
and steel.[65]

It reminds me of seeing daffodils pushing through the asphalt paving at the side of a residential street in Okayama in 1993. I had just come from an interview with a woman who held a responsible civic job. She had managed to introduce changes that she felt were long overdue.

This woman told me that Japanese women were finding room for their talents 'in the cracks' of traditional structures. I turned the image over in my mind. Was it a confining one? Apologetic? Not when daffodil shoots can split asphalt. Not when windswept pines are driving their roots through rock. Interstices of time and space can spread and connect until a structure is transformed. Until the mountain moves.

NOTES

Chapter 1: Is the Mountain Moving?

1 Sumiko Iwao, 'The Japanese: Portrait of Change,' *Japan Echo* special issue 15 (1988): 6.
2 Japan Institute of Women's Employment, *Japan's Working Women Today* (Tokyo: Japan Institute of Women's Employment 1991), 5.
3 Chie Nakane, *Japanese Society* (London: Weidenfeld and Nicolson 1970), 149.
4 Kurt Singer, *Mirror, Sword and Jewel: The Geometry of Japanese Life* (Tokyo and New York: Kodansha International 1981), 60.
5 See Norma Field, *In the Realm of a Dying Emperor: A Portrait of Japan at Century's End* (New York: Pantheon Books 1991), 28-9.
6 Sam Jameson, 'Violence Chilling Freedom of Speech in Japan,' *Los Angeles Times World Report*, 17 October 1992, A8.

Chapter 2: Back to the Future

1 Richard Storry, *A History of Modern Japan* (Harmondsworth, Middlesex: Penguin Books 1960), 245-53. The occupation authorities, in regulations dealing with election laws, pronounced on 17 December 1945 that all Japanese women over the age of twenty would have the right to vote; Kita Kusunose, among others, had spoken out for women's right to vote as early as 1878. In 1946, at the urging of Japanese women, women over twenty-five were permitted to stand for political office. By early 1947, the new Constitution gave women significant legal protection.
2 See Kazuko Tsurumi, 'Women in Japan: A Paradox of Modernization,' *Japan Foundation Newsletter* 1, 5 (1977): 2. Tsurumi draws on the work of folklorist Kunio Yanagita.
3 See Laurence Caillet, *The House of Yamazaki: The Life of a Daughter of Japan*, trans. Megan Backus (Tokyo and New York: Kodansha International 1994), 90. Yamazaki Ikue describes her father as belonging to an era when only the eldest son was treasured: 'We girls held no interest for him' (p. 64).
4 Meiji (1868-1912), Taishō (1912-26), and Shōwa (1926-89) are the posthumous names of the emperors whose rule governed those years.
5 Fumiko Enchi, *The Waiting Years*, trans. John Bester (Tokyo and New York: Kodansha International 1980), 40. All references are to this edition.
6 Sharon L. Sievers, *Flowers in Salt. The Beginnings of Feminist Consciousness in Modern Japan* (Stanford, CA: Stanford University Press 1983), 19.
7 Akiko Kuno, *Unexpected Destinations: The Poignant Story of Japan's First Vassar Graduate*, trans. Kirsten McIvor (Tokyo and New York: Kodansha International 1993), notes that all five girls belonged to the defeated clans that had opposed the Imperial Restoration in the 1860s and that their leaders may have hoped to recover power and influence indirectly through the future husbands and sons of these girls.
8 Ume Tsuda, *The Attic Letters: Ume Tsuda's Correspondence to Her American Mother*, ed. Yoshiko Furuki (New York and Tokyo: Weatherhill 1991), 86-7.
9 See Kittredge Cherry, *Womansword: What Japanese Words Say about Women* (Tokyo and New York: Kodansha International 1987), 41-2: 'Roused to defensive fury, the local police in

the Kyoto suburb where [Kishida] was speaking arrested her for "dangerous, left-wing" agitation and fined her the equivalent of a month's salary.'

10 See Hideko Fukuda, 'People's Rights and National Rights,' in *Reflections on the Way to the Gallows: Voices of Japanese Rebel Women*, trans. and ed. Mikiso Hane (New York: Pantheon Books and the University of California Press 1988), 29-50.

11 Sievers, *Flowers in Salt*, 53. See also Hane, introduction to *Reflections on the Way to the Gallows*, 8; and Mikiso Hane, introduction to Kaneko Fumiko, *The Prison Memoirs of a Japanese Woman*, trans. Jean Inglis (Armonk, NY, and London: M.E. Sharpe 1991): 'The civil code of 1898 gave the head of the extended family virtually absolute authority ... One provision stated that "cripples and disabled persons and wives cannot undertake any legal action"' (p. xi).

12 Baroness Shidzue Ishimoto, *Facing Two Ways: The Story of My Life*, introduction and afterword by Barbara Molony (Stanford, CA: Stanford University Press 1984), 161. The autobiography was drafted in Japanese and turned into English by the author. It was first published in 1935. Ishimoto Katō (b. 1897) has worked throughout her long life for birth control, family planning and women's rights. See also: 'I regarded the birth control movement as the polestar guiding women from slavery and unceasing poverty to personality and culture' (p. 241).

13 See ibid., 278-9. A Japanese man could divorce his wife by means of a short note to her parents. Three and one-half lines were common. Divorce usually meant that the woman lost her children and all economic support. Samurai women could be put to death for adultery, or any suspicion of adultery. Cf. Sievers, *Flowers in Salt*, 4.

14 Sievers, *Flowers in Salt*, 56-7.

15 Patricia Tsurumi, *Factory Girls: Women in the Thread Mills of Meiji Japan* (Princeton, NJ: Princeton University Press 1990), 192.

16 Sievers, *Flowers in Salt*, 56, 57.

17 'A survey of 28 prefectures in 1910 revealed that of 200,000 female workers from villages ... 120,000 did not return home. Some married, but most ... were compelled, by failing health and economic need, to take up prostitution or other kinds of unsavory work. Of the 80,000 who returned home, 13,000 were seriously ill' (ibid., 85). Suicide was also common among mill workers.

18 Caillet, *House of Yamazaki*, 130.

19 Tsurumi, *Factory Girls*, 196.

20 See Junichi Saga, *Memories of Silk and Straw: A Self-Portrait of Small-Town Japan*, trans. Garry O. Evans, illus. Dr Susumu Saga (Tokyo and New York: Kodansha International 1987), 150-4.

21 Akiko Yosano, *Tangled Hair: Selected Tanka from Midaregami by Akiko Yosano*, trans. Sanford Goldstein and Seishi Shinoda (Rutland, VT, and Tokyo: Charles E. Tuttle 1987), 23. *Midaregami* was first published in 1901.

22 See Sievers, *Flowers in Salt*, 15.

23 See Hane, ed., *Reflections on the Way to the Gallows*, 14-5; Sievers, *Flowers in Salt*, 86; and Gail Lee Bernstein, ed., *Recreating Japanese Women, 1600-1945* (Berkeley: University of California Press 1991), 201-4, 208. In the last of these, Margit Nagy notes that in the second decade of this century, women in the Japanese labour force numbered only 3.5 million, or one-eighth of the estimated female population, and that three-quarters of these employed women were classified as manual workers. During the same decade, the 'woman question' became a popular topic in newspapers and magazines, many of which began to use female reporters and writers for features on women's issues (Nagy, 'Middle-Class Working Women during the Interwar Years,' 208).

24 Nagy documents the steady growth in women teachers from 1916-7, 'the World War I years of prosperity for Japan, when many men left teaching to take better-paying jobs in private industry' (Nagy, 'Middle-Class Working Women,' in *Recreating Japanese Women*, ed. Bernstein, 203). The same period saw an increasing demand for female education and a swelling of the school-age population in major cities.

25 See Kaneko, *Prison Memoirs*, 213.

26 Saga, *Memories of Silk and Straw*, 156.

27 Hane, introduction to Kaneko, *Prison Memoirs*, ix.

28 Quoted in Harumi Setouchi, *Beauty in Disarray*, trans. Sanford Goldstein and Kazuji Ninomiya (Stanford, CA: Stanford University Press 1983), 20.

29 See ibid., 191. This early twentieth-century Japanese group has some resemblance to the 'Real Women' who became a political force in America over the last twenty-five years.

30 See Sievers, *Flowers in Salt*, 171.

31 Ibid., 178.

32 See ibid., 183, 187-8.

33 See Gregory J. Kasza, 'The State and the Organization of Women in Prewar Japan,' *Japan Foundation Newsletter* 18, 2 (1990): 9. Cf. Sheldon Garon, 'Women's Groups and the Japanese State: Contending Approaches to Political Integration, 1890-1945,' *Journal of Japanese Studies* 19, 1 (1993): 7-8. Garon's analysis of the growth of politicized women's organizations and their close relationship with the Japanese state both before and after the Pacific War suggests that these two groups shared many common goals. Certainly Article 5 of the Police Law prevented women from joining political parties and from achieving suffrage until 1945. Despite this, the enthusiasm of many women for working with the bureaucracy remained strong.

34 Ibid., 12-3.

35 Many historians of the women's movement in Japan in the 1920s and early '30s identify it with the struggle to attain suffrage, one led by Fusae Ichikawa, leader of the League for Women's Suffrage. Most of the prominent women's leaders, including Ichikawa, collaborated with the militaristic regime during Japan's wars with China and the West, 1937-45. In 1947, Ichikawa was temporarily purged from public life by the Occupation Forces. Defenders insisted that she and other women had collaborated only in order to advance the interests of women during this traumatic period. See Garon, 'Women's Groups and the Japanese State,' 7-8. See also Garon, *Molding Japanese Minds: The State in Everyday Life* (Princeton, NJ: Princeton University Press 1997), chapter 4. Garon emphasizes that women's groups responded favourably to the government's 'moral suasion' before 1945 and for almost two generations after war's end: 'Growing affluence in the 1980s made the populace less receptive to messages of austerity' (p. 231).

36 Shizuko Gō, *Requiem*, trans. Geraldine Harcourt (Tokyo and New York: Kodansha International 1985), 21, 27. *Rekuiemu* was first published in book form in 1973.

37 Interview with Shizuko Gō in her home in Yokohama, 15 June 1990, translated by Shunko Sasaki. In our talk, Gō said that Japanese people did not expect their nation to re-arm and that she was shocked and alarmed by the large defence budget of recent decades. She answered 'Yes' to my query, 'So *Requiem* is not just an historical novel, but a plea for "never again," and a comment on present and future acts?'

38 Sievers, *Flowers in Salt*, 192.

Chapter 3: Culture

1 See Masako Togawa, *The Master Key*, trans. Simon Grove (London: Century Publishing 1984), 80.

2 See Laurence Caillet, *The House of Yamazaki: The Life of a Daughter of Japan*, trans. Megan

Backus (Tokyo and New York: Kodansha International 1994): 'The development of individualism along Western lines, thought to be founded exclusively on selfishness, is one of the favorite themes of the Japanese when they speak of themselves. It ranks high among the list of evils engendered by modernization ... Individualism, whose development is tied to the nuclearization of the family, is also perceived as the principal cause of the solitude of the aged and the sometimes spectacular aggressiveness of the young' (pp. 298-9 n. 4).

3 Chie Nakane, *Japanese Society*, 2nd ed. (Tokyo: Charles E. Tuttle 1984), 29.

4 Caillet, *House of Yamazaki*, 21, where Ikue Yamazaki observes that *ie* (etymologically, 'hearth') means both the house as a structure and the family that occupies it: 'The *ie* ... is the chain of our existence that gives it strength.'

5 Nakane, *Japanese Society*, 8.

6 Ibid., 10, 82-3.

7 See Sumiko Iwao, *The Japanese Woman: Traditional Image and Changing Reality* (New York: The Free Press 1993), 5.

8 Nakane, *Japanese Society*, 34.

9 See Takeo Doi, *The Anatomy of Dependence*, trans. John Bester (Tokyo and New York: Kodansha International 1973), 166 and passim: '*Amae* is, first and foremost, an emotion, an emotion which partakes of the nature of a drive and with something instinctive at its base.' The verb *amaeru* means to presume on someone's goodwill and to act as though one has the right to do so. See also Takeo Doi, *The Anatomy of Self*, trans. Mark A. Harbison (Tokyo: Kodansha International 1986), 138 and passim.

10 See Ruth Benedict, *The Chrysanthemum and the Sword: Patterns of Japanese Culture* (Cambridge, MA: Houghton, Mifflin 1946), chapter 12, 'The Child Learns.' See especially pp. 263-4, where Benedict notes that a small boy may never manifest aggression towards his father, but all his accumulated anger and resentment can be expressed in tantrums directed against his mother and grandmother. See also Kurt Singer, *Mirror, Sword and Jewel: The Geometry of Japanese Life*, ed. Richard Storry (Tokyo and New York: Kodansha International 1981), 31-4, for a very similar portrait of child rearing in Japan.

11 See Joseph Tobin, 'Japanese Preschools and the Pedagogy of Selfhood,' *Japanese Sense of Self*, ed. Nancy R. Rosenberger (Cambridge: Cambridge University Press 1992), 21-39.

12 Benedict, *Chrysanthemum and the Sword*, 263.

13 Geoffrey Gorer, *Japanese Character Structure*, quoted in Benedict, *Chrysanthemum and the Sword*, 274.

14 Norma Field, *In the Realm of a Dying Emperor: A Portrait of Japan at Century's End* (New York: Pantheon Books 1991), 75. Cf. Joan Kabayama, 'Don't Embarrass Your Family,' *New Canadian*, 9 June 1994, E5, where Kabayama recalls the old Japanese value taught to children, never to bring embarrassment to their families, in connection with an incident of spousal abuse, in which a Japanese woman who had stayed in a violent marriage for five years rather than disappoint her parents was saved from probable death by neighbours who overheard a particularly vicious attack.

15 See Nakane, *Japanese Society*, 15

16 See Doi, *Anatomy of Dependence*, 28, 57, 65.

17 Cf. Field, *In the Realm of a Dying Emperor*, 23-4. She finds the hierarchical marking of every speech to be 'oppressive, formulaic humility or arrogance ... The very possibility of intimacy is embedded in the tyranny of language. The luxury of addressing my grandmother without honorifics is inseparable from the obligation to use them with her brother's wife, my greataunt.'

18 See Doi, *Anatomy of Dependence*, 174.

19 See Singer, *Mirror, Sword and Jewel*, 34.

20 Ichiro Ozawa, *Blueprint for a New Japan: The Rethinking of a Nation*, trans. Louisa Rubinfien, ed. Eric Gower (Tokyo and New York: Kodansha International 1994), 9 and passim. In 1994, Ozawa was the secretary general of the Japan Renewal Party, Shinseito.

21 Singer, *Mirror, Sword and Jewel*, 69.

22 Masao Miyamoto, 'Bullying Endemic to Japan,' *Japan Times*, 17 January 1995, 18. This is the first of a two-part analysis of *ijime* in Japanese culture. See also Miyamoto, 'Japan, Inc. Survives on a Mix of Bullying and Envy,' *Japan Times*, 18 January 1995, 17.

23 See Masao Miyamoto, MD, *Straitjacket Society: An Insider's Irreverent View of Bureaucratic Japan* (Tokyo and New York: Kodansha International 1994), 127 and passim.

24 Field, *In the Realm of a Dying Emperor*, 141.

25 See Donald Richie, 'Fighting Flag, God and Emperor,' *Japan Times Weekly*, 25 January 1992, 3.

26 Takie Sugiyama Lebra, 'Sex Equality for Japanese Women,' *Japan Interpreter* 10, 3-4 (1976): 284.

27 See Hiroshi Minami, *Psychology of the Japanese People*, trans. Albert R. Ikoma (Toronto: University of Toronto Press 1971), 50-3, 103. Cf. psychiatrist and comparative culture specialist Noda Masaaki, *Kokka to maronie* [The individual spirit and the state] (Tokyo: Shinchōsha 1993), reviewed in *Japanese Book News* 3 (Summer 1993): 14. Masaaki shows that these attitudes exist currently, as found in a general feeling of malaise in both the society and the individual. Despite economic success, many Japanese feel spiritually unfulfilled. Noda attributes this to the fact that individual awareness is not well developed and a spirit of conformity prevails: witness, he argues, the uniformity of mass media reporting at the time of the death of Emperor Hirohito and the increase in death from overwork.

28 Iwao, *Japanese Woman*, 3, her emphasis.

29 See Nicholas D. Kristof, 'Land of Rising Voices,' *Asahi Evening News*, 14 December 1995, 1.

30 See Jeannie Lo, *Office Ladies/Factory Women: Life and Work at a Japanese Company* (Armonk, NY, and London: M.E. Sharpe 1990), 7.

31 Tomoko Bamba, 'The "Office Ladies" Paradise: Inside and Out,' *Japan Quarterly* 26, 2 (1979): 241-7.

32 See Etsuko Yamashita, 'One of Japan's Leading Novelists Portrays Women Journalists as Media Geisha,' *Japan Times Weekly*, 23 December 1995, 6-7.

33 See Kittredge Cherry, *Womansword: What Japanese Words Say about Women* (Tokyo and New York: Kodansha International 1987), 53; and Bamba, '"Office Ladies" Paradise,' 244. The subliminal threat suggests that women's value is declining from this point.

34 See 'Single Women Face Parental Censure,' *Asahi Evening News*, 26 May 1993.

35 Ozawa, *Blueprint for a New Japan*, 12.

36 Morihiro Hosokawa, 'A Vision for the Twenty-First Century,' *Look Japan* 41, 457 (1994): 4. This is a translation of a speech given by Hosokawa in January 1994.

37 Michael Blaker, 'In Japanese Politics, Oil and Water Are Mixing,' *Los Angeles Times*, 10 July 1994, M4.

38 E. Patricia Tsurumi and Bulletin of Concerned Asian Scholars, eds., *The Other Japan: Postwar Realities* (Armonk, NY, and London: M.E. Sharpe 1988), quoted in Sepp Linhart, 'Paradigmatic Approaches to Japanese Society and Culture by Western Social Scientists,' *Japan Foundation Newsletter* 22, 3 (1994): 10.

Chapter 4: Housewives

1 See Kittredge Cherry, *Womansword: What Japanese Words Say about Women* (Tokyo and New York: Kodansha International 1987), 73-4.

2 See Masatsugu Otsuka, 'Women Pay through the Nose for a Date,' *Asahi Evening News*, 22 June 1994, 9.

3 See editorial, 'Now Is the Time to Snap out of Rabbit-Hutch Mentality,' *Asahi Evening News*, 29 May 1994, 3.

4 Reijiro Hashiyama, 'Rabbit Hutch City,' *Look Japan* 41, 458 (1994): 33. Over 65 percent of Tokyo commuters spend at least two hours a day on trains.

5 See Cherry, *Womansword*, 62.

6 'National Briefs,' *Asahi Evening News*, 30 December 1993, 4.

7 See Cherry, *Womansword*: '*Oku* means not just interior, but the depths far within a building ... As the language makes clear, that is traditionally considered a woman's place ... A man ordinarily refers to his own wife as "house-insider," *kanai*' (pp. 66-7).

8 See Yoshiko Miyaka, 'Doubling Expectations: Motherhood and Women's Factory Work under State Management in Japan in the 1930s and 1940s,' in *Recreating Japanese Women 1600-1945*, ed. Gail Lee Bernstein (Berkeley: University of California Press 1991), 267-95.

9 Keiko Higuchi, 'Women at Home,' *Japan Echo* 12, 4 (1984): 51 and passim.

10 See Yōko Abe, 'Housewives at the Helm,' *Japan Echo* 6, 4 (1979): 96-7. Abe also contends that 'nuclearization' of the family structure has freed the wife from the task of caring for elderly parents, a dubious hypothesis that is contradicted by the majority of research in the field.

11 See Sumiko Iwao, 'The Quiet Revolution: Japanese Women Today,' *Japan Foundation Newsletter* 19, 3 (1991); and *The Japanese Woman: Traditional Image and Changing Reality* (New York: The Free Press 1993), passim.

12 See 'Teenagers Don't Talk to Dads. Kids Spending Less Time at Home, White Paper Says,' *Japan Times*, 29 January 1994, 2. See also 'The Makinos: So Far Away,' *Look Japan* 41, 460 (1994): 'Having a husband who lives far away isn't that much of a change for me ... Even when he lived at home, he would come back late every night or would be gone for long periods on business trips' (pp. 20-1).

13 See Ayako Sono, 'Fuji,' in *Rabbits, Crabs, Etc.: Stories by Japanese Women*, trans. Phyllis Birnbaum (Honolulu: University of Hawaii Press 1982), 18-23.

14 Minako Ōba, 'The Pale Fox,' trans. Stephen W. Kohl, in *The Shōwa Anthology: Modern Japanese Short Stories*, Vol. 2, 1961-1984, ed. Van C. Gessel and Tomone Matsumoto (Tokyo and New York: Kodansha International 1985), 342.

15 Cf. the title of Yūko Tsushima's novel, *Woman Running in the Mountains*, trans. Geraldine Harcourt (Tokyo and New York: Kodansha International 1991).

16 Sumiko Iwao's observes that childhood socialization discourages independent thought; that this is emphasized for girls more than for boys; and that girls learn early to develop a high degree of sensitivity to what is expected of them. In short, deferring to others is desirable behaviour, especially for women.

17 Minako Ōba, 'The Smile of a Mountain Witch,' in *Stories by Contemporary Japanese Women Writers*, ed. and trans. Noriko Mizuta Lippit and Kyoko Iriye Selden (Armonk, NY, and London: M.E. Sharpe 1982), 188.

18 This satire of the treatment of Japanese women by a predominantly male medical profession is also applicable to the West in the nineteenth and early twentieth centuries. See Elaine Showalter, *The Female Malady: Women, Madness and English Culture, 1830-1980* (New York: Pantheon Books 1985), passim.

19 According to an Osaka physician in 1990, families of hospitalized women often pressure doctors to release female patients early because they are needed at home to care for the family. The death of a woman patient who was not expected to recover full health is cause for celebration, not grief.

20 Aki Gotō, 'Where Are Japanese Housewives Heading?' *Japan Echo* 9, 4 (1982): 109. See also Cherry, *Womansword*, 85, where Cherry details the Japanese words that reflect 'a culture where the strongest psychological bond is between mother and child, not between spouses,

for marriage has long been viewed as a primarily economic relationship.'

21 See Keiko Higuchi, 'Women at Home,' *Japan Echo* 12, 4 (1984): 56. Higuchi's overview is followed by a discussion with three other social critics, including Michiko Nakajima and Itsuko Teruoka.

22 Minako Ōba, 'Candle Fish,' in *Unmapped Territories: New Women's Fiction from Japan*, ed. and trans. Yukiko Tanaka (Seattle: Women in Translation 1991), xiii.

23 Gotō, 'Where Are Japanese Housewives Heading?' 104.

24 Yūko Tsushima, *Child of Fortune* [Choji (1978)], trans. Geraldine Harcourt (Tokyo and New York: Kodansha International 1983), 19. See also Yūko Tsushima, 'The Silent Traders,' trans. Geraldine Harcourt, in *Shōwa Anthology*, vol. 2, ed. Gessel and Matsumoto, 401, where Harcourt notes in a preface that Tsushima does not consider herself to be part of the feminist movement but that her stereotype-breaking heroines have a strong appeal for Japanese women readers.

25 See 'Nation's Birthrate Drops to Record 1.46 in 1993,' *Asahi Evening News*, 24 June 1994, 1. The institute forecasts that 20 percent of women in their early thirties will be single in the first decade of the next century, compared with 14 percent in 1990; and that 48 percent of women in their late twenties will be single in both 2000 and 2010, compared with 40 percent in 1990. The birth rate was 1.42 in 1995 and 1.43 in 1996. When the birth rate is less than 2.1, the population declines (*Look Japan* 43, 502 [1998]: 38).

26 See 'Couples without Kids to Double,' *New Canadian*, 23 June 1994, E3.

27 See 'Teenagers Don't Talk to Dads,' 2. The composition of families changed little during the 1980s, with nuclear families staying at 71.1 percent of total households.

28 See 'Teaching Fathers about Raising Kids,' *Asahi Evening News*, 1 June 1994, 9.

Chapter 5: Education in a One-Chance Society

1 See Chieko Irie Mulhern, ed., *Heroic with Grace: Legendary Women of Japan* (Armonk, NY, and London: East Gate Books and M.E. Sharpe 1991), 213-5.

2 See Amano Ikuo, 'The Bright and Dark Sides of Japanese Education,' *Japan Foundation Newsletter* 19, 5-6 (1992): 'Intense entrance examination competition has been a feature of the Japanese education system since its inception' (p. 3). The government harnessed community, regional, and extended family loyalties to encourage people to compete to achieve the goals and standards it had set up.

3 See ibid., 5-6. Speaking of the 'myth' of equal opportunity, Ikuo notes that although entrance to senior high schools and to universities is based on performance in entrance examinations, the majority of those passing these competitive examinations come from wealthy backgrounds. Japan is socially stratified by school background; the level of education attained and the school graduated from play an important role in determining a person's social class. Wealthy Japanese, however, are able to get their children into prestigious preschools and so onto the track towards the most prestigious universities. In this way, class determines education. Hiroshi Ishida, in *Social Mobility in Contemporary Japan* (Stanford, CA: Stanford University Press 1993), confirms this view by demonstrating that social stratification in Japan, as in the United States and the United Kingdom, depends less on education than on class. Universities, in Ishida's thesis, are the means of reproducing inequality from generation to generation. The importance of education rests primarily in the institutional arrangements that link the education system and the labour market. Companies will often hire graduates from particular universities only. Unlike workers in the West, most Japanese youths end their education with a single undergraduate degree; further skill acquisition takes place within companies, hence the necessity to graduate from a prestigious institution. See also Jeff Kingston, 'Education in Japan. Myth of Confucian Meritocracy Exposed,' *Japan Times*, 30 March 1993, 19.

4 See Alex Shishin, 'Inside the Education Monster,' *Asahi Evening News*, 27 July 1992, a review of Bruce Feller, *Learning to Bow: An American Teacher in a Japanese School* (New York: Ticknor and Fields 1992): 'Feller is absolutely right in saying that the purpose of schooling in Japan is to create good servants for the State and the corporations.'

5 See 'Study Shows Educational Gender Gap Limits Girls' Chances in Many Nations,' *Japan Times*, 2 February 1994, 2.

6 See Clayton Naff, *About Face: How I Stumbled onto Japan's Social Revolution* (Tokyo and New York: Kodansha International 1994), 88-9, 286.

7 Mariko Sugahara, 'Five Fatal Symptoms of the Japanese Disease,' *Japan Echo* 21, 2 (1994): 72. In 1994, Sugahara was cabinet councillor and chief of the office for women's affairs in the Prime Minister's Office.

8 Norma Field, *In the Realm of a Dying Emperor: A Portrait of Japan at Century's End* (New York: Pantheon Books 1991), 135. Field, a professor at the University of Chicago, was born to a Japanese mother and American father in Occupied Japan.

9 One reason for the extraordinary degree of popularity of L.M. Montgomery's *Anne of Green Gables* is the relative freedom of 'red-haired Anne,' as the Japanese call the young heroine.

10 See 'Open Pupils' Records, Kawasaki Panel Urges,' *Mainichi Daily News*, 13 October 1992, B12; 'Kawasaki Breaks Taboo. Board Discloses Students' Files,' *Japan Times*, 27 February 1993, 3; and 'PTA Dropout Rate Rising,' *Asahi Evening News*, 4 May 1993, 7.

11 See editorial, 'Society Has an Obligation to Provide Better Child Care,' *Asahi Evening News*, 17 April 1994, 3. Japan's public spending on education accounts for 3.7 percent of gross domestic product, the lowest among twenty industrialized countries.

12 See 'Education Costs Skyrocketing,' *Daily Yomiuri*, 10 August 1992, A2; and 'Parents Paying More for Tutoring: Survey,' *Asahi Evening News*, 10 August 1992. In the early 1990s, when I was speaking in Tokyo to a large group of women about education in Canada, the audience gasped audibly when I mentioned that senior high school was free. They gasped again when I said that Canadian universities, unlike Japan, did not charge students an entrance fee but simply annual tuition fees. Later, many of the questions from the floor concerned *juku*: the cost, the social prestige accorded to it, and so on. These women found it difficult to believe that private coaching for subjects studied in school was considered unnecessary in North America and was relatively rare.

13 See '"Juku" Enrollment Increases Sharply,' *Japan Times*, 30 July 1994, 3.

14 See 'Cram Schools Squeezed,' *Asahi Evening News*, 16 August 1992, 5.

15 See Ikuo, 'The Bright and Dark Sides of Japanese Education,' 3. See also 'Tokyo University Stays No. 1 for Bureaucrats,' *Japan Times*, 12 August 1993, 3; and 'You've Been to a Good University – So What?' *Asahi Evening News*, 16 October 1993. In an attempt to alter people's attitudes, the Ministry of Education announced its intention to stop mentioning a person's educational background in its publications, but a Ministry official said that he doubted whether this would prevent Japanese from judging people according to what university they had attended. See also Mary C. Brinton, *Women and the Economic Miracle: Gender and Work in Postwar Japan* (Berkeley, Los Angeles, London: University of California Press 1993), 190-5, for a further explanation of what she calls the 'extraordinary' significance now attached to entrance to a prestigious university.

16 'Japan's Missing Children,' *The Economist*, 12 November 1994, 46.

17 Field, *In the Realm of a Dying Emperor*, 13.

18 Naff, *About Face*, 87.

19 See Ikuo, 'The Bright and Dark Sides of Japanese Education,' 6-8. Ikuo is a professor of the sociology of education at the University of Tokyo, an institution ranked first in the country.

20 See 'Students May Be Given Another Five-Day School Week,' *New Canadian*, 20 October

1994, E3. The ministry mandated a five-day school week once a month beginning September 1992. By 1994, it was experimenting with a five-day school week twice a month in selected schools. See also 'Primary, Junior High Absenteeism Hit New High in '91 Academic Year,' *Asahi Evening News*, 8 November 1992: 'Even among students who were not absent for extended periods, there is a growing feeling of resistance to attending school.'

21 A junior high school student suffocated after being placed upside down in a rolled up gym mat and stuffed in a closet by fellow students who had been tormenting the youth for some months. See Ryuzo Sato, 'Bullying: Nasty Open Secret at All Levels of Japanese Society,' *Daily Yomiuri*, 11 May 1993, A8. Suicide incidents resulting from extended bullying are not infrequently reported in the major dailies.

22 Field, *In the Realm of a Dying Emperor*, 14.

23 See editorial, 'Japanese Education's Dark Side,' *Japan Times*, 4 February 1993, 20.

24 See 'Bullying a Fatal Flaw in Education System,' *Japan Times*, 18 March 1993, 3. Other Japanese writers have observed that the popular media typically treats each incident of bullying as an isolated event, ignoring the pattern and the underlying causes.

25 See 'Childish Pursuits Signal Society's Failure,' *Japan Times*, 20 March 1993, 19.

26 Brinton, *Women and the Economic Miracle*, 190.

27 See ibid., 201; also Japan, Prime Minister's Office, *Japanese Women Today 1990* (Tokyo: Prime Minister's Office n.d.), 10; and Japan Institute of Women's Employment, *Japan's Working Women Today* (Tokyo: Japan Institute of Women's Employment 1991), 3. Between 1965 and 1990, the percentage of women entering junior college rose from 6.7 to 22.2. During the same period, the percentage of women entering university rose from 4.6 to 15.2. By comparison, the percentage of males entering junior college in the same twenty-five-year period remained constant at 1.7, but the percentage of males entering university rose from 20.7 to 33.4. Men constitute about 70 percent of all university students.

28 Brinton, *Women and the Economic Miracle*, 205. See also Brinton's remark that mothers are more likely than fathers to have university aspirations for sons: 'This is consistent with the popular image of the mother-son bond as the strongest one in the Japanese family ... It also coincides with the image of the *Kyōiku mama* ... This investment of hope in sons makes sense in view of the sex-discriminatory labor market and in view of parental and especially maternal reliance on children in old age' (p. 215).

29 See 'Textbooks Called Sexist,' *Asahi Evening News*, 10 August 1993: 'The fact that women today face a growing range of options in life is not presented in a positive light' (p. 9). In 1993, only one of the nineteen members of the civic committee of the Textbook Examination Council, an advisory body to the Ministry of Education, was a woman.

30 See 'Male Teachers Tune in to Home Economics,' *Asahi Evening News*, 15 November 1992, 4.

31 See 'Home Economics Joins the Real World,' *Asahi Evening News*, 26 April 1994, 9.

32 Ibid.

33 See 'The Name Game,' *Asahi Evening News*, 18 April 1994: 'Nationally, the percentage of schools using mixed rosters may still be between 10% and 20%' (p. 6).

34 See 'School Girls Combine Job of Team Manager and Mother,' *Asahi Evening News*, 28 July 1993, 9. See also 'High School Sports Clubs' Female Managers often Act as "Mother" to Their Male Peers,' *Asahi Evening News*, 25 November 1992, 5. One teacher stated that school is the place where sexual equality should be taught, but the managers' current role as mother reinforces discriminatory views.

35 In 1990, I gave a talk on trends in Canadian education to an adult audience at a community centre in Okayama. After the talk the centre's director, a man of perhaps sixty, expressed astonishment at the large numbers of mature students now studying at Canadian universities. How could they relate to the young students, he asked? What shared ground would they have,

and what could they talk about? I suggested they could talk about the particular course they were both taking. He replied, 'Japanese students don't talk about their courses.' I said that some became friends and could talk about anything. The director said, 'Japanese people cannot be friends with people whose age is not close to their own.'

36 Ichiro Ozawa, *Blueprint for a New Japan: The Rethinking of a Nation*, trans. Louisa Rubinfien, ed. Eric Gower (Tokyo and New York: Kodansha International 1994), 195.

37 Affluent young adults in the 1990s are buying books on assertiveness and the 'search for self.' See Hirokazu Kobayashi, 'Youth Look Inward in Affluent 1990s,' *Daily Yomiuri*, 6 October 1992, A7.

38 See Kathleen Morikawa, 'Waseda Professor Proposes Radical Changes,' *Asahi Evening News*, 7 November 1992, 5

39 See 'Japan Students Exhibit Apathy in Global Survey,' *Daily Yomiuri*, 3 December 1992: 'Compared with college students in other major cities in foreign nations, college students in Tokyo showed low goal-orientation and general dissatisfaction with daily life ... When asked how they spend their time, 63.1 percent of Tokyo students replied, "having fun with friends," the highest of any of the cities' (p. A9). See also Ritsuko Nakamura, 'Indulging a Love Affair with Academia,' *Japan Times*, 31 December 1992, 12. See also Iwao Nakatani, 'Jobs Agreement Has to Go,' *Japan Times*, 23 May 1994, charging that the 'collective discipline' imposed by employers, which forces senior students to hunt for jobs over a set period, shows that Japanese business has little respect for higher education: 'Seniors must spend most of the first half of their last year [in university] looking for jobs ... The employment agreement is but one example of how [highly] the Japanese job market is regulated' (p. 18).

40 This negative view of many students at regular universities was expressed by a woman student who preferred the vitality and love of learning found at the Jiyu Daigaku described below.

41 See David Thurber, 'Competitiveness Called into Question. Industry Seen in Creativity Drought,' *Japan Times*, 12 August 1993, 3.

42 Ozawa, *Blueprint for a New Japan*, 204-5.

43 See 'Survey of Education Programmes on Women and Family Education,' NWEC *Newsletter* 11, 1 (1994): 3-4. This is a biannual publication of the National Women's Education Centre of Japan in Saitama.

Chapter 6: Facing Two Ways

1 Cf. Sumiko Iwao, *The Japanese Woman: Traditional Image and Changing Reality* (New York: The Free Press 1993): 'The central organizations and groups that make up Japanese society are almost exclusively staffed and controlled by men' (pp. 5-6).

2 See Mary C. Brinton, *Women and the Economic Miracle: Gender and Work in Postwar Japan* (Berkeley, Los Angeles, London: University of California Press 1993), 1.

3 See 'Woman Claims Bias, Sues for Full-Time Pay,' *Japan Times*, 24 March 1994, 2: 'There are more than ten million part-time workers, and 14.7 percent of them work full time and tend to become a victim of unstable working conditions.' This statement was made by Tatsue Suzuki, lawyer for the plaintiff. See also Brinton, *Women and the Economic Miracle*, 10. She notes that in 1960, 43 percent of all part-time workers were women, but by 1986, the figure had risen to 70 percent; that the working conditions of these part-time women were inferior to those of regular employees; and that Japan was the only industrial nation where female wages *fell* relative to male wages in 1984.

4 See Andrew Dewit, 'Japanese Tax-System – Updated and Readable,' *Asahi Evening News*, 21 August 1994, 6, a review of Hiromitsu Ishi, *The Japanese Tax System*, 2nd ed. (Oxford and New York: Clarendon Press and Oxford University Press 1994). See also Kittredge Cherry, *Womansword: What Japanese Words Say about Women* (Tokyo and New York: Kodansha

International 1987), 103-5, where part-time women workers are described as the safety valve in Japan's famous lifetime employment system, and the tax system is considered to contribute to the general acceptance by women of very low pay. Women working part time (typically six hours per day) in their homes earned slightly more than half the hourly wage of part timers in offices and factories. See also 'Old Laws Impede Women,' *Asahi Evening News*, 23 July 1993, which refers to a government advisory panel under then labour minister Masukuni Murakami. The panel's report was addressed to the ministers of labour, finance, health and welfare, and home affairs, and called for revisions to tax, social insurance, and wage laws that discriminate against women. It noted that many current laws are based on the old assumption that women are not working full time. Further information on the tax situation for women comes from the author's interviews.

5 See Prime Minister's Office, *Japanese Women Today 1990* (Tokyo: Prime Minister's Office 1990), 13; and Japan Institute of Women's Employment, *Japan's Working Women Today* (Tokyo: Japan Institute of Women's Employment 1991), 6-7. Cf. Brinton, *Women and the Economic Miracle*, who quotes an American scholar at an international conference in 1984: 'The function of Japanese women is to work at low wages, produce 1.9 children, and work at low wages again.' Brinton notes that there was no rebuttal to this succinct summary of women's dual role in the economy.

6 See Brinton, *Women and the Economic Miracle*, 3-6. There are women running their own businesses in Japan, but self-employment is more likely to mean piece-rate work done in the home, assembling parts of consumer goods, often for subcontractors. The Japanese census calls this 'home handicraft,' and such workers are overwhelmingly women: 94 percent of self-employed women are piece-rate workers, while fewer than half of one percent of self-employed men are doing such work.

7 See Tatsumi Shinoda, 'Hey Big Spenders. Miran Fukuda's "Stained Glass" Exhibit Looks at That Indulgent Force in Japanese Society – Young Women Consumers,' *Asahi Evening News*, 6 February 1994, 8. This woman painter adds the illusion of stained glass frames to her iconic and satiric portraits of women.

8 Tomoko Bamba, 'The "Office Ladies' Paradise" Inside and Out,' *Japan Quarterly* 26, 2 (1979): 246.

9 Rodney C. Clark, *The Japanese Company* (New Haven, CT: Yale University Press 1979), quoted in Brinton, *Women and the Economic Miracle*, 15.

10 See Mieko Takenobu, 'Pushing Married Women out of the Workforce,' *Asahi Evening News*, 25 May 1994, 9.

11 See Jeannie Lo, *Office Ladies/Factory Women: Life and Work at a Japanese Company* (Armonk, NY, and London: M.E. Sharpe 1990), 48-9. See also Rachel Swanger, 'Letters/Sexism No Surprise,' *Japan Quarterly* 41, 1 (1994): 'In a society where in most workplaces female employees are still expected to serve tea and, worse, where educated women can be heard agreeing with men that the tea surely tastes better when served by a pretty girl, who could find it unusual that the expression *onnadatera* (unfeminine) is still commonly found in Japanese-language dictionaries? ... Similar examples reflecting Japanese society's tendency to automatically associate women with marriage and home, not to mention chattering, meddling, and other undesirable behaviour, are all too easy to find in dictionaries published in Japan' (p. 4).

12 See Lo, *Office Ladies*, 48-9. *Shigarami* is literally a weir, a fence of brush used to trap fish in a river. One office woman described it as follows: '*Shigarami* is a word commonly used by the Japanese to describe themselves ... It refers to the delicate way in which human relationships hold together. If one bond breaks, then the whole structure falls apart. People are careful not to harm these relationships.' The word, Lo adds, is a metaphor for the underlying structure of Japanese relationships, and is used in a similar way to *amae*.

13 Cf. editorial, 'Time to Destroy Society's Wall between Women, Men,' *Asahi Evening News*, 28 August 1994: 'What is expected of [women] at the workplace is no more than to serve as part-time employees or supplemental workers who are paid low wages and can be fired at any time' (p. 3).

14 See 'City to Stop Staff from Serving Tea,' *Asahi Evening News*, 13 April 1994: 'According to the personnel office, in the past the general belief was that women were basically hired for routine tasks such as clerical work or serving tea' (p. 5).

15 Lo, *Office Ladies*, 18.

16 Barbara Molony, 'The Japanese Debate over Motherhood Protection, 1915-50,' in *Japanese Women Working*, ed. Janet Hunter (London and New York: Routledge 1993), 133.

17 See Alice Lam, 'Equal Employment Opportunities for Japanese Women: Changing Company Practice,' in *Japanese Women Working*, ed. Hunter, 199-200. In 1965, only 6 percent of women entering the job market were graduates of either two-year college or four-year university programs. The figure rose to 27 percent in 1975 and to over 40 percent after the mid-1980s.

18 Cf. 'Women's Rights Law Defended. Former Minister Speaks out against Punitive Measures,' *Japan Times*, 4 March 1994, 3. Eight years after the supposed implementation, Mayumi Moriyama, a former Labour Ministry bureaucrat, described the EEO Law as a very good way of 'educating' society and the business community. Moriyama blamed the recession, not sexism, for the current difficulties experienced by women seeking jobs. Such an explanation ignores the many documented cases of systemic discrimination and of sexual harassment of women workers.

19 See Lam, 'Equal Employment Opportunities,' 210.

20 Molony, 'Japanese Debate over Motherhood Protection,' 142.

21 Only 13.5 percent of mothers with infants manage to carry on full-time work. See 'Japan's Missing Children,' *The Economist* 12 November 1994, 46.

22 See 'Preschool Caters to Working Mothers,' *Japan Times*, 5 May 1994, 3.

23 See Japan Institute of Women's Employment, *Japan's Working Women Today*: 'Under the Health Insurance Law, working women who give birth are given a daily stipend, once their paid vacation is used up, during the period where they are not paid their salary because of leave; the maternal allowance is equivalent to 60 percent of the worker's average daily pay before taking leave' (p. 38).

24 See 'Corporate Japan Not Receptive to Calls to Aid Working Mothers,' *Asahi Evening News*, 20 October 1992. Quite different statistics and attitudes are reported in 'Firms Lure Women Workers by Providing Nurseries,' *Japan Times*, 16 April 1992, 12, where the writer indicates that some manufacturing firms are providing nurseries in order to retain women workers.

25 'Child-Rearing Leave Legal But Elusive,' *Asahi Evening News*, 19 May 1993, 9.

26 See 'Day Care System Criticized,' *Asahi Evening News*, 18 August 1993, 9; letter to the editor, 'Women Weigh Jobs and Children,' *Asahi Evening News*, 15 September 1993, where a housewife wrote to a newspaper as follows: 'Working conditions in Japan are decidedly backward, so much so that it seems our society is denying working women the opportunity of bearing and raising children. I quit my job after I gave birth, but I still doubt whether that was the right choice. Maybe that is because I have an envy and an inferiority complex for working mothers. Now I can pay full attention to my child when he is sick, but ... I often feel empty' (p. 7).

27 The data are used to determine eligibility, and mothers are asked very detailed questions. See 'Working Moms Object to Unequal Paperwork,' *Asahi Evening News*, 29 September 1994: 'Namiko Watanabe, head of the city's women's policy office said the policy is merely a remnant of the days when women were supposed to stay at home. She said the requirements should be changed' (p. 5).

28 See 'Stop Sexism, Ministry Warns,' *Asahi Evening News*, 29 September 1994, 6. Some broadcasting stations made it a rule to give women newscasters only part-time status. Some companies hired only women who could commute from their parents' homes. The ministry had found 260 financial institutions and fifty-one broadcasting stations to be in violation of the EEO Law, including those that imposed unwritten and tacit conditions that women quit their jobs after marriage.

29 See 'Sumitomo Metal Suit Tests Equality Law,' *Asahi Evening News*, 13 September 1994, 4. See also 'Equal Employment Law Put to Test,' *New Canadian*, 22 September 1994, E3. The mediated settlement with Sumitomo will be non-binding; if either side is unsatisfied it can ask the ministry for advice or take legal action. One veteran worker, aged fifty-four, told reporters she had twice received a departmental award for outstanding work and had never missed a day. After marriage, her work evaluations dropped to a substandard C, and she was told by the personnel manager that most women are Cs. The writer of the article took this as a clear indication that gender rather than work performance determines evaluations, which are crucial for promotions. Cf. 'Woman Claims Bias,' 2. In the same Sumitomo dispute, employees also filed a complaint with the Osaka Summary Court urging the Sumitomo labour unions to make public actual salaries paid to male and female workers. The unions had declined to provide such information, citing the need to protect the privacy of members.

30 See 'Career Women Find More Work Overseas,' *Japan Times*, 25 February 1994, 15. In 1993, 547 Japanese women registered, compared with 288 in 1991. Foreign ministry statistics show that 1,052 Japanese women were working in Hong Kong as of 1 October 1992. Cf. 'Women Find Jobs in Hongkong,' *Asahi Evening News*, 1 February 1994, 4, where a job placement firm estimated that 1,500 Japanese women now hold corporate jobs in Hong Kong and that eight out of ten of its women applicants are career oriented. One woman is quoted as saying that working for three years in Japan had shown her that women managers there faced severe discrimination.

31 In 1991, 20 percent of management positions in Hong Kong were held by women, according to *Asian Business*, a monthly magazine published in Hong Kong. See also 'Leaving Japan for a Better Life,' *Asahi Evening News*, 3 September 1994, 5.

32 Keiko Hamada, 'Why Colony Lures Japanese Women,' *Asahi Evening News*, 8 June 1994, 9. See also 'International Organizations' Applications Up,' *Asahi Evening News*, 7 June 1994, 5.

33 See Ryosuke Ono and Shinji Fukushima, 'A Japanese Rush for Green Cards,' *Asahi Evening News*, 6 February 1994, 1. Some Japanese women are applying to emigrate to Canada for similar reasons.

34 See 'Working Women Suffer Stress-Related Illnesses,' *Asahi Evening News*, 10 September 1992, 5. Dr Junko Unihara, who had been treating working women for ten years, found that the number of women suffering mental and physical disorders had increased since 1986. A 1987 survey by the Ministry of Labour shows that human relations were the cause of stress for 60.6 percent of working women.

35 See 'In Slump, Women Cut out of Jobs,' *Asahi Evening News*, 2 June 1994, 5; 'Women Jobhunters Hit Brick Wall,' *Asahi Evening News*, 18 May 1994, 9. Some enterprising university graduates produced job-hunting guidebooks that described company attitudes towards women and workplace atmospheres. See also all of *NWEC Newsletter* 11, 2 (1994) regarding the special difficulties experienced by women university graduates in the 1990s in their search for jobs.

36 See 'Women to Get Right to Use Maiden Names,' *Asahi Evening News*, 23 April 1994, 4.

37 See Reiko Yamanoue, 'Name to Go by Is Serious Issue for Married Couples,' *Asahi Evening News*, 5 January 1994, 9.

38 See editorial, 'Choosing Surnames to Suit the Times,' *Japan Times*, 17 July 1994, 16. In 1990,

slightly more than half of those questioned in a Prime Minister's Office survey objected to the idea of women being allowed to retain their surnames. In 1994, a survey of male and female college students in Kanagawa Prefecture found that nearly three-quarters supported it.

39 See 'Uniforms Cramp Women's Style,' *Asahi Evening News*, 26 January 1994. See also 'Females for and against Uniforms at the Office,' *Asahi Evening News*, 2 February 1994, 9. Some women find them convenient and economical.

40 See 'Maternity Uniforms Buoy Female Spirits,' *Daily Yomiuri*, 5 October 1992.

41 See Hiroshi Hamota, 'Women Clean up at Part-Time Jobs,' *Asahi Evening News*, 8 February 1994, 4.

42 Cf. ninety-nine-year-old doctor Yayoi Koide, who still examines patients and prescribes for them for one-half day each week in Yaesu, Tokyo ('Newspeople,' *Daily Yomiuri*, 15 March 1992, A3).

43 See Choko Arai, 'Problems of Nursing in Japan,' *NWEC Newsletter* 9, 1 (1992): 5; 'Nurses Fed up with Job, Low Pay,' *Asahi Evening News*, 17 November 1992, 5; 'Nurses Leave Their Jobs Due to Physical Strain,' *Asahi Evening News*, 11 August 1992; and 'Nurses Nationwide Stage Walkouts,' *Japan Times*, 14 November 1991, 2. Nurses obtained the right to strike in 1991. Media attention indicates that the problems have been endemic for some time. Hospitals seem unwilling to improve pay and hours, and many Japanese nurses are seeking work overseas. The problems can only get worse until nurses are treated more professionally.

44 Sociologist Chie Nakane, author of *Japanese Society* (1970), was the first woman full professor at the University of Tokyo.

45 See 'More Japanese Women Studying to Become Veterinarians,' *Asahi Evening News*, 22 December 1991; 'Tokyo College Trains Animal Lovers to Become Veterinary Technicians,' *Daily Yomiuri*, 13 July 91, A3; and 'Ueno Zoo Gets First Female Director,' *Asahi Evening News*, 3 July 1992. More than 50 percent of 1990s veterinarians are women.

46 Jocelyn Ford, 'Female for Bench Called Tokenism,' *Japan Times*, 28 January 1994, 3.

47 Editorial, 'Selection of Woman Justice Broadens Top Court's Scope,' *Asahi Evening News*, 17 January 1994.

48 See 'Women Who See Other Paths Blocked Are Flocking to Law,' *Asahi Evening News*, 19 May 1993.

49 See 'Ministry Names 1st Woman Probation Chief,' *Daily Yomiuri*, 16 January 1993, A2. Hashimoto's experience in education and welfare are suited to her new task, she said, adding that volunteer specialists are important in this field and that she hopes to integrate her office with the community.

50 See 'Women Grads Flock to Local Government,' *Japan Times*, 26 June 1993, 17; and 'Second Tier Not Bad Career,' *Asahi Evening News*, 6 October 1992.

51 See 'Women-Only Town Offices Prove Hit,' *Japan Times*, 18 April 1992, 3. One such pioneering arrangement is in Matsue, Shimane Prefecture.

52 See 'Women Climb the Bureaucratic Ladder – Though Slowly,' *Asahi Evening News*, 2 September 1993, 5. Mayumi Moriyama, a Diet member of the Liberal Democratic Party in 1993, recalled that the Labour Ministry was the only government department that employed a career-seeking woman in 1950.

53 See Masaki Tonedachi, 'Women in Demand to Fill Government Positions,' *Asahi Evening News*, 28 January 1994, 5. The exaggerated headline is not an accurate reflection of the obstacles noted in the article: 'The greatest obstacle to women's advancement are the restrictions on membership that require prospective members to hold specific positions, such as governors or speakers of prefectural assemblies, or to be recommended by economic or industry associations. In addition, many seats are traditionally occupied by former bureaucrats who have retired from government service.'

54 See 'National Briefs. First Woman Police Chief Named,' *Asahi Evening News*, 21 January 1994, 4. Rueko Sakurai, aged fifty-eight, superintendent and head of the Juvenile Protection and Guidance Center in Tokyo's Asakura, was appointed chief of the Mita Police Station, to begin 1 February 1994. Tokyo's Metropolitan Police Department at that date had 44,000 officers, of whom 1,700 were women. See also 'Female Police Chief Appointed,' *Japan Times*, 2 February 1994, 2. See also 'MPD's First Women Pilots Take Off,' *Asahi Evening News*, 14 November 1992, 4. Two officers, chosen out of forty-nine policewomen, said they welcomed the challenge, and had made 'an enormous effort to overcome the pressures of being the first female officers to undergo training.'

55 See 'Defense Academy Admits First Women Students,' *Asahi Evening News*, 6 April 1992. The Academy had determined that 'it is possible to maintain Japan's military strength with high-ranking female officers ... News reports said the decision was made chiefly to attract more male students.'

56 See 'National Briefs. SDF Has First Woman Pilot,' *Asahi Evening News*, 22 January 1994, 4. An SDF spokesperson said that women would not be allowed to fly fighter planes 'because of the need to protect the sex that bears children,' a curious but traditional argument in Japan that has not barred women from doing physically demanding and dangerous work in mines, factories, and other areas.

57 See 'Mukai Getting Set for Shuttle Liftoff,' *Asahi Evening News*, 4 February 1994, 13; and 'Woman's Shuttle Flight Set for July,' *Japan Times*, 12 May 1994, 3. Chiaki Mukai, a medical researcher, hoped that her work would encourage those who were unable to break away from 'the limitation of being women.'

58 See 'Japanese Woman Climbs 7 Continents' Top Peaks,' *Asahi Evening News*, 3 July 1992; and Makoto Hattori, 'Japanese Woman Conquers Top Peaks of 7 Continents,' *Daily Yomiuri*, 3 July 1992, A2.

59 See 'Woman to Study Antarctic Penguins,' *Daily Yomiuri*, 10 July 1992; and 'Woman to Join Australia's Antarctic Project,' *Asahi Evening News*, 6 October 1992.

60 See 'Modern Mountain Monks Head for Hills,' *Japan Times*, 30 September 1992, 11.

61 See 'Female Engineering Students Work at Construction Sites in Summer,' *Asahi Evening News*, 18 August 1992. Labour shortages led to a link between female engineering and architectural students and construction companies eager for summer workers. Companies were well satisfied with their women workers, but many of the engineering students were headed for jobs in urban design and environmental protection rather than in construction. Nevertheless, driving heavy trucks and working on building construction is proving popular with women from many educational backgrounds.

62 See 'Japanese Women Making Way into Construction Industry,' *Asahi Evening News*, 28 April 1992.

63 Ibid.

64 Ichiro Ozawa, *Blueprint for a New Japan: The Rethinking of a Nation*, trans. Louisa Rubinfien, ed. Eric Gower (Tokyo and New York: Kodansha International 1994), 193.

65 See 'Japan's Missing Children,' 46.

66 'The government must therefore give public assistance for the care of the elderly and for the care of children' (Ozawa, *Blueprint for a New Japan*, 194).

Chapter 7: The Twilight Years

1 Sawako Ariyoshi, *The Twilight Years* [Kokotsu no hito (1972)], trans. Mildred Tahara (Tokyo and New York: Kodansha International and Peter Owen 1984).

2 See Rieko Saito, 'Japan's Rapidly Aging Society Confronting the Issue of Death,' *New Canadian*, 16 March 1995, E3.

3 See '2007 Called Critical Time in Society's Rapid Aging,' *Japan Times*, 19 February 1993, 3. Infants born in 1992 are expected to maintain average lifespans similar to current statistics (76.09 for men, 82.22 for women). Since 1985, the life expectancy of the Japanese has been longer than that of people in any other nation. See also 'Current Policies to Care for the Elderly,' *NWEC Newsletter* 11, 2 (1994): 8-9.
4 See editorial, 'Birth of Hosokawa's Cabinet,' *Daily Yomiuri*, 11 August 1993, A8.
5 See 'Responsibility for Elderly Care Falls on Female Family Members, Study Shows,' *Asahi Evening News*, 16 September 1989. Cf. 'Sex Linked to Atrophy of the Brain, Study Finds,' *Japan Times*, 2 April 1991: 'A new study ... may indicate women are more likely than men to remain mentally sharp as they age ... The overall rate of brain-cell death, called atrophy, is about three times higher in men than in women' (p. 8).
6 Adrian Waller, 'Three Women, and Human Bondage,' *Japan Times Weekly*, 4 April 1992, 3.
7 See Yoshihiro Otsu, 'Women Face Brunt of "Aging Society,"' *Daily Yomiuri*, 5 May 1993, A9.
8 See Takie Sugiyama Lebra, 'The Dilemma and Strategies of Aging among Contemporary Japanese Women,' *Ethnology* 18, 4 (1979): 'In 1973 Japanese women of 75 and over had the highest suicide rate in the world' (p. 339). See also Yoshimoto Takahashi, MD, 'Seniors' Suicide Seen as Special Problem,' *Japan Times*, 23 May 1991, 17. Takahashi quotes from a study that reports that old people who felt isolated and abandoned within the family committed suicide and that the elderly required a measure of independence to find life worth living.
9 See Reiko W. Sekiguchi, 'Education and the Aged: Social and Conceptual Changes in Japan,' *Educational Gerontology* 11 (1985): 277-93.
10 See Harumi Yamamoto, 'Elderly Society Won't Be All Problems,' *Asahi Evening News*, 4 October 1992, 4.
11 See Akiko Shiozaki, 'Sharing Eases the Burden of Age,' *Asahi Evening News*, 1-2 January 1995, 10.
12 'Bedridden and Lonely Elderly Express Simple Needs.' *Asahi Evening News*, 22 September 1992.
13 See Kittredge Cherry, *Womansword: What Japanese Words Say about Women* (Tokyo and New York: Kodansha International 1987), 135; and Alton Robertson, 'A Language That Eloquently Meets the Changing Needs of Its Speakers,' *Japan Times*, 28 September 1990, 11.
14 See Susumu Matsumoto, 'Elderly Could Help Solve Labor Shortage,' *Daily Yomiuri*, 12 March 1991. Cf. '70% of Japanese Men Want to Work Past 60, Survey Shows,' *Asahi Evening News*, 15 January 1992.
15 'Pressure to Up Pension Age Seen Rising,' *Japan Times*, 16 April 1992, 3.
16 'Pre-Retirement Illnesses: Men Complain of Physical Pains, Tied to Anxiety,' *Asahi Evening News*, 29 July 1992.
17 'A Helping Hand from the Boys,' *Asahi Evening News*, 30 June 1993. A state examination for workers caring for the elderly was established in 1988.
18 See Hideko Sakuma, 'Shortage Hurts Elderly Care,' *Japan Times*, 14 September 1990, 3.
19 See editorial, 'New Course for "Home Helps,"' *Asahi Evening News*, 3 March 1992, 8.
20 See 'Osaka Training Home Helpers to Cope with an Aging Society,' *Japan Times*, 29 January 1991, 4.
21 See ibid.; and 'Women's Groups Honored for Service,' *Daily Yomiuri*, 30 April 1992, A3.
22 See 'Local Care-for-the-Elderly Co-ops to Form Nationwide Network,' *Asahi Evening News*, 31 May 1991.
23 See 'Demand Growing for Two-Family Homes,' *Asahi Evening News*, 16 February 1992.
24 See Min H. Kim, 'Providing Freedom for the Elderly,' *Japan Times*, 7 February 1991.
25 Philippe Pons, 'Aging of Japan Apt to Bring a Lot of Social Change,' *Asahi Evening News*, 17

May 1993. See also Shigehiro Yoshino, 'Some Light at the End of the Tunnel,' *Look Japan* 41, 458 (1994): 9.

Chapter 8: Sexual Politics

1 Anon. review of Kazue Morisaki, *Baishun ōkoku no onnatachi: shōfu to sampu ni yoru kindaishi* [Women in the prostitution paradise: A modern history of whores and childbearers] (Tokyo: Takarajima Sha 1993), in *Japanese Book News* 6 (Spring 1994): 10.

2 Sara Harris, 'A Note to the Reader,' *House of the 10,000 Pleasures: A Modern Study of the Geisha and of the Streetwalker of Japan* (Toronto: New American Library of Canada, Signet Books 1963), 7. Geisha undergo years of training in the arts of music, dance, and pleasing men. They are by no means common prostitutes, yet may be sexually available to special clients.

    Cartoonist Bruce Leigh, long resident in Japan, makes the same point as Harris with regard to the state of repression common to many Japanese men. In a satirical portrait of sexual harassment, with typical exaggeration but more than a grain of truth, Leigh has a fictional psychiatrist observe that Japanese men are forced to hide their deepest desires, fears, and anger: 'I refer to this as cultural entombment. It is not acceptable to express anything in this society, hence the average man seethes with hidden fury.' See Leigh, 'Harassment Sears Women's Lives,' *Japan Times*, 25 May 1991, 22.

3 Harris, *House of the 10,000 Pleasures*, 91.

4 Having a mistress is still considered the mark of wealth and success. In 1991, then-prime minister Uno dismissed a mistress with a small payment and the woman made the affair public. The media seemed to condemn him not for having a mistress but for being ignorant of the proper amount owing. The concept of appropriate payment to a mistress is clear in Toyoko Yamasaki's novel, *Bonchi* [Young master (1959)], trans. Harue and Travis Summersgill (New York: Laurel Books, Dell 1984), where the slightly idealized hero is a generous man. This popular novel was made into a movie and two different films for television, one in 1962 and one in 1972.

5 Ibid., 8.

6 Ibid., 'Translators' Note,' 5.

7 'Kaifu's U.N. Speech Knocked as Sexist, Boastful of Japan,' *Japan Times*, 2 October 1990, 2.

8 See Eric Talmadge, 'NTT Losing Battle against Porno Stickers,' *Asahi Evening News*, 8 April 1990: 'Although prostitution and pimping are illegal in Japan, the country has a booming sex industry with a long history.' A blackly comic misunderstanding was encountered on flights to Japan by the British airline Virgin Atlantic after it began offering free massages in 1989 to business class passengers: 'Soon after we introduced the massage service on our Tokyo route, it became clear that in Japan the implications of offering a massage are distinctly different. After some of our masseuses had been obliged to become adept at rapid but always courteous evasion, to the evident disappointment of some of our passengers, we concluded that we were being seen as offering rather more than we intended to deliver, and we withdrew the service.' There were no such misunderstandings on flights from London to New York, Los Angeles, and Boston. See 'Japanese Misunderstood Massage Offer,' *Asahi Evening News*, 30 September 1993.

9 See Kittredge Cherry, *Womansword: What Japanese Words Say about Women* (Tokyo and New York: Kodansha International 1987), 120-1.

10 See Sally Kobayashi, 'Feminists Protest Public Sexism,' *Asahi Evening News*, 14 December 1991, 5.

11 See John Vachon, 'A Stroll through the Past,' *Asahi Evening News*, 28 July 1994, 13.

12 See Atsuko Shigesawa, 'Bordello Architecture Recalls Images of a Notorious Past,' *Japan Times*, 9 October 1991, 4.

13 Chie Nakane, *Japanese Society*, 2nd ed. (Tokyo: Charles E. Tuttle 1984), 74n.
14 See James Fallows, 'The Japanese Are Different from You and Me,' *Atlantic Monthly* (September 1986): 35-7.
15 Inazo Nitobe, *Bushido, the Soul of Japan: An Exposition of Japanese Thought*, rev. ed. (Rutland, VT, and Tokyo: Charles E. Tuttle 1969), 147.
16 See Tomoko Yamazaki, *The Story of Yamada Waka: From Prostitute to Feminist Pioneer*, trans. Wakako Hiranaka and Ann Kostant (Tokyo and New York: Kodansha International 1985). Sent to America around the turn of the century and forced into white slavery, Waka escaped from a Seattle brothel to a Protestant halfway house and later returned to Japan. She became a leader in the women's movement in the 1910s and 1920s. Yamazaki, since 1954, has concentrated on researching the history of Japanese women.
17 Adrian Waller, 'When Culture Abuses Women,' *Japan Times Weekly*, 9 May 1992, 1.
18 A sample passage of Japanese deletions from *Lady Chatterley's Lover* reads as follows: 'Even the tightness of his arms around her, even the intense movement of his body, and the springing of his seed in her, was a kind of sleep.' See editorial, 'Government Must Keep up with Public Views on Sex,' *Asahi Evening News*, 21 August 1994, 3.
19 Ibid.
20 For the secrecy theory, see Yoshiki Kishi, 'Japan's Sex-Related Industries Worth ¥4.2 Trillion Annually,' *Asahi Evening News*, 28 April 1991, 3. See also Fallows, 'The Japanese Are Different,' 36-7.
21 Derek Sidenius, 'Letter from Japan. Under the Rising Sun, the Media Becomes the Massage,' *Times-Colonist* (Victoria), 27 July 1993, A5.
22 See 'Japan Moving to Tighten Control over Obscene Telephone Services,' *Asahi Evening News*, 4 July 1991.
23 See 'Around Japan. Ōita Used Kids' Art to Battle Sex Ads,' *Asahi Evening News*, 19 August 1994, 5.
24 Fallows, 'The Japanese Are Different,' 37. Cf. Simon G. Capper, letter to the editor, *Japan Times*, 14 October 1992. Capper writes to express shock and disgust at a television show in which ten-year-old girls dressed as adults were paraded as titillating objects before 'drooling' middle-aged men: 'I still can't begin to understand a society that finds candle-dripping S&M schoolgirl rape fantasies to be permissible edification while pubic hair is considered a dangerous obscenity ... [nor] how a reputable TV station can peddle this sick trash as entertainment' (p. 18). Cf. the popularity of *buru-sera* shops, where girls' second-hand underwear and high school uniforms are sold as pornography. See 'Buru-sera,' *Asahi Evening News*, 1-2 January 1994, 9.
25 See Ōtsuka Eiji, 'Culture in Transition: Comic-Book Formula for Success,' *Japan Quarterly* 35, 3 (1988): 287-91. By 1988, *manga* accounted for 10 percent of all Japanese publishing. See Alexander MacKay-Smith IV, 'New Magazine for Language, Culture and Education,' *Japan Times*, 30 October 1990, 14, for the point that the sex-and-violence genre does not represent all *manga*. Cartoons for girls are romantic fantasies, some with historical settings. A young woman cartoonist is presenting the dark side of teenage life through topics such as bulimia, single-parent families, and the bullying of homosexuals: see 'Kyoko Okazaki, Cartoon Artist,' *Asahi Evening News*, 21 August 1994, 2. Also see Frederik L. Schodt, *Manga Manga: The World of Japanese Comics* (Tokyo and New York: Kodansha International 1983), 125-6.
26 See Schodt, *Manga, Manga*, 131-2. By the mid-1990s, after another decade of violent *manga*, Japanese society was changing. See 'Gun-Critical Japan Facing Surge in Armed Crimes,' *New Canadian*, 10 November 1994: 'Japan, often critical of gun-related crime in the United States, is facing a surge in armed crimes at home ... Police admit they are alarmed by signs that Japan is becoming a lawless society' (p. E3).

27 Peter Hadfield, 'Women Are Objects, Good to Rape and Kill,' *Daily Yomiuri*, 23 July 1990, A7. See also 'Women in Adult Videos Can Call Special Hotline This Weekend,' *Asahi Evening News*, 17 June 1992, where a speaker for a human rights group is quoted as saying, 'In recent popular adult videos that depict realistic rape, we believe that actual rapes are sometimes being perpetrated.' A *manga* called *Rapeman* depicts a rapist who is hired by husbands and boyfriends to keep women under control. See Kate Berridge, 'It's Japanese, But Is It Art?' *Spectator*, 21 September 1991, 44.

28 See Aquarius, 'Sexually Explicit Comics under Scrutiny,' *Japan Times*, 9 February 1991: 'The general opinion is that the police should not interfere.'

29 Colin Nickerson, 'Comic Relief. The Japanese Read Them by the Billion,' *Ottawa Citizen*, 10 December 1988, A1.

30 See Berridge, 'It's Japanese': 'Screams and groans were the sounds the torsos made as the men watching slurped beer.' While the men took turns at the live torture, their faces remained 'deadpan, indifferent ... With each other the men had the air of delegates at the first day of a conference, politely passing the props as if they were borrowing pencils rather than whips and syringes' (pp. 43-4).

31 See 'MPD: Thai Women Help Businessmen Close Deals,' *Daily Yomiuri*, 10 October 1992, A3. 'MPD' stands for Metropolitan [Tokyo] Police Department.

32 See Adrian Waller, 'When Culture Abuses Women,' 6.

33 After the mysterious death of a Filipina dancer in Tokyo in 1991, another Filipina was quoted as saying she hoped that Filipinas would not be banned from Japan 'because they should pity the families of workers – many will go hungry.' See 'Women in Manila Protest Filipina's Japan Death,' *Daily Yomiuri*, 19 October 1991, A2. See Steven L. Herman, 'Just Another Tough Night at Work,' *Japan Times Weekly*, 26 October 1991, 13.

34 *Kara* refers to China; *yuki*, to go. See Lisa Louis, *Butterflies of the Night* (New York: Tengu Books, Weatherhill 1992), 156-60.

35 Ibid., 160. Japanese girls and women are also held in forced prostitution, although less frequently than *japayuki-san*: see 'Eight Held in Sale of 16-Year-Old Girls,' *Japan Times*, 25 April 1991, 2.

36 See David Bottorff, 'Illegal Immigrant Women Suffer Anxiety, Depression, Stress,' *Japan Times*, 24 October 1991, 19. See also 'Victims of the Sex Industry. Thai Women Describe Route to Japanese Brothels,' *Daily Yomiuri*, 9 October 1992, A3. Mizuho Matsuda calls these women 'the most vulnerable people in Japan.'

37 See Jeff Kingston, 'The Truth about "Comfort Women,"' *Japan Times*, 17 May 1994, 19. Between 1991 and 1994, Japanese newspapers published hundreds of articles on what quickly became a public scandal. Kingston relates how Professor Yoshimi Yoshiaki of Chuo University, Tokyo, had discovered documents that made it impossible for the government 'to keep on promoting collective amnesia about sexual slavery.' The *Asahi Shimbun*, one of Japan's leading newspapers, printed some of these documents showing that orders for seizing, holding, and supervising the women had come from the Japanese government.

38 See Alex Shishin, 'War Victims Speak out on Sexual Slavery, Forced Labor,' *Asahi Evening News*, 23 January 1994, 6, a review of *War Victimization and Japan: International Public Hearing Report* (Osaka: Toho Shuppan 1993). The first memorial library for the enslaved Korean women was established in Los Angeles' Koreatown: see K. Connie Kang's article in *Los Angeles Times*, 23 November 1994, B1, B4.

39 Enslaved teenaged Burmese women were among those gunned down at war's end. See Alex Shishin, 'Japan's Violent Imperial Legacy,' *Asahi Evening News*, 22 February 1993, 7, a review of Donald Calman, *The Nature and Origin of Japanese Imperialism* (London: Routledge 1992). See also Jocelyn Ford, 'Court Will Hear Untold Story of "Comfort Women,"' *Japan*

Times, 14 December 1991, 3, a report on testimony before the Tokyo District Court that the Japanese military preferred young Korean women because strong Confucian values in Korea 'virtually assured' that such women would be virgins and hence free of sexual diseases. Regulations written by the army's education branch spelled out that the women would provide sexual services from noon to midnight.

40 See Leslie Helm, 'Korean Women Fight Back,' *Daily Yomiuri*, 30 September 1991, A7.

41 See Tokyo (SNS), 'An Imperial Sex-Slave Hunter Speaks Out,' *East Kootenay Weekly*, 25 March 1992, 5. Yoshida described a typical military order from the Army Ministry, 15 May 1943, for 2,000 women to be collected by various prefectural Patriotic Labor Associations. His own order at that time was for 200 women for the 'Imperial Army Relaxation/Korean Women's Volunteer Corps.' Yoshida's claim that Britain and the United States were part of a conspiracy of silence concerning these women in 1945-7 is backed by published declassified American records based on interrogations of 'comfort women' left behind in Burma.

42 See 'Sexist Ads Spark Angry Protests,' *Asahi Evening News*, 12 November 1992, 5; and 'Toyota Ad Angers Australian Woman,' *Asahi Evening News*, 17 March 1993.

43 Masao Miyamoto, *Straitjacket Society: An Insider's Irreverent View of Bureaucratic Japan* (Tokyo and New York: Kodansha International 1994), 64.

44 See Brian Covert, 'Women Fight Makers of Debasing Games,' *Japan Times*, 1 October 1991, 4.

45 See 'Sexual Harassment: It's about Power, Not Sex,' *Asahi Evening News*, 24 October 1991, 3. Examples included women machinists who were harassed more than assembly-line workers, and women holding high-profile jobs as surgeons, lawyers, and investment bankers. Psychologist Dr John Gottman called sexual harassment 'a subtle rape,' more about fear and power than about sex.

46 See 'Japanese Woman under Siege after Harassment Case,' *Independent* (London), reprinted in *Daily Yomiuri*, 14 August 1992, A14; Asako Murakami, 'Politician Takes on Harassment,' *Japan Times*, 5 March 1993, 3; 'Kamamoto City Assemblywoman Collapses while Fighting Sexual Harassment Suit,' *Asahi Evening News*, 19 June 1992; and 'The News in Perspective,' *Japan Times Weekly*, 27 June 1992, 2.

47 See 'Mitsui to Quit SDPJ, Cites Sexual Harassment, Rigidity,' *Daily Yomiuri*, 15 January 1993, A2; and 'Assemblywoman Cites Sexual Harassment before Leaving SDPJ,' *Asahi Evening News*, 14 January 1993.

48 Editorial, 'Another Form of Sexual Harassment,' *Japan Times*, 20 October 1991, 22. Current media euphemisms such as *itazura*, literally 'mischief,' used to refer to both rape and bullying, support this editor's views.

Chapter 9: 'Our Little Noah's Ark Planet'

1 See Kazuko Tsurumi, 'Looking for Ways to Work in Harmony with Nature,' part 1 of 'Man and the Environment,' *Japan Times*, 19 October 1990, 5.

2 Ibid. In Minamata, Kyūshū, cases of a disease attacking the central nervous system were reported from the mid-1950s and finally acknowledged in 1968 to be caused by organic mercury discharged in the effluent of Chisso Corporation, a chemical manufacturer producing fertilizer and related products.

3 See Kunio Nishimura with Hitoshi Chiba, 'Nothing Shakes Hope,' *Look Japan* 41, 470 (1995): 7. This report makes no mention of the gender of volunteers. Noting that democracy has not functioned well in Japan, Kusachi hopes that the response to the earthquake marks a step closer to 'a truly democratic society' (p. 7).

4 Kazuko Tsurumi, 'Women in Japan: A Paradox of Modernization,' *Japan Foundation Newsletter* 5, 1 (1977): 7.

5 'Effective Training Programme for Women's Social Participation,' NWEC *Newsletter* 6, 2 (1989): 1.

6 See 'Housewives Learn to Speak Up,' *Asahi Evening News*, 23 June 1994, 5.

7 See 'Women Discuss Problems, Hopes and Goals for the Future,' *Asahi Evening News*, 28 February 1986, 9.

8 See 'Japan Turning Pale Shade of Green. More People Taking off Blinders and Taking up Conservation Activities,' *Daily Yomiuri*, 22 September 1992, A7.

9 Maggie Suzuki, 'Environmental Groups in Japan Lack National Cohesion,' *Japan Times*, 15 November 1991, 5. Suzuki, who lives in Shikoku, is an American co-editor of the *Japan Environment Monitor*, an English newspaper published monthly in Kofu, Yamanashi Prefecture.

10 See Osamu Yunoki, 'Wild Bird Protection: Ichida Noritaka,' *The Forefront of the Environmental Movement in Japan*, booklet, March (n.p.: Ministry of Foreign Affairs 1992), 4-5. See also Ministry of Foreign Affairs, *Japan's Environmental Endeavours* and *Economic Development and the Environment: The Japanese Experience*, booklets, April (n.p.: Ministry of Foreign Affairs 1992). All three booklets habitually refer to 'citizens' groups' while ignoring that a very large percentage of members of such groups are women. Work done by the 'housewives,' including fund-raising, has been essential to the success of the various environmental movements.

Maggie Suzuki notes that the Wild Bird Society, Japan's largest nature-oriented group, has about 300,000 members or 0.2 percent of the nation's population, while the National Wildlife Federation, the United States' largest, has 4.8 million members or 2.0 percent of the population.

11 See Hitoshi Chiba, 'A Leaf from the Fisherwomen's Book' (part of cover story, 'Nature's Symmetry'), *Look Japan* 41, 471 (1995): 4-6.

12 See Ministry of Foreign Affairs, *Economic Development and the Environment*, 5 and passim. See also Richard Jones, 'Greedy Vandals,' letters, *Asahi Evening News*, 2 July 1994, 8.

13 Anonymous review of Shin'ichi Sano, *Nihon no gomi* [Japan's garbage] (Tokyo: Kodansha 1993), in *Japanese Book News* 6 (Spring 1994): 16.

14 See William de Biase, 'No One Should Go Hungry in Tokyo,' *Asahi Evening News*, 7 July 1990. De Biase, a Franciscan priest who has worked in Japan for twenty-four years, is writing of the attitude of many Japanese towards the homeless who live in or near Shinjuku Station, Tokyo. He qualifies his initial reaction – 'The insiders do not take care of the outsiders' – with many exceptions.

Travelling by train from Tokyo to Kyoto in 1961, I was astonished to see garbage thrown on the train floor, so much garbage that after several hours it was difficult to negotiate the aisle. I knew the Japanese to be meticulously clean with regard to personal property and could not understand such blatant disregard for public property. I later came to see this behaviour as a case of *uchi/soto*. Since the 1970s, in my experience, the floors of express trains have been clean.

Compare the experience of Ryoichi Ogasawara, who saw his own country with new eyes after studying and working in the United States and France. He believes that 'negligence by littering is deeply rooted ... Overall, the [environmental] awareness is still too low in Japan. We have a long way to go there' (Milan Dinga, 'He's Had His Travels, But He's Holding on to His Precious Niche in Rural Japan,' *Japan Times*, 3 June 1990, 11).

15 See Uta Harnischfeger, 'Companies Learning Value of Volunteerism,' *Japan Times*, 22 December 1991, 9.

16 See 'Scrubbing up for the Environment. Kanagawa Co-operative Turns Used Cooking Oil into Soap,' *Japan Times*, 19 July 1990, 18.

17 Kazuko Fujimoto, 'Recycling Group Makes Paper from Trash,' *Japan Times*, 22 April 1990, 10.

18 'Matsuda's Trash Gets Rave Reviews,' *Daily Yomiuri*, 1 June 1990, A3.

19 See 'Tokyo Plans Garbage Plant in Heart of City,' *Asahi Evening News*, 8 May 1990. A curious twist to the matter of recycling milk cartons occurred in 1992, by which time the success of the women's campaign had reduced the share of toilet paper made from recycled newspapers, and the price of old newsprint was falling. A debate on the usefulness of recycling milk cartons took place at Kyoto University between Atsushi Tsuchida, a researcher at the Institute of Physical and Chemical Research, and Akihiro Morizume, an assistant professor of engineering at Osaka University. Evidently Japan has few or none of the newer high-tech newspaper plants that recycle old newspapers into fresh newsprint paper.

20 See anonymous survey in *Asahi Shimbun*, 17 April 1995, 20, regarding the work of volunteers following the Great Hanshin Earthquake, 17 January 1995. According to the survey, conducted by the newspaper, 70 percent of volunteers said it was their first time to do such work, and 80 percent hoped to continue volunteer activities.

21 See also 'More Companies Are Encouraging Employees to Do Voluntary Work,' *Japan Times*, 23 July 1993, 2. Matsushita Electric has encouraged some of its workers to help people with learning disabilities to prepare to leave their group home and to return to society.

22 Yayoi Uchiyama, 'Postwar Portrait: Yukiko Sohma, Veteran Volunteer,' *Asahi Evening News*, 12 April 1995, 5.

23 See Yaeko Mitsumori, 'Japanese Volunteer for Emergency Medical Teams,' *Asahi Evening News*, 13 July 1994, 5.

24 See 'Peddling Family Planning Data,' *Asahi Evening News*, 22-3 September 1994. See also Chapter 2, above, concerning the pioneer work of Shidzue Ishimoto Katō (b. 1897) in family planning. Katō was honoured by the United Nations in 1990 for seventy years of work in this field.

25 See 'Woman Promotes Glaucoma Exams,' *Daily Yomiuri*, 2 March 1991, A3.

26 See Atsuko Shigesawa, 'Group Sets up Shop in Hyōgo to Help Women in Business,' *Japan Times*, 28 May 1991, 4. See also 'Japan Branch of Women's World Banking to Open in Tokyo Thursday,' *Asahi Evening News*, 5 November 1990.

27 Kazuko Shiraishi, *Little Planet*, pamphlet, trans. Allen Ginsberg (Paris: Shoshi Yamada 1985).

28 Kenneth Rexroth, ed., *Seasons of Sacred Lust: The Selected Poems of Kazuko Shiraishi*, trans. Ikuko Atsumi, John Solt, Carol Tinker, Yasuyo Morita, and Kenneth Rexroth (New York: New Directions 1978), 72, 82-3. This is the only volume of Kazuko Shiraishi's work available in English. She returned to Japan with her parents at the age of seven.

29 See H.J. Kirchhoff, 'Novelist, Poet See Readings in Different Light,' *Globe and Mail*, 27 January 1988.

30 Yukiko Tanaka, Introduction to 'Iron Fish' (1976), by Taeko Kōno, in *The Shōwa Anthology: Modern Japanese Short Stories*, Vol. 2, 1961-1984, ed. Van C. Gessel and Tomone Matsumoto (Tokyo and New York: Kodansha International 1985), 348.

31 Makoto Ōoka, *Sanga mugen* [Infinitely mountains and rivers] (1977), trans. Janine Beichman, in 'A Poet's Notebook,' *Asahi Evening News*, 2 September 1990.

32 Cf. Linda Grant, 'Is the Battle Lost If Women Go to War?' *Asahi Evening News*, 6 September 1992, 3. Grant quotes from Jill Liddington's *The Long Road to Greenham: Feminism and Anti-Militarism in Britain since 1820* (London: Virago Press 1989) to connect the pacifist women encamped at Greenham Common in England in the last decades of our century with Ann Knight, a British Quaker who believed that universal women's suffrage and elected female representatives in Parliament would bring peace.

33 See Shuichi Kato, 'Jumping the Gun. Japan Must Decide First How It Wants to Cooperate in World Peace,' *Asahi Evening News*, 14 November 1991, 8.

34 Editorial, 'Blanket Pacifism Can Be Irresponsible,' *Japan Times*, 9 March 1991, 22. Other male politicians and commentators have called Doi's unilateral pacifism 'selfishness.' See also Yoko Hani, 'Texts More Direct on Defense. Students Taught Nation Has a Right to Preserve Its Security,' *Japan Times*, 30 April 1993, 3.

35 See Jill Smolowe, 'A Mountain Moves,' *Time Magazine*, 7 August 1989, 16.

36 See 'Women's Right to Vote Celebrated,' *Asahi Evening News*, 20 September 1993, 4.

37 'Women Still Not Taken Seriously in Politics, Group Says,' *Asahi Evening News*, 23 July 1992.

38 See Flora Lewis, 'Changing the Way of Japanese Politics. The Feminine Factor Strengthens Its Foothold,' *Asahi Evening News*, 15 October 1990, 6.

39 Harue Kitamura, the nation's first woman city mayor, was elected mayor of Ashiya, Hyōgo Prefecture, in 1991. Kitamura ran her campaign on a platform of environmental protection and an improved budget for education.

40 See 'Japan's Second Woman City Mayor Vows to Fight U.S. Housing in Zushi,' *Asahi Evening News*, 9 November 1992, 1.

41 Stephen Hesse, 'Mayor of Zushi Seeks U.S. Cooperation,' *Japan Times*, 24 June 1993, 17.

42 Akiko Shiozaki, 'Zushi's Environmental Mayor,' *Asahi Evening News*, 24 January 1993, 4.

43 See Kyoko Sato, 'Zushi Head Fights to Save Forest,' *Japan Times*, 22 June 93, 3.

44 See David Sanger, 'New Japanese Leader May Prove an Easy Target,' *Globe and Mail*, 31 July 1993, A6.

45 See 'Women Rally at Diet for Testimony,' *Japan Times*, 27 November 1992, 2. More than 100 women rallied outside the Diet with pickets demanding a thorough investigation of a scandal. Muneyuki Shindo, a professor of political science at Rikkyō University, called for a package of anticorruption laws like Britain's. See also Hisashi Inoue, 'Now Is the Time to Get Angry – At Nakasone's Power Concentration,' *Mainichi Daily News*, 16 June 1986, 1, where Inoue, speaking of government corruption, states that people 'have forgotten how to be angry.' Women activists show that Inoue is wrong on that point.

46 See H.O. [Hisako Okamura], 'Women's Advance in Politics,' in English Discussion Society, *Japanese Women Now* (Kyoto: Women's Bookstore Shoukadoh 1992), 65-7.

47 See 'Woman Takes Top Japanese Post,' *Ottawa Citizen*, 26 August 1989, A7. See also Irene Kunii, 'Japan's PM Makes Woman His Top Aide,' *Montreal Gazette*, 26 August 1989, A16.

48 Untitled article, *NWEC Newsletter* 6, 2 (1989): 9.

49 See Okamura, *Japanese Women Now*, 67. The 3.1 percent figure is from a survey by the Fusae Ichikawa Memorial Society, taken 1 June 1991, and represents a 1 percent increase since their last survey, approximately four years before. See also 'Number of Assemblywomen on the Rise,' *Asahi Evening News*, 22 December 1991, 4. The Fusae Ichikawa Memorial Foundation began to monitor the advance of women in politics in 1971; the 1991 survey is the sixth in twenty years. Their surveys show that it is more difficult for women to be elected in small towns, where local and family ties are strong, but that women are making slow gains and that by 1991 'signs of change have gradually begun to appear.'

50 See 'Women Lawmakers Vow to Boost Their Strength to 30%,' *Asahi Evening News*, 17 February 1992. A 1991 international survey of the percentage of female legislators in 130 nations placed Japan 110th, between Algeria and Egypt. Mitsui, a former high school teacher, now a prominent politician, remembers being humiliated by a male teacher for refusing to make tea: see Kumiko Makihara, 'A New Era for Women,' *Time Magazine*, 23 October 1989, 81.

51 See Yayoi Uchiyama, 'Women Reach for Greater Involvement in Politics,' *Asahi Evening News*, 2 June 1993, 9.

52 See Takako Doi, 'Japan Should Follow German Lead,' *Daily Yomiuri*, 24 May 1990.

53 See 'Japanese Women's Group Fetes 45th Anniversary,' *Asahi Evening News*, 28 March 1991.

54 See 'Women's Groups in Japan. Japan Women's Council,' NWEC Newsletter 11, 1 (1994): 9-10.

55 See 'Women Civic Groups Oppose SDF Dispatch,' Asahi Evening News, 19 October 1990; 'Hiroshima Groups Stage Rally against War,' Japan Times, 18 February 1991; 'Citizens Stand against PKO Bill across Nation,' Asahi Evening News, 2 December 1991, 4; and 'Women Key to N-Free World, Panelists Say,' Asahi Evening News, 7 August 1990, 3.

56 See Catherine Pawsat, 'Women Take up the Nuclear Fight,' Japan Times, 24 November 1994, 3. Beatrix Potter's 'Peter Rabbit' was created in England's Lake District, a major Japanese tourist destination and now home to THORP, the Thermal Oxide Reprocessing Plant that has contracted to reprocess Japan's spent nuclear fuel. Reprocessing extracts plutonium and reduces the volume of high-level radioactive waste while increasing the volume of low- and medium-level waste.

57 See James Kirkup, 'Killing People Is Wrong,' review of The Hiroshima Murals: The Art of Iri Maruki and Toshi Maruki, ed. John W. Dower and John Junkerman (Tokyo: Kodansha International 1985), in Asahi Evening News, 8 November 1985.

58 See 'Paintings Depict War Factory. Ex-Teacher's Book Shows Life at Poison-Gas Plant,' Japan Times, 10 August 1990, 10. Reiko Okada's self-published book, Okuno Island: The Story of Mobilized Students, has English and Japanese captions for thirty-six paintings. Okada sent copies of her book to China, where the Imperial Japanese Army used poison gas, to express her apology, and received letters stating that her book had changed the feelings of hostility formerly felt by Chinese readers.

59 See Susan J. Pharr, Political Women in Japan: The Search for a Place in Political Life (Berkeley: University of California Press 1982), passim.

Chapter 10: Firewords

1 See, for example, Noriko Mizuta Lippit and Kyoko Iriye Selden, eds. and trans., Stories by Contemporary Japanese Women Writers (Armonk, NY, and London: M.E. Sharpe 1982); Phyllis Birnbaum, trans., Rabbits, Crabs, Etc.: Stories by Japanese Women (Honolulu: University of Hawaii Press 1982); Yukiko Tanaka and Elizabeth Hanson, eds., This Kind of Woman: Ten Stories by Japanese Women Writers 1960-76 (New York: Perigee Books 1982); Yukiko Tanaka, ed., To Live and to Write: Selections by Japanese Women Writers 1913-1938 (Seattle, WA: Seal Press 1987); Yukiko Tanaka, ed., Unmapped Territories: New Women's Fiction from Japan (Seattle, WA: Women in Translation 1991); and Masao Miyoshi, guest editor, Manoa. A Pacific Journal of International Writing, special issue Japanese Women's Writing 3, 2 (Fall 1991).

2 Shugorō Yamamoto, Japanese Women: Short Stories, trans. Juliet Winters Carpenter (Tokyo: Japan International Cultural Exchange Foundation 1993), 184. Cf. Carpenter, 'Enchi Fumiko: "A Writer of Tales,"' Japan Quarterly 37, 3 (1990), in which Carpenter notes that 'Enchi herself once attributed her success as a writer to the strong presence of certain masculine elements within her that led her to reject a life limited to marriage and child raising and to dream instead of achievement in the largely male provinces of literature and the theatre' (p. 343).

3 See Kittredge Cherry, Womansword: What Japanese Words Say about Women (Tokyo and New York: Kodansha International 1987), 31. See also introduction to Stories by Contemporary Japanese Women Writers, ed. and trans. Lippit and Selden: 'In the modern period too, women writers have been placed in their own group ... and their words have been treated as belonging to a separate category not always regarded as an integral part of Japanese literary development ... The recognition of the female school of literature as a separate and legitimate school backed by a long, brilliant tradition and the existence of educated women readers contributed to the flourishing of women's literature by exempting women writers from full-scale

competition with men writers and from being subjected to the more acute sexist prejudices in literary criticism ... Yet as more women found the means to express themselves and to participate in modern life, the tradition of autobiographical, psychological writing associated with the female-school became a heavy burden ... increasingly restrictive' (pp. xiv-xv).

4 Janine Beichman, 'Yosano Akiko: The Early Years,' *Japan Quarterly* 37, 1 (1990): 37.

5 Ibid., 54, n. 1. As Beichman notes, Doi's allusion initially went unrecognized by a largely male press and political establishment. Amusingly, Doi's reference was also widely misinterpreted 'to mean that the mountain (*yama* can be singular or plural) of the LDP had moved.'

6 Introduction, *Tangled Hair: Selected Tanka from Midaregami by Akiko Yosano*, trans. Sanford Goldstein and Seishi Shinoda (Rutland, VT, and Tokyo: Charles E. Tuttle 1987), 19.

7 See Janine Beichman, 'Akiko's Passion Undying to Life's End,' no. 52 in a long-running series entitled 'Yosano Akiko. Poet of Modern Japan,' *Japan Times*, 28 March 1991, 16.

8 Quoted in ibid.

9 See Janine Beichman, 'Yosano Akiko: Return to the Female,' *Japan Quarterly* 37, 2 (1990): 224. Earlier verses depict the birthing woman as passing through the hospital gate 'as if into an execution ground,' and curse men for not wagering their lives in this way: 'What idlers / they are!'

10 Selected passages from interview with Fumiko Enchi, Tokyo, 11 July 1986, translated by Mayumi Kurokawa. For an English translation of 'Boxcar of Chrysanthemums,' see *This Kind of Woman*, ed. Tanaka and Hanson, 71-86.

Enchi's reference to divorce carries a personal sting. The writer, née Fumi Ueda, married Yoshimatsu Enchi in 1930 and remained married until his death in 1972. However the marriage was not happy, and stale, loveless marriages became a common theme in Enchi's writing. See Carpenter, 'Enchi Fumiko,' 348. Carpenter quotes from *Enchi Fumiko Zenshu* [The complete works of Enchi Fumiko], 16 vols. (Tokyo: Shinchōsha 1977-8): 'When I was married, I had already begun to write after a fashion, and I entered on married life with the express condition that my writing might be allowed to continue; but this concession was a far cry from the understanding demonstrated by husbands of working women today ... We often quarreled; talk of separation came up more than once. Women writers have a record rate of divorce ... The only reason I never divorced my husband was that I lacked the courage to make the leap and live on my own' (vol. 15, pp. 382, 250, trans. Carpenter).

11 Fumiko Enchi, *Masks* [Onna-men (1958)], trans. Juliet Winters Carpenter (Tokyo: Charles E. Tuttle 1984).

12 Black humour, which may include grotesque, tragic, or horrifying elements and yet retain a comic aspect, is associated with twentieth-century literature of the absurd, a philosophical term used by French existentialist writers such as Albert Camus and Jean-Paul Sartre to describe the tone of modern plays and novels by writers such as Alfred Jarry, Samuel Beckett, Jean Genet, Eugène Ionesco, Edward Albee, Harold Pinter, and others. Black humour and irony are common in twentieth-century Western literature after the Second World War.

13 Soon after receiving the Noma Literary Prize for *The Waiting Years*, Enchi wrote: 'Perhaps my works are haunted by the bitterness and resentment of Japanese women oppressed by men long ago, from the era of *The Waiting Years* and before ... I cannot escape the feeling even now that this novel is not mine alone but was produced jointly with numbers of women who lived in the past, women having no connection to literature ... It is the secrets of Meiji women, passed on in a thin stream of hushed voices for dozens of years in novel form' (quoted in Carpenter, 'Enchi Fumiko,' 352-3). Carpenter adds that Enchi agreed with Yukio Mishima's assessment of her as simultaneously moral and deeply immoral: 'She herself suggests that *The Waiting Years* sprang from her virtuous, moral side, while *Masks* depicts the darker, decadent, immoral half' (p. 353).

14 See anonymous, 'Novelists: The Front Lines of Emptiness,' *AsiaWeek*, 11 May 1986, 79. See also Chapter 4, above, for a discussion of *Child of Fortune*.

15 Ibid.

16 From an interview with Yūko Tsushima, Tokyo, 8 July 1986, translated by Shunko Sasaki, taped transcript translated by Mayumi Kurokawa, edited by Patricia Morley.

17 See Manako Ihaya, 'Yumi and Her Baby: Both Are Victims,' *Japan Times Weekly*, 30 November 1991, 15. Babies born to unwed mothers at this clinic were being adopted abroad. It is ironic that Japan, a country concerned about its low birth rate, is exporting babies.

18 Yūko Tsushima, 'The Silent Traders,' in *The Shooting Gallery*, trans. and comp. Geraldine Harcourt (New York: Pantheon Books 1988), 44.

19 See Fumiko Y. Yamamoto, 'Tanabe Seiko,' in *Japanese Women Writers: A Bio-Critical Sourcebook*, ed. Chieko I. Mulhern (Westport, CT, and London: Greenwood Press 1994), 398. The sourcebook includes works available in translation for each writer.

20 Ibid., 400.

21 Interview with Seiko Tanabe, Itani City, Hyōgo Prefecture, 3 July 1986, translated by Professors Miho Shimada and Yasuko Ikeuchi, taped transcript translated by Mayumi Kurokawa, edited by Patricia Morley.

22 See Seiko Tanabe, 'How to Win a Woman Writer,' trans. Geraldine Harcourt, *Winds* 9, 9 (1988): 52-60.

23 See Seiko Tanabe, 'How to Seduce Miyamoto Musashi,' trans. Geraldine Harcourt, *The Magazine* 2, 8 (1987): 48-54; and 2, 9 (1987): 17-22. A frequent theme in Tanabe's fiction is the age-old sparring between the sexes.

24 See Chapter 4, above, for an analysis of three stories by Ōba. Cf. her story 'Sea-Change,' trans. John Bester, *Japanese Literature Today* 5 (March 1980): 12-8, in which two men and a woman are sharing a sexual encounter: 'Before long, all three of them turned into creatures in some unidentified depths, with mouths and shining eyes like squids, and tangled their warty tentacles lined with suckers' (p. 15).

25 See Marian E. Chambers, 'Ōba Minako: Rebirth in Alaska,' *Japan Quarterly* 38, 4 (1991): 474-5; and Michiko N. Wilson, 'Ōba Minako,' in *Japanese Women Writers*, ed. Mulhern, 285-6.

26 Selected portions of my talk with Minako Ōba, Tokyo, 7 July 1986, translated by Shunko Sasaki, taped transcript translated by Mayumi Kurokawa. We talked in English and in Japanese. As I was leaving, Ōba remarked that she disliked being interviewed and that if I did not come on business we could be friends.

27 Minako Ōba, 'Double Suicide: A Japanese Phenomenon,' trans. Takechi Manabu and Wayne Root, *Japan Interpreter. A Journal of Social and Political Ideas* 9, 3 (1975): 344-50.

28 See Sanroku Yoshida, 'Setouchi Harumi,' in *Japanese Women Writers*, ed. Mulhern, 345-53. See also Beverly Findlay-Kaneko, 'The Literary Nun Flying High. Tanizaki Prize Winner Connects Buddhism, Sex and Feminism,' *Japan Times Weekly*, 26 June 1993, 12-3.

29 See Chapter 2, above, for a discussion of the movement, its leaders, and the journal by the same name.

30 See Harumi Setouchi, *Beauty in Disarray*, trans. Sanford Goldstein and Kazuji Ninomiya (Tokyo: Charles E. Tuttle 1993), passim. This dramatic biographical novel focuses on the life of Noe Itō, the youngest member of the Seitō group and the last editor of the journal. However, it includes a dramatic portrait of Raichō, whom Setouchi calls 'a really special person.'

31 Portions of my interview with Harumi Setouchi, Kyoto, 1 July 1986, translated by Miho Shimada, taped transcript translated by Kyoko Watanabe. Setouchi defines the novel as 'an expression of an inner voice of the inexplicable creature called "human being," or of the pains he feels as he vomits, being unable to contain any longer the dark, frustrating part of his life' (*Setouchi Harumi no sekai* [The world of Setouchi Harumi], quoted in *Japanese*

Women Writers, ed. Mulhern, 348). Only two of Setouchi's fictions are in English translation: *Beauty in Disarray*, trans. Goldstein, and *The End of Summer*, trans. Janine Beichman in collaboration with Alan Brender (Tokyo and New York: Kodansha International 1989).

32 In 1949, Chizuko Machida joined a literary coterie and assumed the pen name, Ayako Sono. In 1953, she married writer Shumon Miura. Both before and after it was interrupted by war, her education was at Seishin Joshigakuin (Sacred Heart School for Girls). See Fumiko Y. Yamamoto, 'Sono Ayako,' in *Japanese Women Writers*, ed. Mulhern, 369-77.

33 See Sono's novel, *Satōgashi no kowareru toki* [When a sugar cookie crumbles] (1965). Sono suffered from insomnia for many years.

34 I talked with Ayako Sono in her home in Tokyo on 8 July 1986, assisted by Shunko Sasaki as translator.

35 Yamamoto, 'Sono Ayako,' in *Japanese Women Writers*, ed. Mulhern, 372. See Chapter 4, above, for a discussion of 'Fuji.'

36 Yasuko Harada, *An Elegy* [Banka (1956)] (Boston: Beacon Press 1957). *Banka* won the Women's Literature Prize, held readers spellbound, and stayed on the bestseller list for more than a year.

37 Portions of talk with Yasuko Harada, Sapporo, 26 July 1986, trans. Mayumi Kurokawa.

38 Michiko N. Wilson, 'Harada Yasuko,' in *Japanese Women Writers*, ed. Mulhern, 91.

39 See Yasuko Harada, 'Evening Bells' [Banshō], trans. Chia-ning Chang and Sara Dillon, in *The Mother of Dreams and Other Short Stories. Portrayals of Women in Modern Japanese Fiction*, ed. Makoto Ueda (Tokyo and New York: Kodansha International 1986), 47-69.

40 Ayako Miura, *The Wind Is Howling*, trans. Valerie Griffiths (London: Hodder and Stoughton 1976), 162.

41 From my interview with Ayako Miura, Asahikawa, 13 July 1986, translated by Mayumi Kurokawa and Mitsuyo Miura, tape transcribed by Mayumi Kurokawa.

42 See Ayako Miura, *Shiokari Pass*, trans. Bill and Sheila Fearnehough (Robesonia, PA: OMF Books 1974). Miura's third and only other novel in English translation is *The Freezing Point*, trans. Hiromu Shimizu and John Terry (Wilmington, DE: Dawn Press 1986).

43 Michiko N. Wilson, 'Miura Ayako,' in *Japanese Women Writers*, ed. Mulhern. Wilson adds that Miura finds her kindred spirit in Masao Nangano, a devout Christian and a humanist who stops the runaway train with his own body. Miura 'is considered the best evangelical Christian writer Japan has to offer. The success of her works, proven time and gain, lies in the way she speaks to the reader, unabashed, straightforward, simple and, above all, sincere' (p. 220).

44 Mulhern, ed., *Japanese Women Writers*, ix.

45 Minako Ōba, 'Ai in Japanese Literature: The Awesome Power of Love,' *Japan Foundation Newsletter* 22, 1 (1994). She adds that women poets in these oldest extant anthologies 'are all bright, witty, aggressive women full of vim or vigour' (p. 6).

Chapter 11: Becoming the Flag

1 See Richard Lloyd Parry, 'For the Sake of Tradition,' *Style and Travel*, 25 April 1993, 3.

2 See Bill Powell, 'The Reluctant Princess,' *Newsweek*, 24 May 1993, 28.

3 See Martha Duffy, 'The 21st Century Princess,' *Time Magazine*, 7 June 1993, 54.

4 A senior male news executive observed that Owada must 'give up her endeavour to build up her own character.' See David E. Sanger, 'The Career and the Kimono,' *New York Times Magazine*, 30 May 1993, 48. It appears that the views of women held by older Japanese men and formed before the war have not changed.

5 The words are those of Mizuho Fukushima, a thirty-seven-year-old Tokyo attorney, quoted in Powell, 'Reluctant Princess,' 34.

6 See, for example, the photograph of a subdued Masako in kimono, head down, shown with

an article by David E. Sanger, 'The Molding of Masako-san, Japan's Perfect Bride,' *New York Times International*, 7 June 1993, A2.

7 See Duffy, '21st Century Princess,' 54. See also Charles M. De Wolf, 'The Throne and the Status of Women,' *Asahi Evening News*, 15 January 1995. The Imperial Household law stipulates that only a male heir to the emperor may ascend the throne. In Europe, queens may and do reign. Japan will face a problem if neither Princess Masako nor Princess Kiko (wife of Prince Akishino) bears a son. De Wolf writes: 'By insisting on patriliny, Japan is demonstrating to the world that in a matter of fundamental importance, it still believes in the principle of male supremacy ... It will convey the most unfortunate impression that male chauvinism in this country remains deep-rooted' (p. 7).

8 Cf. the anger felt by young political activists one generation earlier, expressed in Motoko Michiura's tanka: 'Dead of night / returning home exhausted / from the interrogation – / my period begins to flow / like rage' (*A Long Rainy Season: Haiku and Tanka*, ed. and trans. Leza Lowitz, Miyuki Aoyama, and Akemi Tomioka, illus. Robert Kushner, vol. 1 of *Contemporary Japanese Women's Poetry*, Rock Spring Collection of Japanese Literature [Berkeley: Stone Bridge Press 1994], 102).

9 See Kyoko Sato, 'Gender Equality Still Considered a Frontline Postwar Battle,' *New Canadian*, 24 August 1995, E7, reprinted from *Japan Times*, 2 August 1995, 1, 3. Statistics from a 1995 survey by the Recruit Research Company show that there were nearly enough job openings for graduates of both sexes despite the recession: the problem lies in discrimination against women. In 1993, the average woman's wage amounted to 61.6 percent of a man's (Ministry of Labour survey), while women accounted for only 8.5 percent of managerial positions in Japan, as opposed to 41.5 percent in the United States and 41.2 percent in Germany (International Labor Organization survey).

10 See 'Job Doors Close for Women,' *Asahi Evening News*, 8 June 1995, 5.

11 Akemi Nakamura, 'Jobs Eluding Female Grads. Corporate Restructuring, Bias Takes Toll on Recruiting,' *Japan Times*, 30 October 1994, 3.

12 See Kevin Rafferty, 'Tokyo's Graduates Face Testing Times,' *Guardian Weekly* (Manchester), 30 April 1995, 21.

13 Keiko Fukuzawa, 'Women's Hiring Woes,' *Japan Quarterly* 42, 2 (1995): 156.

14 Ibid. Note that *gender* is placed first. Hiring statistics in Fukuzawa, 'Women's Hiring Woes,' show that women graduates of four-year co-educational universities did better than women from four-year women's universities. Graduates of junior colleges, predominately female, fared much worse. Overall, the number of female students who found work is just 56 percent of that of male students.

15 See 'Job-Seeking Women Blast Chauvinism,' *Asahi Evening News*, 28 July 1994, 4. Rally organizers released the 1994 *Job-Hunting Black Paper*, a compendium of horror stories, its title a parody of annual government white papers. See also Mieko Takenobu, 'Readers Speak on Women and Work,' *Asahi Evening News*, 15 June 1994: 'Most of the letters were from women who claimed they too were forced to quit a job upon marriage. They all told of the deep despair and damaged morale they experienced when they found their companies evaluated workers according to sex and marital status rather than individual capacities' (p. 9).

16 Masako Kimoto (pseudonym), 'Job Discrimination,' letters, *Asahi Evening News*, 30 June 1995, 8.

17 See Sato, 'Gender Equality,' E7, E8.

18 The views of Suzuki and Ehara are discussed in ibid, E8.

19 See 'Many Tired of Job Market Search, Female Post-Graduate Applicants Rise,' *Japan Times*, 23 August 1994, 2. The 1992 report on opinions regarding marriage is quoted in Duffy, '21st Century Princess,' 54.

20 Fukuzawa, 'Women's Hiring Woes,' 161.
21 Christine Cunanan, 'Woman in Advertising Has Winning Toughness,' *Japan Times*, 12 February 1995, 12.
22 This was the first all-male Cabinet since 1992. Since 1960 eleven women have held Cabinet posts. A record number of three women were appointed to the Cabinet of Morihiro Hosokawa, August 1993 to April 1994. See 'Men Head Japan's Beijing Delegation,' *Asahi Evening News*, 1 September 1995, 4.
23 See Mayo Issobe, 'Equal Strides,' *Asahi Evening News*, 29 August 1995, 5. Further statistics from this report show Japan standing twenty-third regarding 'ratio of women's earnings to total household income'; fifty-third in 'ratio of women in technical fields'; sixty-third in 'ratio of women lawmakers'; and eighty-first in 'ratio of women in managerial positions.'

The United Nations recommended that the ratio of women in leading positions be raised to 30 percent by 1995. In Japan, 0.8 percent of women held management positions in central government offices in mid-1995. See editorial, 'Japan Must First Act at Home to Ease the Plight of Women,' *Asahi Evening News*, 3 September 1995, 3. The editor found that these figures showed 'how indifferent the Japanese government and companies have been toward realization of equality between the sexes,' and that this situation must change if Japan expects to win international trust.
24 See Mieko Takenobu, 'Vocal Women,' *Asahi Evening News*, 13 June 1995, 5. See also '3 Women Win Back Pay Suit,' *Asahi Evening News*, 17 June 1994, 4. The three women employees successfully contested their company's right to base pay scales on whether an employee was head of a household and was willing to relocate.
25 'Man Who Will Stand out in China,' *Asahi Evening News*, 30 August 1995, 4.
26 See Mayo Issobe, 'Bumpy Stump. Women Are Making Inroads in Japanese Politics, but the Going Is Slow and Uneven,' *Asahi Evening News*, 6 September 1995, 5.
27 See 'Battle for Japanese Women,' *Asahi Evening News*, 28 August 1995, 4.
28 See Issobe, 'Bumpy Stump,' 5.
29 See 'Letter Rips Female-less Cabinet,' *Asahi Evening News*, 19 August 1995, 4.
30 Letter to the editor, *Asahi Shimbun*, 29 April 1995, 5, trans. Dr Mary McCrimmon. See also Kaoru Noguchi, 'State Arrogance,' letters, *Asahi Evening News*, 23 January 1995, where the writer expresses indignation that women are being urged to have more children. This reminds her of the wartime atmosphere when women were encouraged to bear children to become soldiers: 'If the government really wants to increase the number of children, it should strive for small classes, upgraded day-care centers, housing better suited for bringing up children, and the like' (p. 6). Other letter writers echo these convictions.
31 See Kikuo Arai, '"Tying the Knot" in Contemporary Japan,' *Pacific Friend* 22, 9 (1995): 2-9. Statistics are taken from a 1993 survey by the Ministry of Health and Welfare.
32 Seventy-three percent of respondents, both men and women, supported this explanation for late marriages in a 1991 public opinion poll by the Prime Minister's Office. See ibid., 8.
33 See Janet Ashby, 'Best-Selling Authors, Women's Issues and More,' *Japan Times*, 2 June 1995, 16.
34 See Arai, 'Tying the Knot,' 9. The figures are 83.6 percent, men; 89 percent, women.
35 Ibid., 7, 9.
36 'More Women Opt for Younger Husbands,' *Asahi Evening News*, 5 April 1995, 5.
37 Ibid.
38 Ichiro Ozawa, *Blueprint for a New Japan: The Rethinking of a Nation*, trans. Louisa Rubinfien, ed. Eric Gower (Tokyo and New York: Kodansha International 1994), 195.
39 See Tony Jackson, 'U.S. Corporate Glass Ceilings Begin to Crack,' *Japan Times*, 4 April 1995, 16.

40 See 'Education Ministry Loosens Text Grip,' *Asahi Evening News*, 26 July 1994, 9.

41 See Fumiko Yoshigaki, 'School Uniform Debate Heightens,' *Asahi Evening News*, 3 January 1995, 7.

42 Ibid. See also 'More Teachers to be Hired to Reduce Class Size,' *Asahi Evening News*, 12 December 1992. Recent plans to increase the number of teachers over a six-year period beginning in the fiscal year 1993 aim at smaller classes so that teachers can pay more attention to each student. The goal is to reduce senior high school classes to forty students (from forty-five or fifty). Similarly, a gifted student program in mathematics and science begun in 1994 to nurture creativity outside the constraints of the uniform education system gives more attention to the individual: see Kojiro Yamagami, 'A Bid to Develop Math, Science,' *Asahi Evening News*, 13 September 1994, 9.

See also Masayoshi Suga, 'Panelists: Ill Society Causes Youth Violence,' *Asahi Evening News*, 2 July 1994, a report on a symposium co-sponsored by the Goethe-Institut Tokyo and Asahi Shimbun. Shizuo Machizawa is quoted: 'The Confucian system and old family system still exist in Japan. Schools and companies are typical examples of places preserving such values ... [People] lose their identities and thus individualism and freedom fall behind authoritarianism.' Summarizing the keynote speakers, Suga notes that 'today's youths have less chance to socialize because of the managed education system. It is alarming that half of junior and senior high school students think their life is a failure' (p. 5).

These problems are frequently the topic of letters to the editor. See Takahiro Koyama, 'Following the Pack,' letters, *Asahi Evening News*, 11 January 1995, who blames affluence for a current lack of individuality and urges Japan to strive to create 'individualistic children and a society which tolerates them' (p. 8).

43 Masao Miyamoto, MD, *Straitjacket Society: An Insider's Irreverent View of Bureaucratic Japan* (Tokyo and New York: Kodansha International 1994), 147.

44 See Juzo Itami, foreword to *Straitjacket Society*, by Miyamoto, 9 and passim.

45 See also Satoru Ota, 'Bullying beyond the Imagination of Detective,' *Asahi Evening News*, 7 January 1995, 5, a report on the findings of a Tokyo-based private investigator hired by parents to obtain photographic and electronic proof of bullying. Detective Fumio Watanabe found that victims rarely resisted and that some children even feigned smiling. Some boys were egged on by girls who used male bullies as pawns to bully other girls. Teachers were commonly aware of the problems and did nothing to stop them but blamed their superiors. The usual solution was for the bullied child to be transferred to another school. Watanabe's observation that an entire class often took part in the bullying reinforces Miyamoto's analysis of workplace conditions. School violence in the form of corporal punishment by teachers is also endemic in Japan.

46 See Vox Populi, Vox Dei, 'Neighbours must unite before a disaster,' *Asahi Evening News*, 24 January 1995, 8, for reference to this popular usage. After the Great Hanshin Earthquake, it became evident that some Kōbe residents had not known their neighbours and that urban residents were increasingly showing a desire to be left alone. The editor locates the new urban trend in a desire to be free from pressure to conform to the group and warns that catastrophes call for co-operation.

47 See Yamazaki Masakazu, *Individualism and the Japanese*, trans. Barbara Sugihara (Tokyo: Japan Echo 1994), passim. See also Patricia Morley, 'Scholar Denies That Japanese Are Purely Group-Oriented,' *New Canadian*, 14 September 1995, E5; and Bill Kelly, 'Individualism Can Save Japan,' *Japan Times*, 9 August 1994, 17.

48 Eiko Arai, 'Crossing the Great Divide. Portraits of New Japanese,' *Pacific Friend* 22, 5 (1994): 8.

49 Karina Sukarno, daughter of a former president of Indonesia, came to Japan for an extended visit at the age of twenty-seven and was astonished by the 'huge difference' between men and women in Japan. She believes it to be the strongest in Asia: see Patrick Markey, 'Karina Sukarno Returning to Her Roots in Japan,' *Asahi Evening News*, 28 August 94, 5.

50 Arai, 'Crossing the Great Divide,' 9.

51 Mariko Sugahara, 'Five Fatal Symptoms of the Japanese Disease,' *Japan Echo* 21, 2 (1994): 68.

52 Anonymous review of Chizuko Ueno, *Kindai kazoku no seiritsu to shuen* [The rise and fall of the modern family] (Tokyo: Iwanami Shoten 1994), in *Japanese Book News* 8 (Fall 1994): 13.

53 See Genichiro Takahashi, 'Wake-up Call for Workers,' *Asahi Evening News*, 17 June 1994, 5. See also 'Survey: Managers Bitter, Frustrated,' *Asahi Evening News*, 15 June 1994, 5. Asked what they would want to do if they were born again, 34 percent of division and department chiefs in major companies in the Tokyo area said they would like to be self-employed; only 14 percent would choose to be salaried workers. Numerous articles identify severe stress-related problems in male employees who have been laid off or demoted to small affiliated companies during restructuring.

54 Mari Osawa, 'End of Helpful Wives and Normal Men,' *Asahi Evening News*, 21 June 95, 5. These views are still considered radical in Japan.

55 See 'Magazines Teach Dads How to Play with Kids,' *Asahi Evening News*, 8 January 1993. One manual, *How to Dad*, by John Boswell and Ron Barrett, is selling well in Japanese translation (Tokyo: Kodansha International 1992).

56 See 'Survey: Family Takes Priority,' *Asahi Evening News*, 18 July 1994, 4. The survey was taken in December 1993 by the Ministry of Education.

57 See Vox Populi, Vox Dei, 'Tanshin Funin Workers Come Home,' *Asahi Evening News*, 9 January 1993.

58 See 'More Men Joining Courses to "Discover" Themselves,' *Asahi Evening News*, 27 September 1994, 5; and 'A Man's Place Is in the Kitchen,' *Asahi Evening News*, 7 March 1993, 4.

59 See 'For Some Men, Being Male Is No Fun at All,' *Asahi Evening News*, 18 January 1995, 9.

60 See Peter Dowling, 'Rock the Boat of Japanese Complacency,' *Asahi Evening News*, 7 May 1995, 6.

61 See Mitsuko Shimomura, 'Hanae Mori Lives According to Her Own Design,' *Asahi Evening News*, 14 September 1995, 9. Cf. Patricia Pfeister, 'Women Artists/Painters in the Recent Period: Art and Gender,' *Asahi Shimbun*, 6 January 1995, trans. Mary McCrimmon. In her book on this topic, Pfeister expresses her surprise at the freedom, variety, vigour and ability of the work of these Edo-era women artists in the face of social restrictions.

62 See Mayumi Maruyama, 'Women's Group Teaches Internet Techniques,' *Asahi Evening News*, 11 September 1995, 4. The Internet address for Women's Online Media is http://www.suehiro.nakano.tokyo.jp/WOM/.

63 Mervat Tallawy, 'Japanese Women: A New Outlook,' *Look Japan* 41, 479 (1996): 27. Mervat Tallawy is ambassador extraordinary and plenipotentiary of the Arab Republic of Egypt to Japan.

64 See Sato, 'Gender Equality,' 1, 3.

65 Kimiko Itami, in *A Long Rainy Season*, ed. and trans. Lowitz, Aoyama, and Tomioka, 44.

INDEX